THE PATHOLOGY
OF LEADERSHIP

by

HUGH L'ETANG

B.A. B.M. B.Ch. (Oxon). D.I.H.

WILLIAM HEINEMANN MEDICAL BOOKS LTD

First published 1969
Reprinted 1970

© Hugh L'Etang 1969

SBN 433 19220 8

In Memory of John Wycliffe Linnell M.C., M.D.
F.R.C.P.
Teacher and Friend

Printed Offset Litho in Great Britain by
Cox & Wyman Ltd, London, Fakenham and Reading

Contents

Preface

I am greatly indebted to those authors and publishers from whose books I have quoted and to Dr William A. R. Thomson of *The Practitioner*, Dr David Carrick of *Medical News* and Brigadier C. N. Barclay of *Brassey's Annual* for allowing me to reproduce material from my previous articles.

Research on this subject has lasted for many years and old and new friendships have been fostered. A lecture in 1947 by Dr Harley Williams on Woodrow Wilson awakened my curiosity. Major Geoffrey Tylden guided my first efforts in 1948 and Dr Francis Neilson stimulated my interest in the history of diplomacy. Dr Humphry Osmond has spurred and encouraged me for many years with weekly letters whose content would make another, and possibly better, book. Professor Arnold Rogow has provided me with vital information from his classic study of James Forrestal, and my other American friends, Dr William A. Glaser and Dr Mottram Torre, have invariably answered my questions. Sir Basil Liddell Hart and the late Major-General J. F. C. Fuller could not have been kinder; nor could Brigadier John Stephenson, and the library staff of the Royal United Service Institution, and the librarians at the Battersea and West Hill, Wandsworth, public libraries. Mrs Moira Strugnell typed the successive drafts with exemplary speed and impeccable accuracy.

CHAPTER 1

Introduction: Should a doctor ever tell?

One of the more disturbing features of modern life is the daily presentation of news in sensational form. To a certain degree this approach has always been the stock-in-trade of newspapers but their managements, now facing intense competition for the advertising revenue that depends on circulation, must seek a novel angle or twist in the news for a seemingly insatiable public. Trivial, ephemeral events are no longer read and forgotten at the breakfast table or on the 8.20 train but are served again, not once but several times, on radio and television programmes during the course of the day and night. Furthermore the newer media of advertising and public relations, insidious or strident depending on taste or need, can fix attention on any aspect of life and, by distortion and an almost perverted form of creation, manufacture what the Americans call a pseudo-event and at times a pseudo-person. It is hardly surprising that this bombardment of our senses has lead to boredom, insensitivity and an unawareness of the unique. Under these circumstances it is easy to forget that the literary sensation of 1966, whether aided and abetted by the factors that have been mentioned, constituted a landmark in biography; the greatest landmark since Froude departed from the pious and reverential style of Victorian biography and omitted no grisly details in his life of Thomas Carlyle.

The publication of extracts from the diaries of Lord Moran, in newspaper articles and in book form, described his experiences as medical adviser to Sir Winston Churchill from 1940 until 1965.[1] No other physician has written of his patients in such detail or with such perception, humanity and literary skill. If the whole truth and nothing but the truth is a fault then Moran erred. A short, idolatrous study, with a few discreet medical details, would have been widely acclaimed. It was the "warts and all" approach that apparently gave offence and provoked discussion about medical ethics and the Hippocratic Oath. However binding the oath may be, and whatever restrictions are placed on physicians in future, Moran has shown that no study of any historical period can be complete without an intimate and detailed medical history of the personalities of the time.

The first extracts of the diary appeared in a Sunday newspaper on 17 April 1966 and some of the first criticisms appeared in the "Lancet" on 23 April. This particular journal combines an academic approach to medicine with a liberal attitude to social problems but its opinion was conventional and condemnatory. Moran should have avoided clinical details since public trust in their confidentiality was involved. He had created a bad precedent and, although the book was published after Churchill's death, he was reminded that the confidentiality that was owed to the living was "doubly owed to the dead". In a letter that appeared in *The Times* on 25 April, Moran maintained that the obligation to secrecy which was absolute in life was not applicable after death and that he had discussed the projected publication with Churchill. He also observed that Churchill's illnesses would inevitably be discussed by the lay public and there was some compulsion to ensure that the details were correct. Bitter condemnation came from the Churchill family who denied any knowledge of the permission that Moran claimed. For two months the battle was joined in lay and medical Press at times with such catching sub-titles as "Fly on the Wall" (*Economist*), "What the Doctor Saw" (*New Statesman*) and "Moranography" (*Medical Proceedings*: South Africa). It lead to discussion about the Hippocratic Oath, which is not sworn by the majority of doctors, and whose knowledge of its content is sketchy. Indeed versions with slightly different words were discussed in the correspondence columns. Whatever version was chosen it was apparent that if this oath formed an ethical background to clinical practice it allowed a doctor, whether he had sworn it or not, complete discretion about the disclosure of information. He is charged and expected not to reveal what should not be revealed. He is not compelled to keep secret everything that he learns from a patient.

"Whatever, in connection with my professional practise, or not in connection with it, I may see or hear in the lives of men which ought not to be spoken abroad, I will not divulge, as reckoning that all such should be kept secret."

The oath confers no privilege on the physician for a doctor may be compelled to give evidence about a patient in a court of law even if it is on matters which he considers "ought not to be spoken abroad". If the health or safety of the community is involved he may use his discretion, albeit reluctantly, to disclose information which in his patient's view "ought not to be spoken abroad". The compulsion to notify infectious disease to the local authority may be resented by patients if their houses are subsequently visited by a health inspector. The doctor is not influenced by the law, or guided by any rules, when he is confronted by an airline pilot or an engine driver with serious disability. If he cannot persuade the patient to notify the appropriate authorities it is his conscience and judgement, rather than ethical rules and ancient oaths, that must guide him towards disclosure or secrecy. The Hippocratic Oath has been given a mystical significance that was probably not intended by its originator. Confidentiality and secrecy are not the prerogative of doctors but are maintained by all responsible members of a community to avoid the dissemination of tittle-tattle which would make daily living intolerable. Nevertheless there comes a time for discreet revelation when, in the words of Sherlock Holmes faced with requests for publication, "It can't hurt now".

G. M. Trevelyan, a former Regius Professor of Modern History at Cambridge University, persuaded Moran to write the book and another historian, Denis Brogan, approved of it. The support of historians, however eminent, does not answer the charges of those who allege that Moran broke his trust. A letter from Dr R. E. Smith, which appeared in *The Times* on the same day as that by Denis Brogan, indicates the significance of Moran's work and its value not only to historians but to the community as a whole. The following extracts are relevant.

"I do not wish to enter into the vexed question of whether medical details of the living or the dead should be published by their doctors, but I am seriously worried that ill people are allowed to conduct national business."

"When many lives or the national economy are at stake, those in charge should be in full possession of all their faculties."[2]

Subsequent reviews of the book in the *Manchester Guardian*, *The New Scientist* and *The Economist* contained regrets that the news of Churchill's physical state had not been revealed earlier or that Moran had not taken decisive action at the time. The cut and thrust of debate between Moran and the Churchill entourage and between historians and doctors ended abruptly in July. A section of the medical profession had the last word and they expressed it unequivocally at Exeter, during the British Medical Association Conference, on 6 July 1966. Members of the Representative Body decided by 597 votes to 3 that the death of a patient did not absolve a doctor from his vow of secrecy. Moran was not mentioned by name but there was no doubt whom the doctors had in mind. Their veto could not be absolute for, contrary to the opinions of the general public, the British Medical Association is not a Union and a proportion of the medical profession are not members. If a member subsequently broke this rule he might be denied membership of the Association but could not be denied the right to practise, since this authority is vested in the General Medical Council.

Moran is not the first doctor to publish details of a patient's illness but he is a pioneer in a unique exploration of a new dimension of historical biography. The longest and most complete case history that has ever been published will enable any future historian to assess the direct effect of Churchill's physical and mental state on his actions and words and its more indirect effect on the events of his times. It may be argued, as it was by Churchill's son and his private secretary, that Moran was only summoned at times of trouble. This is the experience of every physician but these intermittent examinations do not necessarily preclude a penetrating analysis of the patient's condition between visits.

Nearly eighty years before Moran details of the illness of a

Prime Minister were published in a lay journal called *The Nineteenth Century*. The patient was Benjamin Disraeli and the author was his physician. Dr Joseph Kidd, a homeopath, wrote that Disraeli had Bright's disease, bronchitis and asthma. As an adherent of a special branch of therapy, which advocates drugs in minute quantities that cause symptoms similar to the disease, he was critical of Disraeli's physicians. The ipecacuanha which had been given for asthma merely made him sick and "steel" and that delightful Victorian medication, port wine, caused headache and exacerbations of gout. Disraeli was defeated by Gladstone in the General Election of 1880 and died the following year in uraemic coma. Kidd's article appeared eight years after his death.[3]

In the previous year Dr Morell Mackenzie, charged with incompetence by German doctors, felt obliged to give details of the recently fatal illness of the Emperor Frederick III. Although he acted under extreme provocation his intemperate account was censured by his British colleagues.

Between the two World Wars two European physicians published their reminiscences in which they disclosed clinical information about patients. Professor Otfrid Foerster, a German neurologist, was called into consultation by Lenin who did not trust Russian or Communist doctors. Although Foerster was on the periphery in the last months before Lenin's death in 1924, his book appeared in the following year. Dr Victor Eisenmenger, an Austrian physician, was severely censured when he wrote his autobiography in 1930. The Archduke Franz Ferdinand had been his patient and the doctor's breach of confidence had been to disclose that there never had been any mental or physical abnormality. The denial of pathological findings angered those who maintained that the Archduke's policies before 1914 were influenced by mental disturbance and Eisenmenger, a supporter of the Archduke, was victimized.

Nearly twenty years before Moran the mental and physical condition of a foreign leader was published in some detail. In May 1941 Rudolph Hess, then deputy to Hitler, landed by parachute in Scotland. During interrogation his mental state gave cause for concern and over the next few years he was

examined by a number of psychiatrists and psychologists. In
1947 the senior of these, Dr J. R. Rees, edited a book entitled
The Case of Rudolf Hess. Rees and his seven co-authors admitted
that the publication of medical histories of this type was
"unusual though not without precedent". They justified their
work on these grounds:

> "In this case, however, the importance of showing to as wide
> a public as possible the considerable abnormality of a man
> whose influence on world history has been marked made us,
> after much consideration, override the scruples which as
> medical men we felt. In a world where psychopathic men can
> so easily become leaders and where today they might by their
> own personal whims or decisions launch another war on the
> nations, it is for all of us a duty to study and comprehend the
> nature of such men. It is important to see how morbid
> fantasies can activate political conduct of far-reaching
> importance."[4]

Rees took the precaution of obtaining permission from Hess
to publish the details of his medical history. In restrospect it
might be said that Hess, understandably enough, had his mind
fixed on more serious matters. He signed his agreement on 27
September 1946 as he was awaiting sentence at Nuremburg for
complicity in war crimes.

Hess is by no means the only enemy leader who has been subjected either to retrospective or actual psychological investigation. The relish with which we have attached psychiatric labels
to Hitler, Stalin, Castro and Kassem, to name but a few, is in
striking contrast to the absence of curiosity and inquiry about
our own leaders. It is a deficiency that stems from our individual
habit of attributing mental unbalance to colleagues who irritate
us while sparing our personal friends a searching inquiry. Dr
William Sargant, a London psychiatrist of international repute,
has not suppressed his vision with nationalistic blinkers and has
contemplated the compilation of case histories of some leading
politicians.

> "It would teach posterity how frighteningly large a part can
> be played in British politics by various types of illness and

psychiatric abnormality. Some aspirants to the Highest
Office have had some very peculiar psychiatric quirks and
oddities. . . ."[5]

There are those who argue that an individual whether well or
sick, noble or evil, energetic or lazy, has but little influence on
world events; and that the idea of individual power has been
exaggerated and distorted by the tendency to personalize and
humanize the events of the day or the era. They insist that a
national figure may strut convincingly enough on the stage but
that his actions are controlled by impersonal factors that hold
him in their grip. Even in a dictatorship the leader can be the
tool of external influences such as religion, historical tradition
and economics or of the more direct personal influence of his
followers. Churchill was denied the highest office of State until
May 1940 but, with all his ambition and opportunism, he had
the grace and humility to concede that he spoke and acted for
the people of Britain.

Our other great leader of the twentieth century, David
Lloyd George, would have none of this and stressed the part
that individual personality, will and character could play not
only in the conduct, but also in the shaping and alteration of
world events:

"A gifted and resolute person has often postponed for
centuries a catastrophe which appeared imminent and which
but for him would have befallen. On the other hand a weak
or hesitant person has invited or expedited calamity which
but for him might never have happened or which at least
could have been long deferred."[6]

Thomas Callander views with gloom and apprehension the
power and influence of determined individuals in affairs of
State. He doubts whether even the members of a democracy
have any influence over decisions that are supposedly made in
their name:

"The last word rests with sometimes a single functionary,
sometimes an inner ring, but never with a sovereign people.
Fateful actions determining war or peace have not once in a
century been submitted to or ratified by more than a small

group of autocrats, and the bigger the democracy the more does the iron law of oligarchy prevail."[7]

As individuals it is flattering to contemplate and difficult to decry our personal influence and the effect of our will; or to accept that we are animated dummies floating on the tide of events. Lord Horder, a distinguished physician who studied great men in sickness and health, was certain of their peculiar influence.

"Who knows how much turns on whether a prime minister's pipe is clean or foul, or the head of the Foreign Office has had sufficiency of sleep?"[8]

He echoed those words of Zola who in turn was referring to Napoleon III, a victim of stones in the bladder:

"A grain of sand in a man's flesh, and empires totter and fall!"[9]

Before he went to the State Department in 1961 Dean Rusk had no doubt of the power that was held by leaders of State and, as a consequence, the risks that were run when they were unfit. In 1960 he discussed in an article the contemporary desire for Summit Conferences and stressed the disadvantage of such confrontations which allowed little margin for the type of misunderstanding or disagreement that could more harmoniously be settled by more junior officials with less personal reputation at stake:

"Picture," he wrote, "two men sitting down together to talk about matters affecting the very survival of the systems they represent, each in position to unleash unbelievably destructive power . . . one is impulsive in manner, supremely confident . . . possibly subject to high blood pressure; the other . . . weighted down by a sense of responsibility for the hundreds of millions who have freely given him their confidence . . . a man with a quick temper and a weak heart."[10]

He offered no prizes for identifying these leaders but his clinical descriptions could fit Khrushchev and Eisenhower. He stressed the value of the machinery of diplomacy and its seemingly effete formalities and manners for it helped to remove from negotiations the influences of human frailty, aversion and prejudice. Although he was by no means certain in his own mind he tentatively volunteered the theory that illness of an individual might throw grit in the machinery of government or diplomacy.

Later in his article Dean Rusk "speculated about the extent to which the course of world affairs may have been affected by illness among those holding high public office . . ." and went on to say

". . . the international list of those who have carried great responsibility while ill is a long one and there are fleeting glimpses of decisions which good health might have turned another way."

The list of international statesmen, senior officials and officers who have borne supreme responsibility, while in the grip of disabling and debilitating illness, is certainly long and forbidding. In many cases a plausible case can be made for a link between their physical and mental handicaps and impairment of performance, judgement and powers of decision. Persuasive though the argument may be allowance should be made for the tendency of supporters, or detractors in some instances, to attribute personal failure to illness. The effects of illness may be used to provide a convenient excuse for the results of inherent stupidity, incapacity and incompetence which owe nothing to pathological abnormality. In addition retrospective analysis of events, and in particular of national disasters, often seeks a facile or face-saving explanation which the illness of an individual provides. Analysis of successful government might show that affairs can be usefully conducted by sick statesmen; or even that healthy statesmen make mistakes which, if balanced by other circumstances, have no disastrous effects.

Doctors are inhibited by the customs of their profession and usually have neither the wish nor the training to write history. Historians are inhibited by a lack of medical knowledge but are surprisingly diffident, even after they have obtained medical advice, to make any sweeping conclusions about the health of the subjects under consideration. Surely the time has come for a fresh approach. Not only should the health of an individual be explored in detail when a chance finding reveals abnormality; but the health of all individuals should be explored lest some aspect of their health has affected their conduct and their influence on history.

In the forthcoming chapters the health of some of the statesmen and officials who have held high office in the first half of this century will be reviewed. The extent and depth of individual studies are limited by the evidence that is available. As far as it is possible the consequences of any illness will be related to the events of the time, although almost any conclusion about cause and effect can be dismissed as a *post hoc propter hoc* judgement.

Events over the years will show that illness, whether trivial or mortal, is by no means uncommon in this special group: since 1908 eleven out of thirteen British Premiers and six out of ten American Presidents have had illnesses while in office which have incapacitated them to some degree. Uncontrolled and over-enthusiastic observation can lend a false significance to findings and conclusions. It is conceivable that the leaders of any profession or calling may be the victims of a comparable morbidity trend, although the numbers involved are probably too small for statistical analysis.

The case histories have to be reconstructed from sources which, though freely available, may be criticized by the purist. Apart from Moran's contribution there is virtually no direct medical evidence but the histories, diaries, biographies, journals and newspapers of the period provide the multifarious pieces of a fascinating and intricate jigsaw puzzle. It is true that many of the annotations are made by lay people but the keenness of their observation and the depth of their insight should not be despised. If as is often the case they see patients in the intervals between medical consultations, their views embellish any other clinical details that are available. Their reports on conversations are of value. While doctors pride themselves on their skill in taking a history they know only too well that they themselves may not reveal their full medical history to their own physicians. As patients they are as likely as other invalids to discuss their innermost feelings with a special confidant or friend and, since illness is a subject of prime interest, these revelations are commonly recorded or remembered by lay witnesses.

These chapters contain little or nothing in the way of medical detail that has not already been published and the conclusions, albeit tentative and speculative, may be dismissed as subjective impressions culled from the first- or second-hand remarks of unqualified and untrained witnesses. In some cases such a charge may be valid though the lay observers, including the patient, provide as accurate, though not as detailed, an account of Churchill's illnesses as does Moran.

The study of illness should involve a certain restraint on the part of author and reader. The awareness of illness and death is perhaps barely suppressed in the supposedly healthy and disease has an intense fascination for many of us. In pub or club, street or shopping queue, illness and death is a prominent topic and by pandering to this predilection any writer, while attracting an audience, may stand accused of sensationalism or muck-raking. It is hoped that the present study avoids intentional or unintentional bias and represents a serious approach to an important and hitherto unexplored problem. Over the years, and with every appearance of solemnity, serious concern has been expressed about the mental and physical fitness of men in high office and their competence to take crucial decisions that may affect national and international policies and events.

There seems to be a case for placing the evidence before the public so that they can decide whether illness in this group is an occasional, unlucky accident or whether it occurs at a frequent or even calculable rate. The correlation between a statesman, his illness and his times may indicate the effect of individual illness on historical events. If illness is of no apparent consequence it may indicate that other factors are of greater importance or that Prime Ministers and Presidents are either unaffected by illness or individually have less influence on events than they would care presumably to admit. If illness occurs in these groups in all countries at all times the ill-effects should in the long term affect all countries equally; though if there is substance in the hypothesis it could follow that one country, more appreciative of this hazard, might take steps to ensure that

any unfit representatives were summarily removed from the
firing line.

References

1. Lord Moran. *Winston Churchill: The Struggle for Survival*, Cassell
   1940–65.
2. *The Times*, 2 May 1966.
3. *The Nineteenth Century*, 1889, 26, 65.
4. *The Case of Rudolph Hess*, edited J. R. Rees. Heinemann.
5. William Sargant. *The Unquiet Mind*. Heinemann.
6. David Lloyd George. *War Memoirs*, vol. I, p. 89. Nicholson &
   Watson.
7. Thomas Callander. *The Athenian Empire and the British*. Weidenfeld & Nicolson.
8. Mervyn Horder. *The Little Genius*. Duckworth.
9. Emile Zola. *The Downfall*.
10. Dean Rusk. *Foreign Affairs*, April 1960.

CHAPTER 2

Edward Grey and the First World War:
the light that failed

The events that lead to the outbreak of war in 1914 are sufficiently distant for tempers to have cooled and for dispassionate judgement to have replaced emotional partisanship. The meticulous reconstruction of events, almost on an hour to hour basis, by Fay, Gooch and Albertini in particular, have shown that the European powers involved can be shaded in grey rather than black or white. Each of the contestants must now admit that those they regarded as villains were not so sinister, nor the apparently innocent so guiltless, as they have thought in the past. France wanted Alsace-Lorraine and revenge for 1870. Germany felt inferior to Britain and wanted a Navy and colonies. The Austrians wanted to keep the Serbs in their place. The Serbs in the Austro-Hungarian Empire wanted independence and even the Serbs in Serbia were divided by intrigue. Russia, despite her agreement with France, was apprehensive about Germany. Great Britain felt compelled, reluctantly, uneasily and secretly, to come to an understanding with France and had virtually committed herself to close involvement in European affairs. Her naval supremacy, which had hitherto granted international authority, and allowed her to remain relatively aloof from Europe, was challenged by Germany. Fifty years later it is difficult to forget an image of the assaulting Huns in pickelhaube helmets and to accept that gay, waltzing, music loving, Austria must bear the greatest responsibility. Austria-Hungary was perhaps more guilty of engaging inefficiency and feckless irresponsibility; only an Austrian could say that a situation was desperate but not serious. However, none of the European powers, not even Great Britain, can escape censure. War at some time in some place was inevitable. What none of the powers expected was a Great War, a World War. None could foresee the downfall of dynasties, the destruction of Empires and the ultimate recasting of the map of Europe. Wars in the Balkans were endemic, crowned heads and heirs had been liquidated before, and there was no historical reason for immediate alarm when Archduke Franz Ferdinand was shot at Sarajevo in Bosnia on 28 June 1914. Nor should the charge of instigating the First World War be levelled solely against the phthisical Gavrilo Princep, who pulled the trigger, and the idealistic young intellectuals who brooded and dreamed about Bosnian independence. No statute of limitations can absolve a former Austrian Foreign Minister, Count Lexa von Aehrenthal, from responsibility.

For this was the period of the Old Diplomacy, that Secret Diplomacy, when an editorial writer in *The. Times* asked, "Who, then, makes war?" and went on to write:

> "The answer is to be found in the Chancelleries of Europe, among the men who have too long played with human lives as pawns in a game of chess, who have become so enmeshed in formulas and the jargon of diplomacy that they have ceased to be conscious of the poignant realities with which they trifle".[1]

Foreign Ministers and diplomats, if not autonomous, possessed considerable power and influence and were not yet the mere messengers of Prime Ministers and Presidents. Grey may not be a more unusual name than Brown but greater authority and less public accountability made him the more unusual personality. He and his distinguished counterparts were free to move about Europe and decide its future in fashionable spas and discreet hunting lodges. The world of John Buchan and Phillips Oppenheim was not entirely the fantasy of fiction that it must appear to the modern generation. It was left to Neville Chamberlain to put a stop to all this. When he flew three times to meet Hitler in September 1938, he left his Foreign Minister, the lugubrious Lord Halifax, waving bleakly at Heston. A wag at the Foreign Office and young Edward Heath at the Oxford Union allegedly said of Chamberlain's journeys; "If at first you can't concede, Fly, Fly, Fly again."

Prime Ministers and Presidents have been flying ever since, with or without their Foreign Ministers, who have on occasions come to the point of resignation when their specialized advice has been ignored. The first acts of the drama that ended in a world war hardly give one confidence in the unbridled activities of Foreign Ministers and their officials if for no other reason than that some of the incumbents, when viewed through medical eyes, seem not only frail and vulnerable, but also incapable of withstanding the unexpected and destructive storms unleashed by their policies.

Aehrenthal went to the Ballhausplatz in 1906 with the laudable ambition of increasing the standing and national morale of Austria and of rendering her less dependent on Germany. Worthy as these aims were, as the keystone of national policy, their realization provoked inevitable hostility. His annexation of the provinces under Turkish suzerainty, Bosnia and Herzegovina, in 1908 involved the humiliation and resignation of Isvolsky, the neurotic Russian Foreign Minister. Russia and Serbia were driven closer together and the Pan-Serb movement became stronger and potentially dangerous to the peace of Europe. Two British diplomats had no doubt about Aehrenthal's ultimate responsibility for the outbreak of war in 1914. Nicolson singled him out and Lord Hardinge wrote:

> "It is not too much to say that Aehrenthal, by his policy of annexation, was indirectly the cause of the Great War, since the murder of the Archduke Franz Ferdinand at Serajevo was the sequel to the annexation and the pretext of the Austrian ultimatum to Servia".[2]

Aehrenthal did not live to receive praise or blame, for he died from a disease of the blood cells, variously described as leukaemia or leucocythaemia, on 17 February 1912 at the early age of fifty-eight years. Too little is known about the details of his illness to assess its effect on his powers of judgement and decision. There is no available evidence for that fatal year, 1908. Certain symptoms were first mentioned in February 1910 and the course of the illness was sufficiently severe to warrant sick leave in April 1911. He finally decided to resign on 27 January 1912, but remained in office until the day before his death.

Austria had long been convinced that Serbia, flaunting her independence, could have nothing but a provocative and subversive effect on the Slav elements of the Austro-Hungarian Empire. The murder of the Archduke Franz Ferdinand gave a convenient, almost a legitimate excuse for corrective action which would bring Serbia to heel. Right from the start Count Berchtold, the Austrian Foreign Minister, was determined to make demands of such severity that Serbia would find them unacceptable.

He sent an emissary to Berlin on 5 July 1914 with an outline of his plans and his Ambassador, Count Szogyeni, gave the impression in his telegrams that the Kaiser and the Chancellor approved of immediate action against Serbia. Szogyeni was elderly, could no longer follow or transmit the content of conversations with accuracy, and his successor had already been chosen. He may have given Berchtold a distorted impression of Germany's approval, support and intentions.

Tisza, the Prime Minister of Hungary, objected to this policy but the terms of the ultimatum were decided by the Austrian Ministers on 14 and 19 July and confirmed by the Emperor Franz Joseph on 21 July. For tactical reasons the note, with a forty-eight hour time limit, was not sent until 23 July; by that time President Poincaré of France would have left Russia after his State visit. To the surprise of all, not least the Austrians, the Serbs at one time seemed likely to accept nearly all the terms of the note. Their refusal at the last minute has led to debate about secret promises of Russian support. The Austrians were unequivocally guilty of striking the first blow when they declared war against Serbia on 28 July and bombarded Belgrade on the 29th. The Russians were the first nation to mobilize and, by this act on 30 July, removed any hopes that the conflict might be confined to the Balkans. It was in character that Austria did not mobilize until 31 July. France and Germany followed on the 1st August and Great Britain on 5 August.

The Ministers and diplomats of this period were weak in the widest sense. They played with fire but were not strong enough to fight the flames or contain the conflagration which was to involve the whole world. Their judgement and power of decision were weak. They were weak in body and weak in mind and dissolved into tears at moments of crisis.

Charitably Fay tries to make excuses for them:

"Not only in St Petersburg, but everywhere in the Foreign Offices of Europe, responsible officials now began to fall under a terrible physical and mental strain of overwork, worry, and lack of sleep, whose inevitable psychological consequences are too often overlooked in assessing the blame for the events which followed. But if one is to understand how it was that experienced and trained men occasionally failed to grasp fully the sheaves of telegrams put into their hands at frequent intervals, how their proposals were sometimes confused and misunderstood, how they quickly came to be obsessed with pessimistic fears and suspicions, and how in some cases they finally broke down and wept, one must remember the nerve-wracking psychological effects of continued work and loss of sleep, combined with the consciousness of the responsibility for the safety of their country and the fate of millions of lives."[3]

Perhaps an exception may be made for Nicolas Hartwig, the Russian Ambassador in Belgrade, who died of a heart attack on 10 July 1914. Long experience had given him an intimate knowledge of the Serbian secret societies but towards the end of his life he had tried to restrain the demands of Serbian nationalism. He had immense influence in St Petersburg and Belgrade and it is felt that, had he been alive after 25 July, he would have persuaded the Serbian Government to accept the Austrian terms and thus have prevented the first world war. Scientific proof of a true connection is lacking but an association between intense mental stress and coronary heart disease has been described. Like many men of his age group Hartwig was at the mercy of the various pathological processes that contribute to a myocardial infarction or destruction of heart muscle from deprivation of its blood supply due to a blood clot (thrombosis) or narrowing of the coronary arteries. He died, while working for peace, in a noble cause.

No such indulgence can be granted to Sergei Sazonov, the Russian Foreign Minister, who was mentally and physically

unfit for the high office that he held from 1906 to 1916. He has
been described by G. P. Gooch as a "Feminine type: swayed by
feelings: delicate in health: weak in will: changeable: inexperienced: short-sighted".[4] In April 1911 he had what was
described as a septic inflammation of his throat which was
followed by pulmonary complications. Later in the year he had
an operation for lung abscess. When he came to England in
September 1912, his physical appearance caused concern. "He
was really an invalid, and all his elasticity had gone."[4] He found
that he could no longer control events in the Balkans and, in
October 1913, exhausted by a year of crises, he took an extended
vacation. As events in July 1914 moved to a climax Sazonov,
probably unintentionally, made the critical decision on 25 July
1914. When he advised the Czar to sign an order for pre-
mobilization he may have felt that he was playing for time.
Partial commitment might be a warning to Austria-Hungary.
Unfortunately for the world there was only one mobilization
plan in Russia – full mobilization – and, under pressure from
the General Staff, the Czar gave his assent to this step on 30
July. After the war, like so many Statesmen, Sazonov tried to
justify his actions but he has been fairly judged in these terms:

> "Sazonov's state of mind in 1913–14 contributed greatly to
> that over-agitated handling of the Serbo-Austrian crisis which
> precipitated the final catastrophe during the tragic days of
> July 1914. A little more cool-headedness would perhaps have
> sufficed once more to safeguard the cause of peace."[5a]

Great Britain was by no means an innocent and uninformed
spectator of these Ruritanian escapades. Avoidance of involvement in what at first was merely another Balkan war would have
served her own interests and allowed her to bring the contestants
to order. Unfortunately the freedom of manœuvre that might
have been granted to an aloof and impersonal adjudicator was
denied her. Her Foreign Secretary, Sir Edward Grey, was painfully aware that his own freedom of action, and that of his
country, had been compromised. It was unknown to many of
the Cabinet until 1912, and to Parliament and the electorate
until August 1914, that he had in secret virtually committed
Great Britain to act in accord with France.

Nearly sixty years after these events it is inevitable that the visual images of the foreign ministers and diplomats are almost a caricature. They must be a little larger and clearer, and possibly more distorted, than life. Aehrenthal was aggressive and Berchtold was a foppish playboy; Isvolsky was vindictive and Sazonov was erratic. The passage of time enables the student to understand them if not to sympathize with them, for, however they failed, disappointed and in some cases destroyed their countries, they were men of ordinary size overwhelmed by greater events. Like the ham actors of an old melodrama, they no longer arouse tears or even laughter. At various times many in their ranks have been accused of provoking the war; Grey, alone among them, has been accused of failing to stop the outbreak. He is the one pathetic figure that emerges from these events and his presence elevates the diplomatic gyrations to stark tragedy. The public has formed an image of a Cabinet Minister that borders on fantasy; an unemotional, logical and rational being who, fed with facts and situation reports by a devoted staff of robots, behaves like a flesh and blood computer. He is granted the indulgence of an occasional hot-tempered outburst in the House or even of a mistake, provided he makes an immediate confession and apology. With unfounded optimism he is considered impervious to the mental and physical weakness, the indecision, the fears, the passions and the domestic problems that beset ordinary men. The bare details of Grey's life give an impression of the effortless distinction that came, almost as a right in the Victorian and Edwardian era, to a privileged class untrammelled by the sordid and enervating struggle for existence. He was born in 1862, went to Winchester and Balliol, and succeeded his grandfather, the second baronet, in 1882. In the spirit of the age he combined athletic prowess with public service. In 1896 and 1898 he was amateur champion at tennis; the older "royal" tennis rather than the new lawn tennis. From 1885 he was liberal member for Berwick-on-Tweed, from 1892 to 1895 he was Under-Secretary for Foreign Affairs; and, after the landslide of 1905, he became Secretary of State. For eleven years, the longest consecutive tenure, he remained in office until failing health and a government reshuffle lead to his resignation. He had been raised to the peerage in the summer of

1916 and, although not old in years, he easily assumed the dignified and respected role of an elder statesman. He was sent on an abortive mission to the United States of America in 1919 and later worked for the redevelopment of good relations with France and for the admission of Germany to the League of Nations. The last years of his life brought him the dignity of the Chancellorship of Oxford University and the opportunity to follow pursuits such as ornithology which had long absorbed him.

In September 1933, the month that Grey died, David Lloyd George ruthlessly and mercilessly laid bare the superficialities of the newspaper profiles, the laudatory obituaries and the discreet biographies. Grey, he wrote, ". . . failed calamitously in his endeavours to avert the Great War";[6] his ultimatum to Germany, about the integrity of Belgium, was so long delayed that, by the time of its arrival, the Germany Army was beyond the point of no return. Albertini went even further and said that Grey ". . . abstained from all endeavour to control events"[5b] and maintained that he did not call Germany's bluff early enough for fear of Cabinet and Parliamentary disapproval. Lloyd George attributes Grey's inaction and failure to his social background. As a child of privilege he had gained high office without struggle or effort; as Foreign Secretary he was free from the bitter but salutary controversy of parliamentary life. He had "stepped into generalship without ever doing any soldiering. . ."[6] These strictures have merit but Grey's performance in 1914 was also conditioned and dominated by three other factors; his intellectual limitations, the tragedy of his domestic life and the creeping horror of blindness.

Grey's early performance at Winchester showed academic promise but, failing to gain what he regarded as rightful promotion, he lost interest in his studies. He luxuriated at Oxford in a life of "pure pleasure" and after attaining a second-class in Classical Moderations, he was sent down from Balliol for idleness. On his return he gained third-class honours in law. The superior mind can be bored by the workaday curriculum but one is left with the impression that a second- or third-class degree was a reasonable measure of his ability. Distinguished old boys, when asked to speak at a prize day or similar ceremony, emphasize their own lack of success in the class-room. However, Grey must be the only Chancellor who was sent down from his University for scholastic failure.

Cleverness is mistrusted in British public life but, in a crisis, a Minister must be more than a mouthpiece or a puppet of his faceless advisers. Grey failed to diagnose and treat the symptoms of the European disease in July 1914 and one authority has no hesitation in apportioning responsibility:

> "A perusal of the documents shows that up to 23 July there is one explanation pure and simple; namely Grey's utter failure on the one hand to understand what was going on, what was told him and what was reported from the various Embassies, and on the other to grasp that Austrian aggression against Serbia would bring in first Russia and then Germany and France."[5c]

Handicapped by an ignorance of foreign languages and foreign countries his methods of work were not conducive to cool thought, lucid analysis, or prudent foresight and decision. His own account suggests a reluctance, almost an inability, to find the time to reflect upon, and to solve, the burning problem of the day:

> "Work, incessant, peremptory work, relieves nervous strain; it allows no vacant hours in which anxiety can prey upon an unoccupied mind; it wearies, but by that very weariness helps to ensure sleep sufficient to restore; unless or until it causes exhaustion, it stimulates."[7a]

There has been no appreciation, and certainly no exploration, of the influence of private and domestic circumstances on the capacity and performance of public men. In any walk of life there can be but few men, be they humble or famous, who are not afflicted by some adverse factor that casts a shadow on their lives. The blow that struck Grey in the early days of February 1906 was shattering in its suddenness and unexpectedness. His wife, who was always in his thoughts, a constant companion and adviser in his public as well as his private life, was killed in a carriage accident. His immediate thought was of resignation but the Prime Minister, Sir Henry Campbell-Bannerman, asked him to remain in office.

At first, he admitted, the effect on his work must have been great though he tended to discount any undue influence:

> "The mechanism of the brain began to digest work as that of the body digests food. . . . It does not, however, appear, nor do I remember, that any important decision was taken or required in the interval before I returned to London."[7b]

The fatal decision had been taken just before his wife's death. In talks with Paul Cambon, the French Ambassador in London, on 10 and 11 January 1906 Grey agreed to continue the unofficial exchanges between the Admiralty and War Office on one side and the French Naval and Military Attachés on the other, about the steps to be taken if their two countries were allied in war. On 20 February 1906, very soon after his wife's death, Grey wrote in a private memorandum his conviction that Britain would join France if the latter was involved in a European conflict.

When Sazonov visited England in September 1912, Grey confirmed the existence of an Anglo-French military and naval agreement but he did not inform the bulk of his own Cabinet until November. On 22 November 1912 Grey was required by the Cabinet to exchange letters with Paul Cambon, the French Ambassador, and to emphasize that the military conversations did not commit either England or France and did not restrict their individual freedom of choice about mutual assistance. However the letters went on to state that, in the event of a threatened attack, both countries could discuss common measures, including General Staff plans, to prevent aggression and preserve peace. The equivocation was a noose round Grey's neck and in July 1914 he could neither face Cabinet, Parliament or country because the military staffs had turned the talks into plans for immediate action; nor could he counter the importunate demands of Paul Cambon and his sneering doubts of the British interpretation of the word "honour".

Work was a necessary anodyne but some other occupation would have had less disastrous effects. Grey wrote how the past had become more real than the present and that "thought was arrested and thought crippled".[7b] In June 1906 Lord Rosebery dined with Grey and stated:

"He lives entirely in the past, describes himself as 'waiting'. Waiting for the door that has closed behind her to open for him, hoping it may be soon. His only ease is to immerse himself in the past. His present life is purely mechanical."[8]

For a man who had no interest in the future he was dangerously employed and there is a pathetic truth in his words: "Men cling to a job not so much for ambition or love of power, but for occupation".[7c] His only solace was long, solitary country walks and he would escape from his duties like a boy leaving school. It was from one of these week-ends that he was recalled on 26 July 1914, when officials at the Foreign Office became seriously alarmed at the deterioration in the European situation.

For some years before the outbreak of war Grey was faced by another insurmountable obstacle and unsupportable burden. Always a keen student of nature he had noticed as early as 1910 that he could no longer see "The Wagoner", a small star in the Great Bear constellation. Three years later he found difficulty for the first time in hitting a ball at squash rackets and, though he was not a heavy smoker, an oculist considered that tobacco was affecting the nerves of the eye. In the early summer of 1914 a second oculist found that Grey had advanced degeneration of the choroid and retina in each eye which was responsible for limitation of vision and restriction and impairment in his fields of vision. No treatment was possible and the outlook was gloomy. It is likely that the condition was familial for nothing but an unbelievable coincidence could otherwise account for the deaths of his two brothers; George was killed by a lion in 1911 and Charles was killed by a buffalo in 1928. Impaired vision must surely have been the common factor and a lethal handicap for a big game hunter.

Grey maintained that failing sight did not affect his work until after he left office in 1916 and that he was able to read with moderate ease and speed for another two years. In the summer of 1918 he ceased to be able to read although the prescription of special spectacles a few months later allowed him to read and write again slowly but with effort. He may not have been the best judge of his own efforts at comprehension. A child deliberately spells the individual letters and mouths the words that are formed. The science of speed reading has shown that adults, as a result of experience and integration, can anticipate the content of words and sentences without undergoing this laborious process. Grey was compelled to read an inordinate number of State papers, documents and telegrams which in the best possible conditions might have been accomplished with considerable effort. Mental fatigue, emotional tension and mounting pressure of work could have led to an unappreciated failure in analysis and synthesis of letters and words. No doubt this also contributed to "Grey's utter failure on the one hand to understand what was going on, and what was reported from the various Embassies . . ." It may also explain a significant omission in his speech to the House of Commons on 3 August 1914 for which he has been accused of deceit and dishonesty. The German threat to Belgian neutrality meant that Britain could now honour by deed their secret obligations to France. In giving an account of his stewardship over the previous eight years, Grey had to mention his correspondence with Cambon in November 1912 but omitted the vital words that indicated a virtual commitment to a military alliance by their qualification of the contingency measures:

> "If these measures involved action, the plans of the General
> Staffs would at once be taken into consideration, and the
> Governments would then decide what effect should be given
> to them."[5d]

Such behaviour by a Foreign Secretary would heighten the suspicions and give weight to the accusations of that *Times* correspondent who had stigmatized the diplomats for playing with men's lives. Yet the condition of Grey's eyesight and the painful stress of the moment allows a more charitable explanation. He may have omitted those words because he could not see clearly enough to read them.

Grey is now mainly remembered for the haunting words that he uttered on the eve of the First World War; "The lamps are going out all over Europe . . ." Words that are made more poignant by the knowledge of his failing vision. As the shadows lengthened his miseries were increased by the abdominal pain of peptic ulceration while a brief return to public life was marred by misunderstanding. Sent on a special mission to the United States of America in 1919 he was not granted an audience by the paralysed President Wilson who, not without reason, took exception to a member of Grey's entourage. His last years were dogged by further misfortune. Fallodon, his country house, had been burned down in 1917 and his favourite cottage on the Itchen suffered a similar fate in 1923. His second wife died in 1928 but one final mercy was vouchsafed him. He died on 7 September 1933 in the same week that the War Memoirs of David Lloyd George appeared. Thus he was spared the scarifying criticisms of his former colleague.

References

1. *The Times,* 26 November 1912 (Quoted – *Makers of War,* p. 90).
2. Lord Hardinge. *Old Diplomacy.* Murray.
3. S. B. Fay. *The Origins of the World War,* vol. II, p. 288. Collier–MacMillan.
4. G. P. Gooch. *Before the War: Studies in Diplomacy,* vol. II, pp. 290, 321. Longmans Green.
5a. L. Albertini. *The Origins of the War of 1914,* vol. I, p. 550. Oxford University Press.
5b. Vol. II, p. 643. Oxford University Press.
5c. Vol. II, p. 215. Oxford University Press.
5d. Vol. I, p. 405. Oxford University Press.
6. David Lloyd George. *War Memoirs,* vol. I, p. 93. Nicholson & Watson.
7a. Viscount Grey. *Twenty-five Years, 1892–1916,* vol. II, p. 11. Hodder & Stoughton.
7b. Vol. I, p. 100. Hodder & Stoughton.
7c. Vol. II, p. 260. Hodder & Stoughton.
8. Robert Rhodes James. *Rosebery,* p. 461. Weidenfeld & Nicolson.

CHAPTER 3

Admirals and Generals, 1914-18: no miracle at the Marne

"Peace officers are not always war officers!"[1a]
(Fisher to Jellicoe – 7 February 1915)

Admiral Sir Francis Bridgeman, the First Sea Lord, retired for reasons of health on 2 December 1912. An enterprising newspaper reporter found that he was hunting three days a week and it was rumoured that Mr Winston Churchill, the first Lord of the Admiralty, had used illness as an excuse to dispense with Bridgeman's services. The matter was debated in the House of Commons and, with doubtful propriety, Churchill read out the contents of private letters from Bridgeman which indeed indicated the latter's anxiety about his health. In the subsequent exchanges Churchill defended the peremptory dismissal of Bridgeman even though the alleged medical incapacity was literally debatable: "Sir, it is essential that the First Sea Lord should be thoroughly fit and capable". Churchill went on to say:

> "He (the First Sea Lord) must have good health and strength, not only sufficient to bear the daily strain, but to bear any extra or sudden strain or stress which circumstances may throw upon him."
> ". . . the matter is one which affects the lives and honour of thousands of officers and seamen afloat, and that directly affects the safety of the State."[2]

If Churchill was genuinely precoccupied with the safety of the Fleet and the State he should not have confined his strictures to the health of the First Sea Lord. The health of the political master, the First Lord of the Admiralty, is equally important and that of his own Uncle, Lord Tweedmouth, had been grossly impaired when he had held office a few years before. Tweedmouth went to the Admiralty in 1905 and only the onset of cerebral degeneration can explain his omission to notify his substantial holding of shares in Meux and Co. when that brewery secured the beer contract for the Royal Navy. Early in 1908 the Kaiser wrote to Tweedmouth who, with unbelievable lack of discretion and judgement, gave him details of the Navy Estimates before they had been presented to Parliament. Worse still he gossiped about this correspondence and the Kaiser's letter fell into the hands of one of Tweedmouth's lady friends. In April 1908, though displaced at the Admiralty by McKenna, he became Lord President of the Council. Soon his mental degeneration was painfully made public: his grasp failed in the Lords while paying a valedictory tribute to Campbell-Bannerman. Next month he wrote to Lord Knollys, Private Secretary to Edward VII, and offered the services of a number of young nieces who would be delighted to entertain the King. The progress of cerebral dementia, whatever the cause, could not be stilled and Tweedmouth died in September 1909 at the age of sixty.

Churchill did not practise what he preached. When Prince Louis of Battenburg, who had replaced Bridgeman, was hounded from office in November 1914 because of his German ancestry, Churchill turned to an officer who had long retired. Admiral Fisher was seventy-three years old and Churchill has written how the frenetic activity which began early in the morning could not be sustained.

> "As the afternoon approached, the formidable energy of the morning gradually declined, and with the shades of night the old Admiral's giant strength was often visibly exhausted".[3]

Fatigue and incapacity, rather than misunderstanding and personal antipathy, may have led to Fisher's differences with Churchill over the Dardanelles campaign in 1915, and to his resignation which was disastrous for them both. Fisher might have dealt with the demands of peace but he could not meet the requirements of war and the "extra or sudden strain or stress" which Churchill had discussed in 1912. One cannot cavil with Churchill's diagnosis of Fisher at the time of his resignation:

"I for my part have always adopted the hypothesis of a nervous breakdown . . . hysteria, not conspiracy, is the true explanation of his action".[4]

Admiral Sir Henry Jackson who succeeded Fisher, though younger, was not an ideal choice. He had not served at sea since 1910 because of doubts about his health. Physical impairment made him irascible and unapproachable and anxiety and over-work added to his gloom and depression. It was unfortunate that Admiral Jellicoe who replaced him in November 1916 was also worn out by twenty-seven months arduous service at sea with the Grand Fleet; a period which included a major fleet action at Jutland and several minor actions. From the outbreak of war Jellicoe had worried excessively over his responsibilities which admittedly were vast and daunting. He was concerned about the inadequacy of certain aspects of training and equip-ment in the Fleet and of shortcomings among his Admirals. His second-in-command, Vice-Admiral Burney, was often in poor health and "rheumatism" resulted in depression, pessimism and caution. Jellicoe also had to relieve Admiral Warrender (2nd Battle Squadron) because of doubts about his physical fitness; Admiral Bayly (1st Battle Squadron) worried him con-tinually because of his "curious fits of nerves".

Jellicoe had an operation for haemorrhoids in February 1915 and, towards the end of that year, dental treatment for pyor-rhoea and neuralgia. Focal sepsis was thought to account for certain rheumatic symptoms and a vaccine was prepared. He complained of the strain under which he was work-ing in September 1915 and again, just before the battle of Jutland, in May 1916. He had to be careful with his diet and one naval historian has suggested the possibility of a peptic ulcer.

Preoccupation with the health of their own Admirals did not lead Jellicoe and Beatty, who led the Battle Cruiser squadron, to neglect the health of their opponents. Replying to an inquiry from Beatty, about the background of the German Admirals, Jellicoe gave a clinical opinion of Admiral Hugo von Pohl, the commander of the High Seas Fleet, whom he had met before the war:

> "He does not look very healthy, always very white and trans-parent-looking, but I think he is all right physically."[1b]

Jellicoe was wrong because von Pohl had been sick for some time which may account for his ineffectual leadership. He resigned in January 1916, after a year in command, and died in February 1916 from the effects of an intestinal neoplasm. The next in line for command, Admiral Ritter von Lans, could not be promoted as he was on the verge of a nervous breakdown and the appointment was eventually given to Admiral Scheer.

By the end of July 1914 the European heads of State and their officials had done their best or worst and there was no escape from general mobilization. If this process was delayed a country might find itself defenceless and once started it could not be stopped. Boats, trains and horse transport disgorged their human cargoes and the generals were left to fight the war that had been bequeathed to them by their political masters. These generals cannot really be blamed for failing to solve the strate-gical and tactical problems of the first great or world war. It is not reasonable to expect foresight, imagination or creative genius from elderly men, softened by years of peacetime duties, whose military experience was largely confined to small colonial wars.

The Germans mounted a major attack on their right wing through Belgium. The French, wildly optimistic about their philosophy of the offensive, attacked the German centre. On 17 August 1914 while the British Expeditionary Force concentrated in France, Sir James Grierson, commander designate of II Corps, died from a heart attack. This event, trivial in itself, was to have serious consequences. It deprived the BEF of an officer who had a unique knowledge of the French and German Armies. Moreover his replacement, Sir Horace Smith-Dorrien, was heartily disliked by Sir John French, the C-in-C of the BEF.

On 23 August 1914 the BEF clashed with the Germans at Mons, and, apparently unsupported by the French on either flank, was forced to withdraw. A second trivial episode on 24

August also had important repercussions. Sir Douglas Haig, the commander of I Corps, had an internal disorder and was persuaded to seek medical advice. He was given "something designed for elephants, for the result was immediate and volcanic."[5] Next day he was still shaken and had lost his usual icy self control. Late in the afternoon he was uncharacteristically disturbed by a German attack at Landrecies and ordered the immediate withdrawal of I Corps. He sent an urgent message to GHQ on the receipt of which the Chief of Staff, Sir Archibald Murray, fainted. In his turn Sir John French was affected by the alarm and despondency and feared for the safety of the BEF. While Haig, in a weakened state, became apprehensive, Smith-Dorrien stood firm. He appreciated that II Corps was too exhausted to retreat any further and fought a successful rearguard action at Le Cateau. This only served to increase French's wrath and he eventually secured Smith-Dorrien's dismissal in 1915. Sir William Robertson, a former ranker of humble origin, was deputed to break the news which he did with the words "'Orace, you're for 'ome".

By that time French was a sick man. He had a severe heart attack in November 1914 and Haig, after seeing French on 18 December 1915, wrote in his diary, "He did not look very well and seemed short of breath at times."[6] Haig took over from French and subsequently recorded an admission from French that in 1915 "he was then in bad health and not fit to carry out the terrific duties which at that time rested upon him."

As the BEF and the French forces, on the left of the allied line, fell back it began to be realized that they were facing the main German attack. The 1st Army on the German right wing was commanded by the aggressive and impetuous von Kluck who was held in sufficient regard by the BEF to earn himself the nickname of "Old one o'clock". Although he was aged sixty-eight at the time he was tireless and soon outpaced the 2nd Army on his left which was commanded by the more sedate von Bulow. Von Kluck first disobeyed an order to follow behind von Bulow and later, responding violently to French pressure on his right, he allowed a gap to appear between the 1st and 2nd Armies. From 6 September onwards the French 5th and 6th Armies and the

BEF moved forward and on 9 September the Germans moved
back towards and over the Marne.

The credit for victory at the Marne has been given to Joffre,
the French C-in-C, to Gallieni who transported the French IV
Corps in the Paris taxi-cabs, to General Franchet d'Esperey and
to Sir John French. Some have given credit to more remote
agencies and have talked of the miracle of the Marne. There
was nothing mysterious or supernatural in the German defeat
though von Kluck's impetuosity may have made the German
right wing vulnerable. The German withdrawal on 9 September
was simply due to the fact that General von Moltke, the Chief
of the General Staff of the German Army, lost his nerve.

Helmuth von Moltke was aged sixty-six in 1914 and had been
under medical care in Karlsbad since 1911. He had enlargement
of the heart and impairment of kidney function and was warned
by his physician in 1913 that his condition was serious. He
disagreed with this opinion which implied that he was unfit to
be Chief of Staff and, when he returned to Karlsbad early in
1914, consulted another physician. He had neither the character
nor the desire to be Chief of Staff and only took the post in 1906
at the Kaiser's bidding. He had a quiet, reflective and sensitive
temperament and may well have earned the nickname of
"gloomy Julius". He inherited the plan for the attack in the
west from his formidable predecessor, von Schlieffen, but lacked
the courage and gambling instinct that were necessary for
success. Before the campaign he altered the plan and failed to
make the right wing really strong. During the course of the battle
he sent more forces from this wing to fight on the Eastern Front
against the Russians. In his debilitated and anxious state he
remained at too great a distance from the front and completely
lost control of the German Armies. Finally he delegated to a
Staff Officer, Colonel Hentsch, the task of deciding between
8 and 9 September whether the Germans should withdraw.

No account of the battle of the Marne is complete without an
appraisal of the part played by Hentsch, a minor figure who
mingles with the great in the history books. Some have blamed
him for the withdrawal of the German Armies over the Marne
in September 1914; others say that he was made a scapegoat. He
only received verbal instructions on 8 September 1914 but

insisted later that these gave him the authority to visit the
Armies and co-ordinate any withdrawal. Von Bulow of 2nd
Army, whom he held in great respect, had independently
decided to withdraw. Hentsch said that his only choice then
was to ensure that von Kluck conformed and that the Chief of
Staff of 1st Army had already made the decision. A court of
inquiry in 1917 concluded that he had not exceeded his instructions, but his critics state that a more determined officer would
not have agreed so readily to the withdrawal of the two Armies.
They argue that 1st Army was in a favourable position and, on
receipt of this news, Hentsch should have reversed his decision.
It is unfortunate that General von Moltke, physically and
mentally debilitated as he was, should have selected an officer
for this vital task who was in a similar state due to cholelithiasis
(gall stones). Hentsch had an attack of jaundice on 5 September
1914, three days before his mission, and died before the end of
the war after a perforation of the gall bladder.

Von Moltke was not the only invalid in the German Army.
Von Bulow had a toxic goitre (enlargement and over-secretion of
the thyroid gland) and arteriosclerosis while von Lauenstein, his
Chief of Staff, who also had a history of toxic goitre, died in
1917 of aortitis and cardiac failure. At the vital conference at
2nd Army Headquarters on 8 September he did much to persuade von Bulow, who admittedly needed little persuasion, to
retire. Between 7 and 8 September von Hausen, the commander
of the 3rd Army was severely affected by gastroenteritis.

Invalidism does not necessarily militate against sound
generalship. Intellectual ability and powers of good judgement
and decision are not invariably lessened by physical or mental
disability. This is exemplified by General Gallieni who, after a
distinguished career, had reached the retiring age of sixty-five in
April 1914. On the outbreak of war he was made military
governor of Paris and was earmarked as Joffre's successor. Later
in August the French 6th Army came under his control and,
whatever were Joffre's intentions, Gallieni did much to persuade
him to start the general advance on 6 September.

All through this period Gallieni was in acute discomfort from
a prostatic disorder. Lloyd George met him just after the battle
of the Marne and remarked on his "sallow, shrunken and

haunted" appearance and added that "death seemed to be chasing the particles of his life out of his veins".[7] Gallieni was asked to join the French Cabinet as Minister of War in April 1915 but resigned from ill-health in March 1916. After a second operation on his prostate he died on 27 May 1916.

If there was no actual miracle at the battle of the Marne, General Gallieni's performance in the circumstances verged on the miraculous.

On 14 September 1914 the Kaiser removed von Moltke from his command on grounds of ill-health but the official announcement was not made until 3 November. Von Moltke and Haig, though divided on the battlefield, were curiously united by their alleged mode of death. Dr Hermann of Karlsbad could have made no mistake about the cardiac enlargement and albuminuria that he found in von Moltke. His reasons for the cause of these disorders rest presumably on contemporary aetiological concepts. He insisted, long after von Moltke's death at a memorial service in 1916, that his patient had endocarditis and myocarditis due to a therapeutic massaging of inflamed tonsils in 1910 which caused septicaemia.

Haig was somewhat preoccupied with his health. A tendency to bronchitis and asthma led him wisely, and in anticipation of later discovery, to give up smoking. He was a food faddist and at various times devoted himself to sour milk, wholemeal bread, sanatogen and oranges. Like von Moltke he was told that dental sepsis had affected his heart muscle. Four days before he died in 1927 he was hunting; his horse threw up his head, struck Haig in the mouth and loosened his front teeth. Death was attributed to heart failure as a result of septicaemia from the loosened teeth. Fashions change in medicine as in other walks of life. Developments in the last forty years would persuade most physicians today that both von Moltke and Haig died of heart failure resulting from coronary artery disease rather than from focal sepsis.

On other occasions and in other theatres the exigencies of war ruthlessly exposed both the physical and the military deficiencies of the commanders. The addition of another environmental hazard, such as the 120° F. temperature of Mesopotamia, increased the strain. General Barrett took the 6th Division there in November 1914 and resigned from ill-health in April 1915. He was replaced by General Townshend who was compelled to have medical and surgical treatment in India between June and August of the same year. General Sir John Nixon, the Corps Commander, had to limit his activities after September 1915 and illness compelled him to resign in January 1916. On 15 January 1916, General Aylmer, then commanding the Tigris Corps, advised that General Townshend, who was besieged in Kut, should break out and march towards his advancing forces. On 17 January, Nixon curtly dismissed any suggestion of evacuation and condemned Townshend's forces to the ignominy of surrender and to the brutal horrors of imprisonment. On the next day, 18 January, Nixon was evacuated because of illness. His successors fared no better for General Lake also battled with sickness until August 1916, and although his replacement, General Maude, brought the campaign to a successful close, the latter died of cholera in the hour of victory.

Logistic failures, for which Nixon amongst others was blamed, caused our wounded to undergo appalling hardship. General Sir Beauchamp Duff, the Commander in Chief, India, under whom the force was administered, was allotted a share of the responsibility. During his stay in India in 1915 Townshend had noticed that Duff was exhausted. Closely guarded and protected by his staff his slow decline was not immediately realized even by the Viceroy of India. He died in June 1918, a few months after Maude's final victory.

The same dismal story can be told about the leaders at Gallipoli. The preliminary bombardment of the Narrows had been begun early in 1915 by the Royal Navy under the command of Admiral Carden, then aged fifty-seven years. This officer was not the first choice, but had been taken from the post of superintendent of Malta dockyard, and had already spent a trying winter at sea. Under the increasing strain of the naval operations, and pressure from the Admiralty, certain abdominal symptoms grew worse and he was unable to eat a normal diet or sleep at night. On 15 March 1915 he resigned on medical advice. Nor were some of the subsequent Army selections any more fortunate. Lieut-General Stopford was sixty-one years old when he arrived for what was to be a brief stay in July 1915. Too weak to lift his own dispatch case, a knee injury hindered his mobility. General Egerton (52nd Division), described as "highly strung and apt to be excitable under stress",[8] duly collapsed and was evacuated. General Hammersley (11th Division) had a thrombosis in the leg and left in August. The optimistic, and aggressive General Hunter-Weston (29th Division), labelled with diagnoses of "enteric", "dysentery" and "sunstroke", went away in July; he turned up on the Western Front a year later as a Corps Commander, where his ebullience once again led to heavy casualties. Illness had an influence on the most critical decision of all. Late in 1915, General Monro was sent out by the War Office to size up the situation and to advise on future operations. He asked the three Corps Commanders in turn their views on evacuation. As General Byng said "yes", and General Birdwood said "no" the casting vote was left to General Davies (VIII Corps). He was ill in bed and, to make considered judgement more difficult, was woken by a staff officer in the middle of the night. If he favoured evacuation he should give an oral answer; if he opposed evacuation he was to give his reasons in writing. In fact he gave an answer in writing; he agreed to evacuation.

It is easy enough to blame elderly and ailing generals for the opportunities that were lost at Gallipoli and even General Hamilton wrote in his diary on 12 August 1915, that Lord Kitchener, the Secretary of State for War "is not capable of understanding how he has cut his own throat, the men's throats and mine, by not sending young and up-to-date generals."[9] Kitchener had to send the generals that were available and, if one examines conditions in the German Army, it is by no means certain that younger generals would have done any better.

History has been called the story of great men. It is true that they gain a place in the history books when their enterprises are successful despite the fact that they may have been advised, helped or even influenced by their juniors. They can argue that they bear the sole responsibility for victory or disaster as reflected on the one hand by honours and fame and on the other by obscurity or even disgrace. It is usually some tragedy or disaster that shines a light on the usually obscure lives of minor figures who, in times of triumph, remain in the shadows while their masters take the credit.

The role of Colonel Hentsch at the battle of the Marne has already been examined. Illness may have contributed to the malign influence of two other colonels.

The suicide of an Austrian Staff Officer in 1913 not only shows that Russian agents have long been adept at blackmailing homosexuals but that officers of middle rank may exert a profound influence on national and international affairs. Colonel Alfred Redl, Chief of the General Staff of VIII Corps, shot himself in the early hours of 25 May 1913 at the Hotel Klomser, Vienna. Early reports gave the conventional excuse of overwork but it was later disclosed that Redl had given secret information to a foreign power.

Redl was born in 1864 and had risen, by diligence and ability, through Cadet School, Regimental duty, and the Staff College to a position in the Intelligence Bureau where he served almost continuously from 1900 to 1911. Early in this period his debts, incurred through dissipation, came to the knowledge of Batjuschin, a Russian intelligence officer, who forced him to supply information. Not to be outdone Redl came to terms with Batjuschin and, by the mutual betrayal of their agents, they each added to their own reputation.

Redl lived a double life for thirteen years until, desperate for money, he was forced to collect a package from the General Post Office in Vienna. He did not realize that the forwarding address was watched by counter-intelligence agents and, when he was traced, his horror was only matched by that of the Austrian authorities.

A post-mortem examination took place on the day of his death and the findings were carefully recorded. There was thickening of the meninges, myocardial enlargement, and chronic inflammation of the aorta. Adenomatous tissue was found in the thyroid gland and a "new growth" in the right suprarenal gland. Hydatid cysts were present in the liver. The gall bladder was inflamed and contained gall stones. The seminal vesicles were chronically inflamed and there was a right inguinal hernia.

It was concluded that the cumulative effect of these pathological changes might have had an adverse influence on his conduct for many years. The postmortem report clearly states that there was thickening of the meninges. One can only speculate about the involvement of the cerebral cortex but it is reasonable to assume that he may have been affected by loss of judgement and intellectual deterioration which led him into further acts of treachery and debauchery. The harm that Redl caused may have been exaggerated for much of it could have been remedied by August 1914. It is difficult to assess to what extent the Russian victories over the Austrians in 1914–15 can be attributed to Redl's treachery.

Redl betrayed his country. Hentsch, conscientious and well-meaning, may have failed to save his country. Colonel d'Alenson, out of ardent patriotism and ambition, almost ruined his country. At the end of 1916 General Nivelle convinced the English and French war leaders that, with his new methods, he could avoid a repetition of the slaughter that had occurred on the Somme and at Verdun. Many soldiers criticized his plans but, by his persuasive personality and linguistic skills, he impressed the allied politicians. The French offensive began on 16 April 1917 and, during the first ten days, 34,000 men were killed, 90,000 were wounded, and 20,000 were posted as missing. The easy success that had been promised became a disaster, the morale of the French Army was undermined, and mutiny broke out in a number of units.

Before the attack it was realized that General Nivelle and other officers at French GQG were dominated by Colonel d'Alenson, the Chief of Staff. This officer was dying of tuberculosis and Sir Edward Spears provides a vivid clinical picture of his physical and psychological state. Spears describes the tall frame, thin face and sunken eyes and suggests that d'Alenson was perhaps unconsciously determined to live in history. He feels that d'Alenson, though responsible for the disaster, bears little guilt because he genuinely believed that he would save France. d'Alenson was obsessively preoccupied with the offensive and relentlessly overcame the criticisms of the soldiers and the uncertainties of the politicians. He did not long survive the failure of his plan for he died a few weeks later "a Napoleon devoid of genius".[10]

Incompetence, caused by illness, may explain and even excuse national disasters.

Caporetto is a place name that will haunt the Italians for years to come. As a consequence of the retreat the honour and courage of the Italian soldier has long been vilified and it was not until after the Second World War that the editor of *Military Operations* was able to write:

"The nature of the retirement of the Italian Second Army after the first collapse near Caporetto has been to a large extent misunderstood".[11]

Italian intelligence predicted that the German and Austro-Hungarian offensive would start in the last week of October 1917. The attack began on 24 October and, on the first day, the German 14th Army shattered the Italian IV Corps. The whole Italian defence system crumbled and, in a headlong retreat, the Italians had to go as far back as the river Piave before they stood and fought in the first week of November.

There is no doubt that panic started in the IV Corps of II Army as a result of a gas attack, and may partly be explained by the fact that the Italian gas mask gave little or no protection. The administrative services in the rear areas failed and local withdrawals gave all the signs of a general retreat. Depots, stores and dumps were set on fire and, worse still, road and mountain paths were blocked by troops and civilians who were struggling to get away. The supply services of II Army ceased to function and hungry soldiers left their units to find food. The Italian High Command and Staff, and in particular General Luigi Capello of II Army, bear a heavy responsibility for the chaos.

Capello defied his C-in-C's directive to fight a defensive battle and planned an offensive-defensive of his own. On 10 October General Cadorna, the C-in-C, had ordered Capello to withdraw XXVII Corps to the west bank of the river Isonzo. This move was not carried out and more than half the infantry and much of the artillery were trapped by the Germans on the east bank. How much Capello's state of health excuses his actions cannot be determined. He was taken ill on 4 October and retired to Padua on 20 October. On the eve of the German attack he returned to his Headquarters although he still had a severe fever. The disasters of 24 October could not have improved his condition and, on the 25th, he dictated the orders for withdrawal before he retired sick once more. Confusion became worse confounded when his successor informed Cadorna later in the day that withdrawal was not immediately necessary.

Erich Ludendorff was the very model of a modern German general. His photographs, which show an arrogant face, protuberant eyes, a bristled moustache, short cropped hair, bulging neck and the inevitable eyeglass, are almost caricatures. He is John Buchan's von Stumm, a Raemaeker cartoon, come to life.

Ludendorff entered the Prussian Army, at the age of eighteen, in 1883 and joined the General Staff in 1894. After distinguished service in the operations and mobilization sections, where he planned the attack on France and Belgium, he might have expected a more senior appointment, in August 1914, than that of Quartermaster-General of II Army. Not to be outdone he seized the opportunity, offered by detached service, and was largely responsible for the capture of the Liege forts. Further recognition came in the form of a high decoration and, better still, the appointment as Chief of Staff of VIII Army on the Eastern Front. General von Hindenburg was brought out of retirement at the age of sixty-six, and made Commander in Chief, almost as an afterthought, and the two officers moved hastily eastwards to replace two generals who had failed.

Two Russian Armies were by now threatening the eastern frontiers of Germany but, in a classic campaign between 26 and 31 August 1914 these were routed at Tannenberg. Ludendorff has received more than his fair share of credit for the victory. Colonel Max Hoffman, of the VIII Army Staff, had anticipated Ludendorff's orders to defeat Samsonov's Army in the south, and then, by a rapid transfer of forces, attack Rennenkampf's Army in the north. Hoffman knew that Rennenkampf would never come to Samsonov's aid for he had heard they had brawled on Mukden railway station during the Russo-Japanese War. He said later that "if the battle of Waterloo was won on the playing fields of Eton, the battle of Tannenberg was lost on a railway platform at Mukden."[12a] Samsonov was beyond any aid. A victim of asthma, and on sick leave when the Russian Army mobilized, he did not reach the front until 12 August. Deserted by his staff in the hour of defeat, he committed suicide.

Hindenburg has been incorrectly regarded as a mere figure-head, for only he could control the situation when Ludendorff was paralysed by anxiety and panic. Such an incident occurred on 26 August when an air patrol reported that Rennenkampf's forces were moving south towards Samsonov. These emotional outbursts were a disturbing characteristic of Ludendorff's personality and disorganized the German High Command. Hoffman wrote on 21 October 1914: "Ludendorff has become frightfully nervous, and the chief burden lies on me"[13a]; and again on 10 October 1915: "Ludendorff is getting nervy and loses his temper unnecessarily".[13b] When the British attacked at Arras on 9 April 1917, Ludendorff was "pale with apprehension", "a prey to nervous anxiety",[12b] and Hindenburg, the older man, reassured him yet again.

What Winston Churchill called the HL combination left the Eastern Front in 1916 and took control of the entire German war machine on 29 August. Early in 1918 Ludendorff decided that Germany must seek victory by one last, bold stroke and that the British should be attacked on the Western Front. Operation Michael began, after a surprisingly short bombardment, at 9.40 a.m. on 21 March 1918. The German infantry, using new tactics, slipped through the British defences in the morning mist, and made startling progress. On 23 March, Ludendorff, instead of exploiting the one major breach, chose three new lines of advance, and altered his plans once more on 25 March. The Michael offensive ground to a halt but with neurotic intensity Ludendorff launched Operation Georgette on 9 April and further offensives on 27 May, 9 June and 15 July.

All were doomed to failure and Ludendorff, at the end of his tether, quarrelled in public with Hindenburg. This was the high tide of the German offensive and from then on, as the Allies recovered and cautiously advanced, Ludendorff's powers deteriorated. Indecisive, anxious, obsessed by trivial details, bedevilling the Staffs with orders and counter-orders, he could control neither his nerves nor his Armies. He described the Allied attack on 8 August 1918 as "the black day of the German Army in the history of this War" and offered his resignation. On 29 September, Hindenburg and Ludendorff advised, perhaps prematurely, that an Armistice should be sought. The loss of morale which resulted from this hint of defeat prevented further effective resistance and reasonable peace terms. Ludendorff, who had been under psychiatric care, was in a state of collapse. One account mentions the possibility of a stroke, another suggests "hysterical paralysis". His resignation was finally submitted and accepted on 26 October 1918.

After the war his actions were so bizarre that it was thought that his reason was affected. He was associated with the right-wing movements of Kapp and Hitler and was both anti-Semitic and anti-Catholic. He built altars to Thor and Odin in his garden. In 1925 he stood as a National Socialist Candidate and was bottom in the poll for President.

It was not until after the Second World War that the possible reasons for Ludendorff's strange behaviour were disclosed. In November 1926 he consulted the celebrated surgeon, Ferdinand Sauerbruch, who noticed a swelling in the neck. The effects of a toxic goitre go far to explain his restless energy, nervous tension, sudden fears and physical exhaustion, which had been apparent since 1914. Ludendorff may have been correct when he said, after a thyroidectomy, that, if the operation had been performed earlier, Germany would have won the first War.

Indeed it is fortunate that General George Marshall, who became the American Chief of Staff in 1939, had a toxic goitre removed before his country was at war. As far back as 1913 Marshall noticed feelings of tightness and tension and an inability to relax. Between the wars a nervous tic, which had started in France in 1917–18, grew worse. Finally irregularity of his pulse was attributed to a toxic goitre which was removed in December 1936.

Ludendorff himself summed up the problem of sickness in senior officers, and provided a suitable epitaph, with these sentences: "A general has much to bear and needs strong nerves"; ". . . the Commander of an Army is faced with decisions daily and hourly. He is continually responsible for the welfare of many hundred-thousands of persons, even of nations".[14]

References

1a. *The Jellicoe Papers*. Ed. A. Temple Patterson, vol. I, p. 142. Navy Records Society.
1b. Vol. I, p. 157.
2.   Official Report. *Fifth Series Parliamentary Debates, Commons 1912*, vol. XLV, 20 Dec. 1912. 1875.
3.   Winston Churchill (1939 and 1959). *Great Contemporaries*. Thorton Butterworth.
4.   Winston Churchill. *The World Crisis*, vol. I. Thorton Butterworth.
5.   John Charteris. *At G.H.Q.*, p. 17. Cassell.
6.   Robert Blake. *The Private Papers of Douglas Haig, 1914–1919*. Eyre & Spottiswoode.
7.   David Lloyd George. *War Memoirs*, vol. I, p. 154. Nicholson & Watson.
8.   Robert Rhodes James. *Gallipoli*, p. 231. Batsford.
9.   Ian Hamilton. *Gallipoli Diary*, vol. II, p. 95. Arnold.
10. Leon Wolff. *In Flanders Fields*. Longmans Green.
11. *Military Operations Italy, 1915–1919*.
12a. John W. Wheeler-Bennett. *Hindenburg: The Wooden Titan*, p. 22.
12b. pp. 97–98. Macmillan.
13a. Max Hoffmann. *War Diaries and other Papers*, vol. I, p. 47.
13b. p. 90. Martin Secker.
14. General Ludendorff. *My War Memories*, vol. I, p. 53. Hutchinson.

CHAPTER 4

Woodrow Wilson and Warren Harding: the breaking of two Presidents

The rooms and halls of the College of Physicians in Philadelphia are graced by the portraits of those who have added lustre to the name of American medicine and have helped to shape the destiny of their country. These were the physicians who treated the influential men of the day and the striking pictures that are left provide another view and further understanding of the history of their time. Here we are faced by William W. Keen, a pioneer in the surgery of the brain, who at the peak of his career successfully removed a malignant growth from the jaw of President Cleveland; and who, in the evening of his days, failed to realize that Franklin Roosevelt had poliomyelitis. There we can see the handsome de Schweinitz who realized that the loss of vision noticed by Woodrow Wilson in 1906 was due to arterial degeneration. Brooding over all these physicians, with the inscrutable look of a Buddha, is Silas Weir Mitchell, who was not only the leading American neurologist of his time but a poet and novelist of distinction. De Schweinitz advised Wilson to live in retirement while Weir Mitchell, who examined him in 1913, doubted if he could complete his first term as President and retain his health. In the short term their prognosis was too guarded and gloomy. Woodrow Wilson maintained reasonable health until the Armistice in 1918 but thereafter his rapid deterioration was a personal tragedy and an international disaster. An all or none law applies to politicians and the electorate must realize that they are likely to retain power, for better or worse, and in sickness and health, if not unto death, at least until they are well past their best. Voters and supporters would be unrealistic if they thought they could retain their man in his prime and avoid the disadvantages of his decline. Politicians are no wiser than boxing champions in selecting the moment to hang up their gloves. Those who are driven by ambition, ideals or unrealized and undefined psychological tensions are often careless of rules and risk. The world would be poorer without men who defy the odds and achieve the impossible; the world might be better off if these men did not regard waning mental and physical vigour as another challenge to be faced and conquered.

Thomas Woodrow Wilson, the 28th President of the United States of America, was born at Staunton, Virginia in 1856. The periods of his life are in some way reflected in the names that his intimates used. Tommy in his youth; Woodrow in the Presidential years at Princeton and in the White House; and Woody, to his dominating and over-protective second wife, in his last years as a crippled invalid. His medical history is long and involved and goes far to suggest that he was a chronic invalid. Twelve illnesses between 1874 and 1910 hardly suggest the presence of presidential timber and, admittedly in retrospect, examination of the nature of the illnesses gives cause for disquiet. An unrequited love affair with a cousin led to a breakdown in 1880. Although his first marriage in 1885, and translation to the faculty of Princeton University in 1890, brought him happiness there were further breakdowns in 1895 and 1899. On these occasions he took refuge in the English countryside which invariably provided solace and refreshment. Election to the Presidency of Princeton in 1902 neither quietened his inner compulsions nor eased his external tensions. He was determined to raise academic standards at Princeton and to introduce the tutorial and college system of Oxford and Cambridge. The old and new alumni bitterly opposed him and his attempt to abolish the University clubs, as examples of exclusive privilege, earned him particular hatred. Moreover it led to opposition by one of his intimates, Professor Hibben, and the loss of a valued friendship for Wilson who was quite unable to compromise or concede when he considered that principle was involved. The bitter wound was responsible for yet another attack of "neuritis", diagnosed when it first appeared in 1896 as writer's cramp, which necessitated convalescence in Bermuda in January 1908 and another blissful visit to England later in the year. If most of his absences appear to have a psychiatric or psychosomatic background there were two episodes of overt organic disease. Early in 1905 he had an operation; one account states this was for the repair of a hernia but Dr Grayson later stated that it was for the treatment of haemorrhoids. The retinal haemorrhage and visual impairment in his left eye for which he consulted de Schweinitz in May 1906 was a serious portent for the diagnosis of arteriosclerosis suggested that irrevocable changes had already occurred in his arteries. A second opinion gave grounds for optimism for Dr Stengel thought the arterial trouble was only of moderate grade and that there was no suggestion of progression. Double talk of this nature is justified if it encourages optimism and prevents invalidism in patients. Arteriosclerosis, or hardening of the arteries, is an inevitable degeneration which may begin in early adult life. It is always progressive and the changes that were noticed in Wilson at the early age of forty-nine years, though apparently minimal, should not merely have been dismissed by a warning from Dr Stengel and a recommendation of rest for three months.

An assessment of Wilson, as he was inaugurated as President of the United States on 4 March 1913, shows that his assets were reassuring. He had an outstanding intellect and an exceptional command of the spoken and written word. His life as a college professor had not blinded him to the harsh realities of the outside world and, as Governor of New Jersey from 1910 to 1912, he had first outmanoeuvred and then dominated the professional politicians. Indeed the lack of opposition by the personalities in the State capital was in startling contrast to his clashes with the members of the academic faculty which had marred the later years at Princeton. His health was broken as well as his friendship when he severed relations with Professor Hibben after the "battle of the Quads". His defeat by Dean West, over the site of the new Graduate College at Princeton, was even more traumatic. Wilson's intellectual superiority had usually enabled him to gain mastery of situations without having to indulge in the rough and tumble of life's arena. One only has to look at West's picture to realize that if he carried the fight to Wilson he would win; muscular and aggressive, one can do no better than to liken him to an irascible field officer from an English county

regiment. Nevertheless it was the defeat by West that lead
Wilson to take the paths to the Governor's Mansion in Trenton
and to the White House. As he stood on the threshold of the
White House it is now obvious that certain traits of temperament, as well as the early signs of degeneration in his arteries,
carried the seeds of destruction. Due to his rigid personality, and
strict religious principles, Wilson equated compromise with
failure and even sin. Such a temperament is a liability in the
political jungle where absolute integrity is an indulgence that
can rarely be afforded.

He brought with him his therapeutic armentarium which
included a stomach pump for the treatment of his gastro-
intestinal symptoms, and a box of analgesic tablets which he
used presumably to relieve the pains of "neuritis" and the
recurrent headaches which afflicted him. On inauguration day
his sister had an accident and his attention was drawn to a
young naval doctor who treated her. Inquiry revealed that his
name was Cary T. Grayson and Wilson asked that he should be
appointed as his physician and naval aide. For nearly eleven
years Grayson was in daily contact with Wilson and, following
the traditions of the true family doctor, he was in addition a
wise counsellor and a good friend. He was not content merely to
treat Wilson's symptoms but stressed the value of regular hours,
adequate relaxation and daily exercise. Indeed it must have
been Grayson who removed the stomach pump and the "quart
can of some sort of coal-tar product"[1a] because the analgesic
tablets were apparently affecting Wilson's kidneys. Grayson's
empirical observation was never publicized and it was not for
another forty years that the medical profession became aware
that the constituents of many analgesic mixtures, phenacetin,
salicylates, the antipyrine group and caffeine, might have a toxic
effect on the kidneys.

In spite of Weir Mitchell's gloomy prognosis, Wilson's health
was satisfactory during his first term of office, when he strove
desperately to keep America out of the war, and during the first
part of his second term when Germany's unrestricted submarine
campaign compelled him to declare war on 6 April 1917. The
death of his first wife from kidney disease on 6 August 1914 was
a severe blow but, after a hectic and emotional courtship, his

second marriage in December 1915 to a wealthy widow, Edith Bolling Galt, restored his happiness and peace of mind. Her single-minded determination to serve her husband's best interests was tarnished by her personal prejudices and, perhaps naturally envious of his friends, she may have alienated him from those whose only wish was to serve him.

Just as the military leaders were planning bigger and better campaigns for 1919 the collapse of some of the minor members of the central powers started a chain reaction. Less embittered and involved than other allied leaders, who wanted vengeance and recompense, Wilson planned a just and lasting settlement. Even the Germans, desperate as they were in the autumn of 1918, trusted him sufficiently to ask for an Armistice on the basis of his "fourteen points". On Friday, 13 December 1918, which some may regard as a day of ill omen, Wilson landed in Europe and was greeted as a saviour. Kings, Queens, Presidents and Statesmen paid tribute and the peoples of Europe lined the streets wherever he went. Yet when he left Europe for America on 29 June 1919, after the Peace Treaty had been signed at Versailles, his popularity had waned for admiration had given way to hatred and gratitude to complaint. None of the delegates at Versailles had got from Wilson what they considered was their due. Wilson was more than ever convinced of the rightness of his cause and with all his old obstinacy and rigidity insisted that the United States Senate must ratify not only the Peace Treaty but also the Covenant of the League of Nations. An appearance if not the actuality of compromise might have mollified the less extreme Republicans but he may have seen in Henry Cabot Lodge, their leader and spokesman, the reincarnation of his old Princeton adversaries. His principles drove him on while the Republicans, irritated at having been ignored by Wilson's one-man band in Europe, were by now uncompromisingly determined to block America's admission to the League of Nations with its inherent and menacing possibility of involvement in foreign wars. It was not only the Europeans who showed ingratitude to Wilson but his own people who were now tired of high ideals and noble words. The spirit of self-sacrifice which is so often present in wartime had quickly changed to the self-seeking and self-indulgence of peacetime. But Wilson too had changed and this was not entirely due to the exhausting and exasperating struggles with the allied negotiators in Paris. All through the war he had "blinding headaches"[2] but, apart from a minor illness after his re-election in 1916 and ten days absence with a cold just before America declared war, there appeared little amiss. It was Colonel Starling, the head of the Secret Service detail, who first noticed signs of change in December 1917. Wilson was uncharacteristically abusive to a watchman who objected to the presidential chauffeur ignoring a "stop" sign at a pedestrian crossing. Starling took particular note of this incident which was unlike Wilson's normal conduct and years later he realized that it was a serious portent. Further errors in human relations could neither be dismissed nor rectified. On 24 October 1918 Wilson made a plea through the medium of the national Press for the election of democrats to Congress on 5 November. This partisan approach to a nation which had sunk political differences for the duration of the war shocked and enraged the Republicans. An attempt has been made to excuse Wilson by suggesting that the letter was written in a period of utter exhaustion "when his nerves were taut and his intellectual sentinels were not on the lookout for danger"[3] and when "he was tired and absent-minded".[1b] He exacerbated the resentment in November when he failed to include either a Senator or a prominent Republican in the Peace Commission that would accompany him to Paris. His protracted stay in Paris has been regarded as the greatest mistake of all. It was his remoteness and apparent disinterestedness that had led the world to hope that he might secure a lasting peace. By lowering himself to the level of the victors who were squabbling over the spoils he lost his prestige and influence.

As has been stated the change in Wilson was not solely due to the long hours that he worked in Paris or to the frustrating and exasperating problems that were never properly resolved. Nor was it entirely due to the burden of responsibility that he assumed for the young lives that had been lost although the twitching of his facial muscles reflected his anxiety over the protracted and tortuous negotiations which made a mockery of the ideals which sustained him. If any one factor stands out it was an episode early in April 1919 when Wilson was prostrated by an illness, the nature of which has never been entirely or satisfactorily explained. In the notes that were found after Grayson's death in 1938 he described an attack of influenza that was followed by asthmatic coughing and insomnia. There were additional symptoms for in a letter to Wilson's secretary at the time, he mentioned vomiting and diarrhoea and, far from an easy diagnosis of influenza, he had considered the possibility that the President's food had been poisoned. Retrospective diagnoses are notoriously unreliable and hindsight is often erroneous in linking cause and effect. His personal staff are unanimous in their view that this episode, for long labelled as influenza, marked an irrevocable and lamentable change in his personality and behaviour. Irwin Hoover, Chief Usher of the White House, thought that Wilson had become mean and suspicious and that "he was never the same after this little spell of sickness".[4] Colonel Starling stated that, following the illness, Wilson "lacked his old quickness of grasp, and tired easily".[5a] Even a short and uncomplicated attack of influenza may be followed by prolonged physical prostration and profound mental depression. Nor could a rapid restoration to health be expected since Wilson continued to negotiate from the bedside and failed to allow a proper interval for recovery and convalescence. There are those who would concur with Lloyd George's opinion that Wilson "had something like a stroke in March 1919"[6] and weight is added to this theory by the subsequent medical history. However, Herbert Hoover, President of the United States from 1928 until 1932, has recently reviewed the history of the period and dismissed the suggestion that Wilson had a stroke: "But though he was a very tired man, his mind and judgement were clear".[3] Following a talk with Dr A. R. Lamb, physician to the American Mission in 1918, Herbert Hoover revealed what Grayson had concealed. Wilson had an infection of his prostate and bladder and this diagnosis is substantiated by the fact that prostatis, though not normally a complication of influenza, was unusually common during the 1919 pandemic. One can argue indefinitely and probably unprofitably about the exact nature of the illness or illnesses; suffice it to say that an exhausted man of sixty-two years, under immense strain for a long period, had an infective illness that may or may not have been accompanied by a stroke. Even if one allows that the first stroke did not occur until the autumn of the same year we must agree that an increasing and crushing load of responsibility on a mind and body no longer allowed time for respite and recovery could lead to a significant deterioration in conduct and behaviour. The supicion, mentioned by Irwin Hoover, unfortunately led Wilson to doubt the integrity of his faithful friend and supporter, Colonel House, who for a number of years had acted as his observer and had won the confidence of European statesmen. Avid for influence rather than power, House knew his way through the European jungle but a suggestion that he was becoming too powerful, a suspicion that he was substituting expediency for principle, lead Wilson to deprive himself of his major source of independent advice. He fought on alone and must carry the responsibility for some serious mistakes; the agreement on a security treaty between Britain, France and America in advance of his Senate's approval; his unwise assent to the addition of the allied pension bill to the reparations; and his clumsy handling of the Italian question which led to that nation's withdrawal from the Conference shortly after his illness in April. Nevertheless the Peace Treaty was signed at Versailles on 28 June 1919 and Wilson embarked next day to face his opponents in America. If he had not secured all that he had hoped for he had established the idea of a world organization to preserve peace. He had helped to establish the International Court of Justice at the Hague and the International Labour Office at Geneva. He had insisted that many of the people of Europe be granted political independence and self-determination, though he had unwittingly sowed the seeds for other tyrants to reap and use for their own destructive purposes.

On the second day of the voyage home the observant Starling noticed that on three consecutive occasions Wilson stumbled on the same iron ring while walking on deck. Fatigue is a possible explanation although spasticity from a previous stroke cannot be excluded. On 10 July 1919 he faced a hostile Senate and as the summer wore on he determined to by-pass this opposition and appeal in person to the American people. He had appealed to them to elect a democratic Congress in November 1918 and had failed. Now his advisers warned him that, in view of his health, such a barnstorming tour should not be contemplated. In defiance of Grayson and other well-wishers the President and his staff left Washington on the night of 3 September 1919: exactly twenty years later the lasting peace that he strove for was brutally shattered. The cavalcade ranged round America and Wilson grimly kept pace with the exhausting programme of speech making and meetings, though the severe headaches and asthmatic attacks deprived him of sleep and rest. The end came in Colorado on 25 September at Pueblo, a name that was to ring round the world nearly fifty years later.

Wilson stumbled on a step and practically had to be lifted to the platform.

"Much of his speech was mumbled; he mouthed certain words as if he had never spoken them before. There were long pauses. He had difficulty following the trend of his thought. It was a travesty of his usual brilliant delivery and fine logic."[5b]

Dr Walter Alvarez heard the halting speech on the radio and realized that Wilson had been seized by a stroke. By the early hours of the following morning the issue was no longer in doubt, though Grayson left no details in his account. Tumulty, his secretary, describes the scene at 4 a.m. on 26 September; Wilson, seated in a chair, and barely able to talk.

"His face was pale and wan. One side of it had fallen, and his condition was indeed pitiful to behold."[7]

On the evening of 26 September Starling talked to Wilson and noticed that "the left side of his face seemed to have fallen a little" and that when he smiled "only the right side of his face responded to his command".[5c]

The ill-fated tour had by now been cancelled and the sad party returned to the White House where on 2 October Wilson had another stroke of such severity, involving the left side of his body, that he was virtually a cripple for the rest of his life. His doctors understandably put patient before country and advised against premature resignation for Dr Dercum was frightened lest loss of office would remove the will to live; a dilemma that would face Moran when Churchill was similarly afflicted.

On 6 October 1919 Robert Lansing, the Secretary of State, discussed with Tumulty the provisions of the Constitution with regard to the removal, death, resignation or disability of a President. Tumulty said that only he or Grayson could provide the evidence and, not only would they never do this, but they would stop any outsider obtaining it. He hinted that Wilson might take action if he heard about Lansing's inquiries. The hint was not taken and, after a bitter exchange of letters in February 1920, Wilson demanded Lansing's resignation for convening the Cabinet without permission.

From October 1919 until March 1921 the Presidency was sustained by a self-elected council of three: Mrs Wilson, Joseph Tumulty and Dr Grayson. It was not so much that the machinery of government was halted, that documents could not be signed, that Ambassadors could not be met, that officials could not be appointed or even discharged; it was that Wilson, isolated by his intimates and handicapped by increasing obstinacy, mental deterioration and failure of judgement, destroyed any hope of attaining even some of the objectives for which he had ruined his health.

He was determined that the Senate would approve the Peace Treaty and the Covenant of the League on his terms and he ordered Hitchcock, the Democrat minority leader, to vote against Cabot Lodge's reservations. On 19 November 1919 the grisly roll call began. Lodge's resolution, for a treaty and a league with his reservations, was defeated by 55 to 39. The Democratic motion for unconditional ratification was defeated by 53 to 38. Since neither party could secure the necessary two-thirds majority the contest was resumed on 19 March 1920. Once more Lodge put forward his resolution with reservations; 49 in favour, including 21 democrats, and 35 against still did not constitute a two-thirds majority and the Peace Treaty and League Covenant were still not ratified by the Senate.

Even this did not deter Wilson. On 13 April 1920 he attended the first Cabinet meeting since his stroke and David F. Houston, the Secretary of Agriculture, reported that he looked "old, worn, and haggard" and that "his jaw tended to drop on one side".

". . . he would not or could not take the initiative. One member brought up the railroad situation, and Wilson seemed to have difficulty in keeping his mind fixed on it."[8]

Furthermore against all the medical evidence and all the odds he seriously sought the Democratic nomination for the third time in the summer of 1920. He evolved a scheme to win over the delegation at San Francisco and, when he heard of its failure, he "unleashed a tornado of masterful profanity."[5d] Nor should his persistence be necessarily attributed to those innate qualities of obstinacy, rigidity and wilfulness which, following brain damage, had become more accentuated and unrestrained. Nor need it have been due to the ingrained habit of a lifetime which forced body and mind to overcome the next obstacle round the corner. A recent study by Dr Edwin Weinstein suggests the possibility that one of the effects of his strokes may have made him unaware of the seriousness of disability. Brain damage following a stroke or trauma may be succeeded by anosognosia, which is a term used to describe the lack of knowledge of a disease. The patient may appear to be unaware of, or fail to accept, the presence of paralysis, blindness or loss of speech. The denial of crippling symptoms is a form of self-defence and they may be attributed to an incorrect and less serious cause or imaginary situations may be invented to account for them. History teaches us that it is difficult to remove a statesman from office when he has some knowledge of the nature of his disability; when the nature of the disability removes any insight about the disability the task of management may be well-nigh impossible.

Nothing could have halted the Republican landslide in 1920, not even Wilson; certainly not Governor Cox or young Franklin Roosevelt, the nominee for Vice-President. Against all the evidence Wilson had a touching faith that the American people supported his aims and their crushing endorsement of Warren Harding on 2 November 1920 was yet another bitter blow. Over three years of incapacity and frustration were left to him: and if they were not years of contentment they may have been eased by the acceptance that the ideals for which he had striven could not be realized in his lifetime. He died on 3 February 1924: he had outlived his successor, Warren Harding, by six months and Henry Cabot Lodge, the man who had shattered his dreams, only survived him by a mere eight months.

No physician would have been rash enough to suppose that Wilson would outlive his successor. As they rode together to the Capitol on 4 March 1921, Warren Gamaliel Harding, strikingly handsome and seemingly healthy, made the crippled Wilson look even more pathetic. Yet Harding died suddenly and unexpectedly on 2 August 1923 at the age of fifty-eight years.

Harding had abdominal pain and fever on his return from a visit to Alaska in the summer of 1923. At first these symptoms were attributed to the ill-effects of crab. meat though it had never appeared on the presidential menu. He continued to fulfil his engagements and when he arrived in San Francisco on 28 July the abdominal discomfort was localized in the region of the gall bladder. On 30 July his temperature was over 100° F., his pulse rate varied from 100 to 125, and the respiratory rate was 44. Clinical signs, confirmed by chest X-rays, were indicative of consolidation in the right lung. His general condition improved on 2 August and gave grounds for optimism so that his death, later in the day, surprised his physicians. Part of the statement they made at midnight was accurately reported in the black-edged *New York Times* on 3 August. "President Harding dies suddenly; stroke of apoplexy at 7.30 p.m."

In retrospect the medical history they revealed now permits, as a result of the medical advances that occured in the decades after Harding's death, an alternative diagnosis. It is true that Dr J. B. Herrick had published papers on sudden obstruction of the coronary arteries in 1912 and 1916, although the first cases were not reported in Great Britain until 1925. The description of the characteristic electrocardiographic changes by Dr H. E. B. Pardee in 1920 provided a diagnostic tool which led physicians to realize subsequently that the condition was more common than they had supposed.

The physicians said that for some years Harding's systolic blood pressure had been in the region of 180 mm. Hg. and there was evidence of an enlarged heart, arteriosclerosis and renal impairment. Their observation that he had a history of pain and oppression in the chest is significant for in the immediate future the realization that such symptoms suggested disease of the coronary arteries would no longer be confined to heart specialists, but would spread to general physicians and practitioners. There is no evidence that any electrocardiograph studies were made on Harding either before or during his fatal illness. The possibility of cardiac involvement is confirmed unwittingly by lay observers. Starling, still the faithful Presidential bodyguard, found that Harding was short of breath when he lay flat and could only sleep when propped up with pillows. When Harding was making what must have been his last public speech on 27 July, Herbert Hoover noticed that he faltered, dropped his notes and grasped the desk; a manifestation that recalls Wilson at Pueblo and could have been the precursor of a stroke. Equally well it could have been a warning of pathological change in the coronary, rather than the cerebral, arteries. Myocardial infarction cannot be excluded as a cause of his death but his doctors should not be blamed for failing to consider such a diagnosis in view of the lack of knowledge and awareness at the time.

If mental stress and physical overactivity can overtax a vulnerable cerebro-vascular and cardiovascular system it is possible that such factors shortened the lives of Wilson and Harding. Both Presidents subjected themselves, or were subjected, to pressure that literally was more than flesh and blood could stand.

Wilson's indomitable will and egocentricity would not permit his body and mind to rest. Harding, easy going and easy living, found to his horror that his associates had entangled him in corruption and scandal. His private indiscretions could no longer be concealed and on many counts he faced public exposure. On the journey to Alaska he tried to calm his anxieties with alcohol and endless card games but it is difficult to deny that the burden of guilt and a sense of personal inadequacy and failure may have precipitated his final illness.

References

1a. William Allen White. *Woodrow Wilson*; the man, his times and his task, p. 276. Houghton Mifflin & Co., 1924.

1b. p. 366. Houghton Mifflin & Co., 1924.
2.   Edith Bolling Wilson. *My Memoir*, p. 116. Bobbs—Merrill 1938.
3.   Herbert Hoover. *The Ordeal of Woodrow Wilson.* The Museum Press.
4.   Irwin Hood Hoover. *42 Years in the White House*, p. 99. Houghton Mifflin.
5a. Edmund W. Starling. *Starling of the White House*, p. 138. Simon & Schuster.
5b. p. 152. Simon & Schuster.
5c. p. 153. Simon & Schuster.
5d. p. 157. Simon & Schuster.
6.   Harold Nicolson. *Diaries and Letters 1930–39*, p. 123. Weidenfeld & Nicolson.
7.   Joseph P. Tumulty. *Woodrow Wilson as I Know Him*, p. 446. Doubleday Page.
8.   T. A. Bailey. *Wilson and the Peacemakers*, p. 295. Macmillan (New York).

CHAPTER 5

C-B, Squiff and the Welsh Wizard: the rise and fall of the Liberals

Attainment of high office is as much a matter of chance, availability and compromise as of merit, ambition, decision or intention. It depends as much on the demands and convenience of the party as on the needs of the country. The call, when it comes, cannot be declined or ignored and its acceptance is invariably attributed to patriotism or duty rather than to personal ambition or a desire for supreme power.

London was shrouded in an old-fashioned fog of pea-soup consistency on 11 December 1905 when the Ministers of the new Liberal Government were summoned to Buckingham Palace to receive the seals of office. The fog was of such density that it persisted next day and ruined the 'varsity rugger match at Queen's Club. Grey found that he had merely felt his way around Queen Victoria's statue under the impression that he was making steady progress towards the Foreign Office. Haldane had no greater success in a hansom cab; attempting to lead the way on foot he lost the cab. Nor was the meeting particularly illuminating for the new Prime Minister, Sir Henry Campbell-Bannerman. He was aware, from previous conversations with Edward VII earlier in the year, that he was by no means the first choice. Lord Spencer was being considered, on the grounds of long service and a distinguished record, but had in the interval been disabled by a cerebro-vascular accident. The King shared the general concern about Campbell-Bannerman's health and suggested that he should take a peerage so that, while conducting the business of government, he could avoid the hurly-burly of the Commons. The King's opinion was reinforced later by Dr Ernest Ott, a Viennese physician; too late unfortunately for Campbell-Bannerman to reconsider his decision to remain in the Commons. Ott was appalled at his attitude and warned him that at the age of sixty-nine years, and in view of his state of health, the results of overwork would be serious.

The power and complexity of the Government machine drives a remorseless treadmill which, despite every form of human and mechanical aid, outlasts and outrages the human machine. Even a younger Minister, giddy with the opportunity to initiate reform and generate change, may find that the speed of the machine is beyond his capacity; the old Minister is only too painfully aware that the passage of time marks his incapacity to keep pace.

Campbell-Bannerman was worn down in addition by a domestic burden that sapped his energies and distracted his efforts. His wife was dying and he conceived it his duty to nurse her and sit by her side day and night. From June 1906, until her death on 30 August, he scarcely left Downing Street and only attended the House of Commons for questions. During the first seven months in office his sleep was interrupted nearly every night. Devotion and care of this order was only to be expected. He had shown both sympathy and understanding over Grey's tragedy in February 1906 and had dissuaded him from resignation.

On 2 October 1906 the state of his heart gave cause for concern though the news was kept from the public. His biographer makes a reference to "blood pressure", and this was presumably raised for the condition of "cardiac asthma" is also mentioned.[1] His return to Downing Street on 19 October heralded the first shots in the protracted struggle between Lords and Commons. His heart was under close and continuous observation and, during a debate in July 1907, his Secretary, armed with the appropriate drugs, waited anxiously in the official's box.

Over the years the Government machine forces the Minister to conform to its revolutions and in addition subjects him to subtle variations of pace and stress; it drives at different speeds at different intervals, now fast, now slow. Regularity in the various aspects of life, and in diet, sleep and exercise in particular, is a practice that is commended by the physician. Regularity is a luxury denied to public men. They must be prepared for long and arduous conferences and debates that extend far into the night often for nights on end; they must be prepared for unexpected and wounding attack and censure, they must be prepared to consume with every evidence of appreciation, unaccustomed food and drink in amounts, and at times, that are quite unphysiological. Trained as he may have been to accept such an irregular way of life, events in November 1907 took an irremediable toll of Campbell-Bannerman's cardiac reserve. The upheaval was caused by the visit of the German Emperor to Windsor. Campbell-Bannerman met him there on the evening of 11 November and returned to London for a meeting next morning; he was at Windsor that day for the State Banquet returning to London the same night. On 13 November he attended a Civic luncheon at the Guildhall but travelled to Bristol later in the day for another banquet at which he spoke for one hour. Returning to his host's house he joined a party in the billiard room and, a few hours later, was found in a state of collapse.

On this occasion the news of his illness could not be concealed. His depression was profound but, despite another attack of cardiac asthma on the way to Biarritz, his convalescence was undisturbed save for occasional visits by the King's Messengers. His improvement was deceptive for, at the end of January 1908, he became anxious about his brother's health and he himself had another heart attack on the night of 12/13 February. For the rest of his life he was confined to Downing Street where at first he made every effort to retain the reins of office. He read State papers and dealt with documents that required his signature as long as his incapacity permitted even this limited activity; meanwhile the remorseless machine raced on and could only be controlled by other drivers:

"but the physical prostration and distress did not admit of more than occasional concentration on business, and, needless to say, his colleagues spared him all possible cause for work and anxiety. For many weeks the Government of the country was carried on with the sick Prime Minister unable to see or consult with his colleagues. Cabinets were summoned without reference to him and decisions taken with such consultation by deputy or in writing as circumstances permitted, and often none was possible."[1]

If most patients lack insight into the severity of their condition, and if statesmen are, if anything, less likely to admit to incapacity, Campbell-Bannerman conducted himself as well as could be expected. Gradually he forsook responsibility or let it pass from his hands. He allowed his other ministers, and Asquith in particular, to take over the Government. Would that President Wilson, or the second Mrs Wilson, had been as understanding and magnanimous nine years later. Then Robert Lansing, the unfortunate Secretary of State, was summarily dismissed for acting as conscientiously as Asquith in maintaining the continuity of Government.

As late as 2 March, Campbell-Bannerman attributed his disability to the effects of influenza but early in April any hopes that he may have had were dispelled. On 3 April he sent his resignation to the King and he died on the 22nd of the same month.

Campbell-Bannerman was failing before he attained the highest office and his life was probably, though not necessarily, shortened by the duties that were thrust upon him. Whether the arduous toil would have ground down a healthier man is a matter for debate.

Herbert Henry Asquith, who succeeded Campbell-Bannerman at the age of fifty-five years, had the temperament and the physique for the post. His outstanding intellect enabled him to establish a mastery over his equally distinguished colleagues while his civilized attitudes did much to contribute to his ease of mind and body. He had the time, or found the time, for friends and conversation, for long week-ends and country walks, for bridge and letter writing. The eight years that he spent in office must verge on the limits of human tolerance and only one other Prime Minister, Lord Liverpool, has had a longer tenure. It may be significant that Liverpool had to resign in 1827, after fourteen years in office, because of a cerebro-vascular accident at the comparatively early age of fifty-seven years. It is an oversimplification and a superficial judgement to say that Asquith's two years as a wartime Prime Minister broke him; that he was essentially a peacetime Minister and, as an old-fashioned Liberal, hated war. The days between 1908 and 1914 were not lit by everlasting sunshine and the peaceful scenes at Lords, Henley and in country houses were deceptive. There was strife between Lords and Commons, between Protestants and Catholics in Ireland, between men and women over the vote, and railway, coal and dock strikes. There were threats of war when the Kaiser sent his gunboat to Agadir and there were two wars in the Balkans.

It was not merely the conduct of war that broke Asquith although in 1914 the Government machinery that existed was naturally enough unprepared to conduct a world war. It was not the unbridled attacks of the newspaper proprietors who abused the freedom of the Press that brought him down; nor the politicians like Churchill who wanted to be soldiers, nor the soldiers like Henry Wilson who wanted to be politicians. Conscious of his great gifts he could ignore the intrigues and disloyalty of lesser men; he was far too patient and tolerant and his abhorrence of histrionics led the uncritical to accuse him of weakness and ineffectiveness.

Asquith was broken by a domestic tragedy. On 15 September 1916, Raymond, his eldest son, was killed while serving with the Grenadier Guards in France. Lloyd George observed:

"Then came the personal tragedy which shattered his nerve. The death of his brilliant son, Raymond, came upon him with stunning effect, and he visibly reeled under the blow."[2a]

Whether he could ever have stooped to contest the machinations of his opponents is doubtful. Some were genuinely concerned about the efficient administration of the war machine and Lloyd George hardly deserved the opprobrious title of "the snake in goat's clothing".[3] Unfortunately in the first days of December 1916, as criticism increased, Asquith was laid low by what was probably an upper respiratory tract infection. Domestic tragedy and an attack of influenza had broken another Liberal Prime Minister, Lord Rosebery, who held office from 1894 to 1895. The death of his wife in 1890 had induced a profound and persistent depression associated with insomnia. His capacity to deal with a Cabinet crisis early in 1895 was impaired by an attack of influenza which has lead a biographer to write:

> "Any plans which the Prime Minister (Rosebery) may have had to impose his will upon his colleagues were irretrievably destroyed by an illness whose seriousness has not been sufficiently appreciated by historians".[4]

On the 29 November 1916, Asquith wrote that he had been struck down by a severe infection and the evidence suggests that the effects were to continue over the next few, but critical, days. Certainly his analysis and judgement of events were sadly at fault. On 1 December he rejected Lloyd George's proposal that he should be excluded from the new War Committee which was to include Lloyd George and two others. On 3 December he sadly misinterpreted a message from the Tory Ministers in the Coalition. He failed to realize that they were supporting him and, swinging the other way, he fell in with Lloyd George's original demands. On 4 December, fortified by the horrified protests of the Liberal ministers in the Coalition, he veered again and found a suitable excuse for going back on his agreement with Lloyd George. The latter resigned on 5 December and Asquith made a final and fatal miscalculation when he took the same step. He was sure that neither Lloyd George nor Bonar Law, the Conservative leader, could form an administration. In the event Bonar Law recommended that the King should send for Lloyd George and Asquith found himself outmanœuvred and out of power.

David Lloyd George seized office at the comparatively early age of fifty-three years: indeed in this century only Harold Wilson at forty-nine years has been younger on appointment. He was avid for power and confident that he alone could find the men and the means to win the war. He had energy and imagination and his uncanny powers of intuition enabled him to manipulate his political colleagues. After two years of war and four years of peace the political blunders which preceded his fall from office might justifiably be attributed to the cumulative **strain of endless toil and trouble.** Minor effects of strain were apparent in earlier years when his resilience enabled him to withstand the shocks that would have broken lesser men; but in 1922 the recuperative powers of his middle years had been dissipated.

As Chancellor of the Exchequer he introduced his first budget on 29 April 1909. Many of the measures that he proposed, health insurance schemes, an increase of income tax and death duties, surtax, are controversial today; at that time they were revolutionary. The finance bill was debated with acrimony for seventy-two days and Lloyd George, a victim of "neuritis", appeared with his arm in a sling. The battle for health insurance in 1911 was even more bitter and a rest in the South of France, after an attack of "clergyman's throat", led to· rumours of cancer or tuberculosis. Lloyd George feared it was "something terrible".[5] Two years later he was embroiled in the Marconi scandal. Rufus Isaacs, later Lord Reading, had bought American Marconi shares and had sold some to Lloyd George at the same time as the Government was entering into contractual arrangements with the British Marconi Company. When viewed over the years by later generations, scandals that rock governments seem trivial if not unintelligible. As experienced Ministers the conduct of Rufus Isaacs and Lloyd George was stupid; their half-truths and attempts at concealment aroused the suspicions of the Conservative opposition, the Press and the public. A committee of the House of Commons investigated their conduct and they were exonerated. A few months later, for political convenience, Rufus Isaacs was made Lord Chief Justice and created Baron Reading of Erleigh; an appointment that prompted Rudyard Kipling to publish his scarifying poem "gehazi" though none dare sue him. The effects of the case on Lloyd George were less happy:

"He lost weight, lost vitality, fell ill again, and his black hair grew grey, the lines began to mark his face, and for the first time in public he was seen to use spectacles. A great life poised on the edge."[6]

Minor illness, as a reaction to crisis, was to form a regular pattern in his life. In May 1913 he attributed a severe pain in the leg to a nervous reaction of the mental stress that had dogged him since boyhood. The more robust Asquith remarked with acerbity in 1914:

> "Lloyd George was kept at Walton Heath by one of those psychological chills which always precede his budgets, when he does not feel altogether sure of his ground. . . . (He) would like to see me take his budget for him. . . ."[7]

The campaign in which he succeeded Asquith proved too much for him and he had to retire to bed for several days. He became "restless and agitated" during the Passchendaele offensive and retreated to Criccieth on 6 September 1917 with "neuralgia".[8]

His illnesses in 1921 and 1922, the years of his political decline, may well have been related to political crises; how much they may have affected his capacity in the first place and have been the cause rather than the effect of crisis is difficult to assess. Lloyd George was not the last Prime Minister to act as a one man band. A threatened strike in the coal mines in March 1919; Lloyd George averted it by appointing a Royal Commission. A railway strike in October 1919: Lloyd George organized a compromise settlement. Failure in the house building programme: Lloyd George removed the Minister of Health, Dr Christopher Addison, who incidentally had helped him to gain power in December 1916. Violence and terrorism in Ireland; Lloyd George organized a settlement with the Sinn Fein leaders on 6 December 1921. The Turks were getting out of hand again; Lloyd George rattled the sabre. To the Conservatives in the Coalition, traditionally opposed to Home Rule for Ireland, the settlement with the Sinn Feiners was bad enough; the threat of war with Turkey was the last straw. This marked the end of the Coalition which had governed since December 1916 and, though it was not realized at the time, the beginning of the end of the Liberal Party as a force in British politics. Lloyd George left Downing Street on 23 October 1922 and, although as late as 1940, he intervened with devastating effect in the Commons to blast Chamberlain from office, he never secured supreme power again.

Early in June 1921, Lloyd George was seeking to make a scapegoat of Dr Addison and on the 7th of the month he wrote to Bonar Law.

"I have had a temporary breakdown . . . much to my disappointment it is only temporary. . . ."[9a]

In August Lord Dawson advised him to convalesce at Gairloch. There was concern about a dental abscess and pyrexia which, in the days before antibiotics, could have been dangerous. He wrote to Dawson on 24 October 1921, that he "came back really rested and invigorated"[9b] but this view was not shared by Lord Buckmaster who met him in the same month:

"I have only seen Lloyd George once since 1916 and that was two days ago. . . . It is remarkable to see what a change these few years have effected in the man. To me it seemed as though the inspiration he once possessed was gone and I found myself talking to a man uneasy in manner and trying rather to evade events rather than to control them."[10]

In March 1922 his intimates were concerned and doubted whether six months rest would enable him to initiate fresh programmes, policies and campaigns.

"I do not mean to say he is getting old but his great work of the last few years must have told upon him more than he and we realize. . . ."[9c]

In the same month came a plaintive cry from Lloyd George:

"It is difficult to rest with all these 'crises' hurtling about your head. I have had today a return of those neuralgic pains that worried me."[9d]

Lloyd George left Downing Street with a flourish and enjoyed his years as a young "elder statesman", his writing and his country pursuits at Churt. Never a man to reject innovation he consulted Voronoff, whose therapy was much in vogue at the time, and was a willing recipient of hormones and vitamins.

What proved to be the last chance of a return to the arena was denied him by illness. Whether he would have taken his place in Ramsay MacDonald's "National Government", after the financial crisis of September 1931, is a matter for speculation. A prostatectomy, a few weeks previously, put him out of the running. His health had been noticeably impaired and Dawson observed that a portrait, painted by Philip de Laszlo before his operation, showed unmistakable signs of illness. He was unlucky with his portraits. Augustus John caught him in a grim mood in 1915 due to a combination of severe toothache and bad news from the Serbian front. There was talk of giving him a Ministry, or even the Embassy at Washington in 1940, but Dawson advised him to decline the offers.

On reflection it may have been the virulence of bacterial rather than human organisms which sealed the fate of the Liberal Party as a major factor in British politics. Mr Percy Illingworth, the Chief Liberal Whip, died of typhoid fever in 1915. He might have kept the Liberal Party first from splitting into Asquith and Lloyd George factions and then from breaking up altogether. Lloyd George later wrote:

"A rotten mollusc poisoned the whole Liberal Party for years and left it enfeebled."[2b]

Then there was the monkey who found a place in the history books. He bit King Alexander of Greece who died of blood poisoning on 25 October 1920 and Lord Beaverbrook has described the subsequent chain of events. King Constantine was recalled and Venizelos, the Prime Minister, aware of his enmity, fled. As a result the French transferred their allegiance from the Greeks to the Turks who were thus in a position to defy the British. The Conservatives in their turn defied Lloyd George, the Coalition dissolved, and Lloyd George's fall sealed the fate of the Liberal Party.

References

1. J. A. Spender. *The Life of the Right Hon. Sir Henry Campbell-Bannerman.* Hodder & Stoughton.
2a. David Lloyd George. *War Memoirs,* vol. II, p. 1109
2b. Vol. II, p. 746. Nicholson & Watson.
3. Lady Kennet. *Self Portrait of an Artist,* p. 149. Murray.
4. Robert Rhodes James. *Rosebery,* p. 369. Weidenfeld & Nicolson.

5. Lord Riddell. *More Pages from my Diary 1908–14*, p. 33. Country Life.
6. Frank Owen. *Tempestuous Journey*, p. 236. Hutchinson.
7. Roy Jenkins. *Asquith*, p. 337. Collins.
8. Thomas Jones. *Lloyd George*, p. 121. Oxford University Press.
9a. Lord Beaverbrook. *The Decline and Fall of Lloyd George*, p. 264.
9b. p. 283. Collins.
9c. p. 293. Collins.
9d. p. 138. Collins.
10. R. F. V. Houston. *Lives of the Lord Chancellors*, p. 289. Clarendon Press, Oxford.

CHAPTER 6

Conservatives and others, 1922-40:
the sickness of the "guilty men"

One biographer has called Andrew Bonar Law "The Unknown Prime Minister":[1] a contemporary has written that Law's "sceptical outlook was tinged with melancholy".[2] His personality, reserved, introverted and modest, sets him apart from his political contemporaries and their histrionics, intrigues and appetite for self-aggrandisement. His character, together with the scars of personal and domestic tragedy, made him above all a reluctant Prime Minister. His wife had died in 1909, two sons were killed in the First World War, and in September 1918, just after his sixtieth birthday, he was at low ebb. Tearful and broken he confided to Lord Riddell.

> "It is useless to conceal that I am nearly at the end of my tether. I do my work from day to day because I have certain powers of endurance, but they are growing less and less. You can see the condition I am in. If it were not so I should not give way like this. Ever since the death of my sons I have gradually been growing worse and worse."[3]

After the Khaki election in 1918 he continued to serve in Lloyd George's Coalition but he resigned his offices of Leader of the House and Lord Privy Seal on 17 March 1921. There was talk of hypertension and influenza but Sir Thomas (later Lord) Horder indiscreetly informed the editor of *The Sunday Times* that Bonar Law was not ill: only he could no longer face the anxieties of the Irish situation and an excuse had to be made to get him out of the country and send him to the South of France. He returned to England with his health restored in September of the same year. A year later Lloyd George had lost his grip and the Coalition was in ruins: even so Bonar Law was in no way anxious to attend the meeting at the Carlton Club on 19 October 1922 when the Conservatives severed their connection with the Coalition. He hoped that he would be found medically unfit but Horder could find no reason why he should not take office again. Bonar Law may have had a premonition that was denied his physician. He had become Prime Minister on 24 October 1922 and, during the subsequent election in November, he noticed discomfort in his throat and difficulty with his speech. The Christmas season was an unhappy one for he lost the use of his voice; he ate little and smoked a lot and returned to work unrefreshed. Lord Beaverbrook wrote:

"After Christmas was over Bonar Law returned again to the strife and turmoil of Downing Street. He was not happy. His tasks were bearing heavily on him. His responsibilities oppressed him and he has become gloomy and sad."[4]

He attended sittings of Parliament in April 1923 although he was unable to speak. On 1 May 1923 he went on holiday and on the 17th of the month a carcinoma of the larynx was diagnosed. He resigned forthwith and died on 30 October 1923.

Thomas Horder, had been called in consultation when Campbell-Bannerman was failing in 1908; Bertrand Dawson was an intimate of Lloyd George. Over the next twenty years the services of Dawson and Horder were required with distressing frequency by the Prime Ministers of the day. Cloaked in the formal garb of the period, their moustaches gave them a superficial resemblance, but any appearance of conformity was illusory. Dawson, the older man, was more the courtier and the politician and in addition to the usual conventional honours was made a Privy Councillor in 1929 and a Viscount in 1936. Horder received no more than a Barony in 1933 and the Presidency of the Royal College of Physicians, which Dawson held for several years, sadly eluded him. Dawson excelled in the personal and psychological understanding of his patients while Horder was almost certainly his superior in the technical and scientific aspects of clinical medicine. We have no record of their professional attitude to their political patients. Horder may have regarded Prime Ministers in the same light as his other patients but there are glimpses, mere flickerings on a screen, which suggest that Dawson may have assessed his patients' health in relation to the responsibility of the office and to the needs of the country.

James Ramsay MacDonald was Prime Minister for nine months in 1924 and from 1929 until 1935. Leonard Woolf had met him towards the end of the First World War and later wrote:

> "(Ramsay MacDonald) had the kind if iron constitution which is the first and, when I think of the Prime Ministers I have known, perhaps the only necessary qualification or asset which a man must possess if he is to become Prime Minister."[5]

Iron rusts and metal fatigue is now a recognized condition. An iron constitution may enable a man to reach the top but may keep him there when he is long past his best. MacDonald was failing some years before he formed his second administration in 1929 at the age of sixty-three years. In October 1930 he forgot the name of the Canadian Prime Minister, who was his guest at Chequers, and exclaimed "my brain is going".[6a] He could get no more than two hours sleep at night.

The financial crisis of 1931 with its inevitable consequences of pay-cuts, retrenchment and unemployment were sufficiently painful for a Socialist. The bitter enmity that he incurred from many in his party, and the accusations of traitorous conduct, over the formation of the National Government, marred the remainder of his life. From this time, not necessarily because of the events of the time, his deterioration was rapid. Lord Swinton wrote:

> "When I sat in MacDonald's Cabinet after 1931, I found him rather woolly; and his physical and mental powers weakened all too rapidly."[7]

MacDonald was not the only casualty and his financial advisers, who must bear responsibility for their policies, were in poor shape. Philip Snowden, the Chancellor of the Exchequer, was depressed and sick in December 1930. The exact nature of his illness has never been precisely disclosed but in March 1931 an infection of the bladder was diagnosed. One writer attributes the infection to the presence of stones but an enlarged prostate seems a possible cause. Snowden had to undergo an operation and needed daily nursing attention for the rest of his life. He was able to introduce his postponed budget on 27 April but there is no doubt that his health was impaired.

Furthermore at the height of the financial crisis in August the Governor of the Bank of England, Montagu Norman, was absent from his post. Earlier in the summer he could not face the ruin and failure of his personal policies. He collapsed at a meeting and was sent on a sea voyage for recuperation. Indeed the decision to leave his cherished gold standard was taken in his absence.

Lord Salter has referred to a serious illness that had affected MacDonald during a visit to America and to the fact that his eyesight deteriorated. He had glaucoma and, as with Grey, reading became difficult; his handwriting also was noticeably affected. MacDonald had no cause to conceal his feeling from an old friend like Salter who recorded his impressions in June 1933.

> "He (MacDonald) was already no longer in a mental and physical condition to be capable of the continuous and exacting responsibilities of high office."[8]

A few months before a disorder of perception may have been present for he was seen to look nervously over his shoulder while speaking in the Commons. He explained later that he was sure that a man in the gallery was about to shoot him.

In February 1934, Tom Jones, formerly Lloyd George's private secretary, whose diaries do much to illuminate this period, had gloomy news of MacDonald:

> "He has lost all grip and moved from one vagueness to another. There is some rumour that Horder has ordered Ramsay [*sic*] to return to Hampstead to sleep at nights and to restrict himself to 2 or 3 hours work per day".[9]

Emmanuel Shinwell met MacDonald at Frognal during the second administration and noted that "his back was bent and the characteristic upright gait was gone".[10] Clement Attlee has described MacDonald's decline and remarked that "his speeches became increasingly incoherent and for the last years of his life he was only a melancholy passenger in the Conservative ship".[11] Winston Churchill conceded nothing to the inexorable advances of pathological ageing and degeneration: he called MacDonald a "boneless wonder". Muddled and verbose as he was in public MacDonald retained sufficient mental clarity and judgement to be aware of the menace of a resurgent Germany. He was ahead of some of his contemporaries in realizing that Germany was an immediate enemy and in contemplating and initiating rearmament. He retired from the Premiership on 7 June 1935 but remained in office as Lord President of the Council. In the autumn he confessed that he began sentences and forgot what he was going to say; by December 1936 even a former supporter was forced to admit that he was "inane and gaga".[6b] He died at sea on a cruise liner in August 1937.

On 3 March 1908, a few weeks before Campbell-Bannerman's death, Stanley Baldwin took his seat in Parliament as the member for the Bewdley division of Worcestershire. His impact as a back-bencher was unremarkable and it was the downfall of Asquith's administration in December 1916 which brought him to the public eye as parliamentary private secretary to Bonar Law. He became joint Financial Secretary to the Treasury in June 1917 and entered the Cabinet, as President of the Board of Trade, in 1921. His record gave no hint either of burning ambition or even of hidden fires but it was he who dominated the meeting at the Carlton Club in October 1922 and, defying the Conservative members of Lloyd George's Cabinet, he persuaded his party to break away from the Liberals and seal the fate of the Coalition. Baldwin became Chancellor of the Exchequer in Bonar Law's administration and, as much due to Curzon's unpopularity as to the difficulties that would have been caused by his position in the Lords, he was invited to form a Ministry when Bonar Law died. This was short-lived but he was Prime Minister again from 1924 to 1929 and from 1935 to 1937: and, as Lord President of the Council in MacDonald's National Government from 1931 to 1935, he commanded considerable power and influence.

The image that Baldwin projected, perhaps subconsciously, unfortunately created a superficial and deceptive impression; it was a caricature of an English country squire with a large pipe and a preoccupation with cricket and pigs. If in one small aspect of his interests he was Lord Emsworth come to life the other facets of his character were long unknown and ignored. His literary and cultural interests were wide. His humane attitudes might now be curtly dismissed as patronizing paternalism, but he had a genuine concern for individuals, whether in the family business or in the Labour opposition. He had greater faith in the decency and virtues of the ordinary man than in the greater ability of romantic adventurers like Lloyd George or of egocentric individualists like Churchill and the first Lord Birkenhead.

The face that Baldwin presented to the world was that of the typical Englishman. In repose it gave no sign of the hidden tensions and fears which at times of stress would distort the mask. Hearing his calm and youthful voice it was difficult to believe that he became pale and nauseated and sweated before a speech; and that once, when Prime Minister, he nearly ran in panic from a Cathedral when he was to read the lesson. He was frightened to travel by car in foggy weather and he never went by aeroplane. A visit to the dentist induced pallor and he fainted easily. In April 1927 he attended a dinner at the Royal College of Surgeons and, as post-prandial entertainment, the guests were shown the museum. Baldwin collapsed but the ubiquitous Dawson managed to put him in a room away from the other guests and return him discreetly to Downing Street. Next morning Dawson, in the vernacular of the period, "overhauled" him and with less than his usual tact said that "it was merely a case of the heart of a very tired man going on strike . . ."[12]

Baldwin's mannerisms and tics were surely a sign of nervous tension. In Parliament he used to smell his notes and lick their edges. He scratched himself persistently so that red excoriations were visible on his head and face. He would half close his eyes and move his head and later he developed, like his father, a facial twitch involving his nose. He found it difficult to remain still and would restlessly fiddle with his pipe or walking-stick. Indeed he is a medical riddle and we have to be content with the comments of one of his intimates in the *Dictionary of National Biography*:

"His lethargy was often a mask to cover impulsive, emotional, and exhausting spurts of nervous energy."
"He was incapable of prolonged continuous effort."[2]

He had such a collapse just before the General Strike in 1926 and, according to a colleague, "as soon as the strike began, Baldwin was a passenger".[13]

Although the miners were still on strike in August 1926, Baldwin was ready for his annual holiday in Aix-les-Bains. King George V was shocked that the Prime Minister could leave the country at such a time and expressed his displeasure through his Private Secretary. Baldwin objected to any constraint in his movements and his aides, making use of the procedures adopted by the humblest in the land, tried to obtain a certificate of medical incapacity. Most of the leading consultants were themselves on holiday but at last a certificate was obtained and probably neither the King nor Baldwin realized that it had been signed by a gynaecologist. This administration lasted until 1929 and he did not become Prime Minister again until 1935. During his final period in office which lasted until 1937, one can learn much about his health from the diaries and letters of an intimate friend.[9b] The following extracts begin in the year that Hitler reoccupied the Rhineland:

February 21, 1936. Yesterday I breakfasted with the P.M. and found him rather sorry for himself. . . . There is nothing wrong beyond an inclination to get tired sooner than usual.
April 25, 1936. *Daily Mail* mentioned P.M.'s deafness as a contributory reason for resignation. I dare say in Cabinet with a large group around a big table it is a serious handicap.
July 7, 1936. He quotes Baldwin as saying "I am too tired for any fresh effort. . . . How long do you want me to go on?"
July 24, 1936. Downing Street Secretaries are concerned about the state of Baldwin's health. It is impossible to get a decision about anything out of him.
September 18, 1936. I reported (to Lord Dawson of Penn) that the patient (Stanley Baldwin) was distinctly better, more

PLATE 1

Roosevelt, February, 1945, Yalta ". . . there was a far-away look in his eyes" (Churchill)
(Reproduced by permission of Keystone Press Agency Ltd.)

Kennedy, 20th January, 1961. It was alleged that the puffiness of his face was related to therapy with steroids
(Reproduced by permission of United Press International (UK) Ltd.)

PLATE 2

Hitler, 20th July, 1944. After the bomb attempt "a back-side like a baboon".
(Reproduced by permission of United Press International (UK) Ltd.)

Hopkins and Stalin
(Reproduced by permission of Radio Times and Hulton Picture Library)

PLATE 3

Macmillan, 2nd October, 1963, "A few days before his illness"
(*Reproduced by permission of United Press International (UK) Ltd.*)

Eden, 1st November, 1956; "The Suez crisis"
(*Reproduced by permission of Radio Times and Hulton Picture Library*)

PLATE 4

Churchill, 8th October, 1954, "his speech . . . was poorly delivered"
(Reproduced by permission of Radio Times and Hulton Picture Library)

Acheson, Bevin and Schuman, 11th May, 1950.
(Reproduced by permission of Radio Times and Hulton Picture Library)

alert and interested but showing little mental resilience, and already brooding apprehensively on coming burdens and responsibilities.

October 16, 1936. The P.M. is back at No. 10 very much rested. . . . There is nothing organically wrong with him. He lost his nerve and every burden became a nightmare. He will last till the Coronation we all hope, but if the foreign situation becomes very difficult he may break under it.

February 19, 1937. On Monday I had lunch with the P.M. . . . "I shall sleep for a week when I get out of this," he groaned.

On 12 November 1936 Baldwin had to reply to Churchill during a Defence Debate which lead a Conservative official to comment: "This will take three months energy out of him."[6c] Superficially his handling of the Abdication crisis in December was effortless and brilliant but his emotions were deeply stirred. After a painful interview with Edward VIII he asked for a whisky and soda so that he could drink to the King's future happiness; both dissolved into tears. Baldwin did last until the Coronation and spent his last night at Chequers on 14 June 1937. His retirement was immediately spoiled by "nervous exhaustion" and increasing incapacity due to arthritis. He survived for ten more years and stoically bore the bitter recrimination and vilification of those who blamed him for neither checking Hitler's rise to power nor for preparing Britain's defences against the totalitarian threat.

A story is told, doubtless apocryphal, of an aeroplane accident in which fortunately there were no casualties. The inquiry revealed that over a period of years the two pilots, if not actually incompetent, had shown skill and attainments that were modest in the extreme. The directors of the airline privately admitted their foreknowledge of the limitations of the two individuals but had made no provision against the possibility that they might both be in the same aeroplane together. It was a singular misfortune for Great Britain, for Europe and for the world that Baldwin, as Premier, and Samuel Hoare, as Secretary of State for Foreign Affairs, were co-pilots in the Abyssinian crisis during the closing months of 1935.

In the summer of 1935, Mussolini's threat to Abyssinia was unmistakable but the approach to the problem divided political parties and the electorate. Surprisingly enough Winston Churchill and Robert Vansittart, the Permanent Under-Secretary at the Foreign Office, were reluctant to antagonize Mussolini unnecessarily and drive Italy into the arms of Germany. The left wing and the Liberals wished to make the Abyssinian question a test case for the League of Nations. The second policy carried a risk of war which neither the Government nor the people really dared to face. On the 11 September 1935, Hoare, hobbling to the rostrum with the aid of a stick, spoke before the full Assembly of the League of Nations at Geneva. There was an element of bluff in his call for collective security which was, rather unexpectedly, rapturously received by the democratic countries.

On 3 October 1935, the Italians invaded Abyssinia and the League hastily condemned Italy as an aggressor and recommended economic sanctions. By the time these took effect half of Abyssinia had been occupied and there still was a reluctance by individual countries to apply oil sanctions. Deprivation of oil would have crippled the Italian war effort. At the same time it would have adversely affected those countries, particularly Great Britain, whose economy depended on their role as a supplier of oil and allied products. Although the Conservatives won the General Election in the autumn of 1935, they came under considerable Labour pressure in the House and were forced to concede the principle of an oil embargo with a provisional date of 12 December. By that date any plans to confront Mussolini were ruined. Samuel Hoare, *en route* for a convalescent holiday in Switzerland, stopped in Paris during the week-end of 7–8 December for what he regarded as private talks with Pierre Laval, the French Prime Minister. Their conversations which leaked, or were leaked, to the Press had apparently dealt with concessions, rather than resistance, to Italy and the partition, rather than the restoration, of Abyssinia. Public reaction in Great Britain was unpredictably violent despite the fact that France and Britain, in the form of Laval and Hoare, had been charged by the League of Nations to bring Italy and Abyssinia to the council table. Baldwin was forced to dismiss Hoare. Far more than the enforcement of oil sanctions was lost, far more than Abyssinia was lost. Faith in the League of Nations vanished and faith in the ability of the great nations to protect the smaller nations was markedly diminished. From then on only ever-increasing concessions could buy temporary appeasement and England and France eventually had to wage war without the allies that they had lost or ignored.

On 7 January 1936 Baldwin discussed the Hoare-Laval pact and said:

"Hoare was bent on going on a holiday: he was seriously overworked. He had some fainting fits . . . he was tired out."[9c]

Later in the same year he referred to the Hoare-Laval conversations:

"They knocked me endways. For two days I did not know where I stood."[9d]

Hoare had been in poor shape since the summer. In August he was crippled by an attack of arthritis in one foot. Worse still he had a number of blackouts; at a cinema, at Glyndebourne, and in the Commons. Early in December his doctor ordered a period of convalescence in Switzerland and he was in no mood for any work or discussions, least of all a talk with as dextrous a politician as Pierre Laval. As Hoare confessed later:

"It may be that I was so pulled down by overwork that my judgement was out of gear."[14]

His biggest blackout followed on 12 December when he fell and broke his nose on the ice. As the storm raged he returned to England and in answer to Baldwin's presumably solicitous question about his health he replied "I wish I were dead". He made his resignation speech on 19 December 1935, his nose and face encased in plaster, but it is a commentary on the times that his fall from power was but a temporary set-back. He was back in office again, at the Admiralty, in the following year. That the onus of blame was seen to fall solely and unquestionably on Hoare may have been due to the fact that Stanley Baldwin did his best to evade any responsibility over Abyssinia. The Italians were concentrated on the Abyssinian border in August but

Baldwin insisted on his usual holiday at Aix-les-Bains. It required considerable effort by Hoare and Neville Chamberlain to persuade him to return in September. Indeed the whole story begins and ends with Baldwin. After meeting Laval in Paris, Hoare sent a dispatch to Baldwin who was spending that week-end at Chequers. The box reached Baldwin on the Saturday afternoon but, immersed in a detective story, he forgot about it until Monday morning. Would an earlier perusal have prevented the storm that broke that week? Could Hoare have been saved and, more important, could a compromise have been reached over Abyssinia?

Arthur Neville Chamberlain succeeded Baldwin in June 1937 and promptly discussed sanctions against Italy as the "very midsummer of madness". His experience had prepared him for departmental rather than supreme authority and for national rather than international problems. After a youthful failure at sisal planting in the Bahamas he made steady progress in the family firm. Local government had a great appeal for him and he was a successful Lord Mayor of Birmingham in what a captious critic called a lean year. In contrast his entry into central government as Director of National Service in 1916 was unsuccessful. Lloyd George never forgave or forgot this failure, attributed it to Chamberlain's small cranial capacity, and contemptuously referred to him as a pinhead. Nothing daunted he returned to the Government in 1922 as Postmaster-General and, after brief tenures of both offices, was outstanding both as Minister of Health from 1924-9 and as Chancellor of the Exchequer from 1931 until 1937. Baldwin was inexperienced and disinterested in foreign affairs and avoided them if he could. Chamberlain was equally inexperienced but what became an embracing interest was accompanied by a profound disregard of professional opinion. Appeasement arose partly from recognition of the tragic consequences of the Treaty of Versailles and partly from realization that Germany was a lesser evil than Russia. Thirty years of bitter history has not altered the analysis of the much maligned politicians of the nineteen thirties. In striving for peace, however, they give the dictators the impression that the democracies were effete and would avoid war at all costs and under any threat. Hitler who

had a secret and sneaking admiration for the British Empire
sadly underrated the underlying determination of the essentially
civilian figure who flew three times to Germany in September
1938. Mussolini largely misunderstood the nature of the visit
that Chamberlain and Lord Halifax paid him in January 1939.
He thought that such an approach could only result from weakness and said, with some prescience, that it indicated the end of
Britain as a world power. All who remember the Czechoslovak
crisis and the Munich agreement in September 1938 must
admire Chamberlain's fortitude although many may criticize
his judgement. The dry, passionless and unemotional attitude
was achieved at some cost for early in October of the same year
he went to Chequers for rest and refreshment and later
admitted:

> "I came nearer there to a nervous breakdown than I have ever
> been in my life. I have pulled myself together, for there is a
> fresh ordeal to go through in the House."[15a]

In his pathetic broadcast on 3 September 1939 Chamberlain
made it clear that the declaration of war was the end of all his
hopes and all his efforts. The qualities that made him such a
successful Minister in peace were not those required for the
ruthless prosecution of total war. The disastrous campaign in
Norway in April 1940 was followed by what was for him an even
more disastrous debate in the House of Commons. He resigned
on 10 May 1940, became Lord President of the Council in
Churchill's new administration, but died on 9 November of
the same year.

Chamberlain died of a neoplasm of the bowel but the exact
onset of symptoms and sign is obscure. The visit to Mussolini
early in 1939 proved no strain and that same indefatigable
diarist wrote:

> "He takes more open air exercise than his Father and drinks
> less than his brother. Why with his gout he should drink wine
> at all is a mystery to me."[9e]

Picking the ides of March as was his wont Hitler struck again
in 1939 and the remainder of Czechoslovakia was swallowed by
the third Reich. This was too much for Chamberlain who almost

cast around for countries to protect against future aggression.
Poland, Roumania and Greece were given guarantees that, in
modern parlance, lacked credibility. Worse still Hitler regarded
our arrangement with Poland as a blank cheque to encourage
future hostility and deliberate provocation.

Another diarist of the period, one who records facial
appearance with an almost clinical precision, wrote on 31
March 1939:

"Chamberlain comes into the House looking gaunt and ill.
The skin above his high cheekbones is parchment yellow. He
drops wearily into his place."[6d]

And again on 26 April when the Prime Minister made a
statement about the unprecedented introduction of conscrip-
tion:

"One sees signs of extreme exhaustion and profound mental
suffering."[6e]

The fact that this diarist notes that Chamberlain looked ill on
3 September 1939, the day that Great Britain and France found
themselves at war with Germany, may explain why the latter
consulted Lord Horder in November for gastro-intestinal discomfort and exacerbations of gout. Chamberlain's biographer,
from a study of his personal diaries and letters, remarks on
changes in personality and attitude in December 1939:

"Yet it is possible to detect a weariness, an added sensitiveness,
a disposition to identify criticism with faction. Some of this
may have come from the physical machine slowing down for
the letters speak of much gout and minor ailments."[15b]

Ironside, the Chief of the Imperial General Staff, recorded
that the Cabinet agreed on 10 September 1939 to plan for a
three-year war and that Chamberlain rested his head on the
table for several minutes and looked ghastly when he raised it
again. On 18 November he appeared "just a weary, tired old
man".[16] On 24 April 1940, Lady Halifax said that Chamberlain "seems to shrivel before one's eyes". Channon noted on 8
May that Chamberlain was "heart-broken and shrivelled" and
on 4 June that he was "tiny and fragile".[17]

On 16 June 1940 his diary mentions "considerable pain".[15c]
There are ominous tones in the words he wrote after a farewell
visit to his beloved Chequers in the same month:

> "We have had some happy days there, but they are over any-
> how, and it is difficult to see how there can be much more
> happiness for any of us."[15d]

Horder advised an exploratory operation on 24 July which
was followed by a more extensive procedure as a neoplasm of
the large bowel had been found. He returned to work in
September and it is ironic that one of the last duties of this man
of peace was to approve the establishment of Special Operations
Executive which was designed to set Europe ablaze. It is sad to
recall that as the curtains fell he thought that Great Britain
would be defeated and confided his fears to the ready ears of
Joseph Kennedy, the American Ambassador. During the
troglodyte existence of September 1940, introduced by the air-
raids, Churchill noticed sandbags being placed on the opposite
side of Downing Street. On inquiry he found that a private
room had been set aside so that Chamberlain could have the
medical treatment that would be impossible in a communal
shelter. This was too much. Kindly but firmly Churchill
insisted that Chamberlain should retire to the country where for
the last few weeks of his life he received State papers and
remained on duty. He died on 9 November 1940: "Malice may
have killed him. All his hopes gone: nothing more to live for."[17]

An increased prevalence of gout has been noted in many men
of distinction and recent studies suggest that senior business
executives, when matched with the general population, have
higher levels of serum uric acid; levels may also be higher in
individuals anticipating a distressing situation. Chamberlain
had a strong family history of gout and a closer study of his
diaries and letters might show whether exacerbations of gout
resulted from exacerbations of political turmoil; or whether
indeed exacerbations of gout were the cause of political complications and difficulties.

The natural history of neoplasm is inevitably unclear. A
shrewd lay observer reported signs of illness in March 1939 but
Chamberlain did not take medical advice until November. The

presence of unsuspected illness may have contributed to his maladroit handling of the debate in the House on 7–8 May 1940 which sealed his fate, but the dramatic and rapid deterioration thereafter is sufficiently remarkable to invite comment. One biographer, Iain Macleod, has drawn attention to the possible relationship between psychological trauma and the spread of cancer. This is dangerous ground on which even the boldest of psychiatrists only dare to walk on tiptoe. An extensive study in New York on patients with cancer in different sites showed to a significant degree that cancer was preceded by "loss of the central relationship and a sense of utter despair, and a conviction that life held nothing more for them".[18] Sir Heneage Ogilvie has written that "The happy man never gets cancer".

Cancer also handicapped an Ambassador in an important and vulnerable post. Sir Nevile Henderson was sent to the Berlin Embassy in 1937. It is not clear whether he was instructed to seek an understanding with the more moderate Nazis or whether a personal predilection for authoritarian governments led him to exceed his instructions. If he was not an appeaser he was a ready tool of the appeasers. Hitler's duplicity and ruthlessness in September 1938 shattered Henderson's illusions who later wrote:

> "I was already feeling very unwell at the time of a malady which was to put me *hors de combat* for four months in the winter;"[19a]

He returned to Britain in October for he had then been ill for six months. A well-known cancer surgeon operated on his abdomen and he could not return to Germany until February 1939. To quote his own words:

> "Physically I was still unfit but morally I was somewhat recovered from the pessimism and disgust which I had felt after the conclusion of the work of the International Commission which had defined the frontiers between Germany and Czechoslovakia . . ."[19b]

The Germans were well aware of his physical incapacity and took advantage of it. They would keep him waiting all evening at a reception and then grant him an interview in the early hours of the morning. Goering would invite him to his hunting lodge, tire him out with a day's shooting and a heavy and presumably alcoholic dinner, and then summon him to an important diplomatic discussion.

Perhaps nothing could have stopped the Nazi war machine from going into action at any time in any place. Nevertheless Nevile Henderson was not in the best state to win friends and influence people between February and September 1939; or to take part in frantic negotiations and meetings in an effort to avert war in August 1939.

Nor was another of Chamberlain's appointees to a key ambassadorial post in any better shape. Lord Lothian was made British Ambassador in Washington in 1939. By 1940 he was tired, but the post was one of exceptional responsibility. One section of American opinion was isolationist; a second section supported the allies, was critical of their puny efforts, but was as yet reluctant to go to war; a third section, probably a minority, was anxious to help the Allies. Lothian's task required tact and delicacy as Roosevelt, for a number of somewhat mixed motives, edged his divided people towards active participation.

In June 1940 it was noticed , though there was no unusual comment or action, that Lothian would fall asleep while dictating or even on public occasions. When he returned to England he fell asleep, no mean feat this, when dining with Winston Churchill. On his return to America in November 1940 he waited for the Clipper in Lisbon and our Ambassador noted that he fell asleep at meals. On landing in America on 23 November he was disastrously indiscreet. He told reporters: "Well, boys, Britain's broke; its your money we want."[20] This remark was highly embarrassing for President Roosevelt and his Administration who had manipulated the law to aid Britain; and it rightly earned Lothian a rebuke from his own Government.

Within two weeks Lothian was dead and, because he was a Christian Scientist, the lack of conventional medical evidence resulted in some mystery about his death. It is now known that he died of uraemia, the poisoning that follows failure of the kidneys, and which is characterized in its later stages by apathy, drowsiness and stupor.

It is the fashion now to decry the political leaders of the nineteen thirties and to call them the "guilty men" who failed to stop the dictators rising to power in Europe. All the evidence suggests that they were sick men rather than sinners. MacDonald, Baldwin and Chamberlain were beyond the then accepted age of retirement when they took office for the last time. It was their misfortune, and their countrymen's loss, that they had to face unprecedented stresses that neither their previous experience nor their mental and physical reserves could combat.

References

1. Robert Blake. *The Unknown Prime Minister*. Eyre & Spottiswoode.
2. Thomas Jones. *Dictionary of National Biography*.
3. Lord Riddell. *War Diaries*, p. 360. Nicholson & Watson.
4. Lord Beaverbrook. *The Decline and Fall of Lloyd George*, p. 228. Collins.
5. Leonard Woolf. *Beginning Again*, p. 219. Hogarth Press.
6a. Harold Nicolson. *Diaries and Letters 1930–39*, p. 56.
6b. p. 283. Weidenfeld & Nicolson.
6c. p. 278. Weidenfeld & Nicolson.
6d. p. 393. Weidenfeld & Nicolson.
6e. p. 400. Weidenfeld & Nicolson.
7. Earl of Swinton. *Sixty Years of Power*, p. 94. Hutchinson.
8. Arthur Salter. *Personality in Politics*, p. 64. Faber.
9. Thomas Jones. *A Diary with Letters*, p. 151.
9b. p. 175 and following. Oxford University Press.
9c. p. 158. Oxford University Press.
9d. p. 228. Oxford University Press.
9e. p. 425. Oxford University Press.
10. Emmanuel Shinwell. *Conflict without Malice*, p. 119. Odhams.
11. C. R. Attlee, *As It Happened*, p. 87. Heinemann.
12. Nourah Waterhouse. *Private and Official*, p. 342. Cape.
13. G. M. Young. *Stanley Baldwin*, p. 116.
14. Viscount Templewood. *Nine Troubled Years*, p. 177. Hart-Davis.
15a. Keith Feiling. *The Life of Neville Chamberlain*, p. 377. Collins.
15b. p. 430. Macmillan.
15c. p. 448. Macmillan.

15d. p. 448. Macmillan.
16. R. Macleod and D. Kelly. *The Ironside Diaries, 1937–40.*
     Constable.
17. Robert Rhodes James. *Chips,* pp. 242, 245, 256, 275. Weiden-
     feld & Nicolson.
18. *The Times,* 26 August, 1966.
19a. Nevile Henderson. *Failure of a Mission,* p. 145.
19b. p. 183. Hodder & Stoughton.
20. J. R. M. Butler. *Lord Lothian,* p. 307. Macmillan.

CHAPTER 7

Franklin Roosevelt: A puzzling
diagnostic problem

The election of Franklin Delano Roosevelt in 1932, as the 32nd President of the United States, was a tribute to his remarkable powers of physical and political rehabilitation. As a result of poliomyelitis in 1921 he was virtually paralysed from the waist downwards. He never walked normally again nor could he stand without supports. Fitted with clumsy steel braces he moved like a man on stilts. In an era, when a cripple was neither expected nor even permitted to live a normal life, his national acceptance was a triumph of personality, persuasion and self-confidence. In modern parlance he projected an image of physical and mental vitality which not only convinced his supporters but also reassured those who could remember the recent past. Within the previous eleven years the paralysed Wilson had been pushed around the White House in a wheelchair and Harding had died in office. The brevity of public memory is a boon to public figures. Immediately after the First World War the American people were only too anxious to forget Wilson and his inconvenient calls to duty and responsibility in faraway countries. Nor did they wish to be reminded of Harding who had pursued his pleasures both incontinently and indiscreetly.

Roosevelt was a magnificent candidate in spite of his physical imperfection. A member of an old and distinguished family, his wealth and good fortune had not led him into a life of ease and pleasure. He had enjoyed varied political experiences in New York State, both as Senator and Governor, and had served as Assistant Secretary of the Navy. In 1932, Presidential campaigns could not be so rigorously and statistically analysed as they are today but one intangible and immeasurable factor may have contributed to his success. The good times and the parties of the jazz age had gone and millions of unemployed constituted a monstrous American hangover. As a consequence, this crippled nation may have turned to a crippled man as a result of mutual sympathy and understanding. Roosevelt was a fellow victim who had overcome that fate and adversity that was all too common in their miserable lives, and who might understand their difficulties and those of their country. Set apart from his contemporaries by illness he was a different man who might succeed with different measures.

In his youth Roosevelt was physically neither stronger nor weaker than any other aspirant for high office. In his liability to illness he did not differ from the man in the street. Throughout his life he was afflicted by nose, throat and sinus infections. He had scarlet fever at school and a humiliating attack of measles prevented him from volunteering with other classmates for service in the Spanish-American War. He married Eleanor, a fifth cousin once removed, in 1905 at the age of twenty-three and their honeymoon in Europe was marred by the fact that he had several attacks of urticaria, variously attributed to fleas and white wine. In July 1907 his wife found to her horror that he walked in his sleep and had to lead him away from the bedroom window. He had typhoid fever in 1912, later claimed to have had it twice, and maintained that it was less unpleasant than paratyphoid fever. He had an appendicectomy in 1915, and pneumonia, after a tour of the Western Front, in 1918.

Contemporary photographs show that he was a splendid physical specimen, confirmed by his devotion to sailing, swimming and golf. Such was his passion for bodily fitness that in 1917 he arranged for members of the Cabinet to have physical training in Potomac Park. This had disastrous consequences for Franklin Lane, the Secretary of the Interior, who had a heart attack. Meanwhile his career proceeded apace. He had been elected to the New York State Senate as a Democrat in 1910 and was re-elected in 1912, although he played no part in the campaign because of typhoid fever. In March 1913 he became Assistant Secretary of the Navy, a post which fulfilled his ambitions and enabled him to indulge his genuine love for ships and the sea. In the 1920 elections he stood as a Vice-Presidential

candidate and perhaps was not too disheartened when the
Democrats were defeated. The republican tide was rolling in and
there was ample time in the future to allow him to wait for the
turn.

The infection that struck him in 1921, at the age of thirty-
nine years, was neither unknown to him nor even unexpected.
For some years he had shown an unusual interest in poliomyelitis. He may have been more fearful for his children than for
himself but three letters, written between July and September
1916, bear witness to this preoccupation. The events of 10
August 1921, when he was on holiday on Campobello Island,
are well known. A day of violent exercise on land and sea;
exposure to the heat of a forest fire and to the ice-cold waters of
the Bay of Fundy; an unnecessary wait in cold, wet bathing
clothes followed by shivering, fever, pains and loss of movement.

His local practitioner called in the celebrated octogenarian, W.
W. Keen, who was on holiday near by. Keen, one of the foun-
ders of American neurosurgery, made a preliminary diagnosis
of thrombosis of the spinal cord. Like many a good doctor he
later changed his mind and, in a letter to Eleanor dated 18
August, said there might be inflammation of the spinal cord.
He also rendered his account for 600 dollars. Poliomyelitis
was mentioned for the first time on 23 August following an
examination by Dr Robert Lovett. On 13 September 1921
Roosevelt was literally smuggled from Campobello to the
mainland and did not return to the island until 1933 when he
was President.

Of the two problems that now faced him, the struggle to
recover the use of his paralysed limbs was by no means the most
daunting. He had to overcome the efforts of his formidable
Mother, who wanted him to retire from politics and lead the life
of a country gentleman at Hyde Park. Much has been made of
the encouragement of Eleanor Roosevelt and Louis Howe and
their indulgence towards his seemingly hopeless desire to return
to public life. Probably Roosevelt did not need as much encouragement as they and others thought. The capacity to overcome obstacles and set-backs distinguishes the exceptional man
from the mass of ordinary men. The apparent influence of fate
or destiny on an individual is often nothing more than a refusal

by that person to accept defeat. Paralysis, like his former political opponents, could be conquered by effort and determination. If he could no longer play golf, and he never mentioned that sport again, he could swim and he became convinced that the waters at Warm Springs, Georgia, had special curative properties. He spent long periods there and followed his own progress and the state of his fellow victims with such enthusiasm, that he came to be called Dr Roosevelt. He organized a Foundation at Warm Springs, which became a second home and, in later years, a second White House.

By 1924 he was sufficiently recovered to return to politics. He became manager of Governor Al Smith's pre-convention campaign for the Democratic Presidential nomination and was asked to make the main address. On 26 June 1924 he was brought to the rostrum on a wheelchair and used crutches to reach the speaker's desk. During the 1928 convention he performed a similar service for Smith but by this time the crutches had been replaced by a cane. Shortly afterwards he gave up any illusions that he may have had about regaining the use of his legs. Originally he was reluctant to accept the Democratic nomination for the Governorship of New York State for he had hoped to continue regular medical treatment at Warm Springs. Once he had been persuaded he seized the chance of election to the office that offered the best stepping-stone to the Presidency. During his second term as Governor in 1931, he tried to dispose of any doubts about his fitness by releasing to the public the details of a medical examination. Such revelations were unusual at that time and, apart from the paralysed legs, the details did not attract adverse comment. It is only hindsight that underlines certain findings in a man of forty-nine that apparently held no significance at the time: a systolic blood pressure of 140 mm. Hg., a diastolic of 100 mm. Hg. and an electrocardiograph tracing which was interpreted as showing left ventricular preponderance and an inverted T wave in lead 3. In the absence of information about the other two leads it is impossible to say whether this tracing was suggestive of underlying abnormality.

As 1932, the year of the next Presidential election, grew near, Roosevelt became increasingly sensitive to comments about his health. On 29 December 1931, he wrote to the editor of the

Butte Standard, objected to his editorial entitled "The Wheel Chair at Albany", and denied that he had a wheel chair. On 20 May 1932 he wrote to the publisher of the *New York Sun* and complained of a reporter's suggestion that while a Governor could go to Warm Springs for treatment, without interference with duty, a President could not. Neither poliomyelitis nor paralysis could be denied and they always provided ample scope for differential diagnosis by the uninformed, the malicious, the paranoid and the rumour mongers. During the 1932 elections, it was said that he was crippled by syphilis, and on another occasion that he had been a victim of encephalomyelitis rather than poliomyelitis. His buoyant self-confidence and arrogant cocksureness was, and still is, attributed to euphoria resulting from cerebral degeneration. It was due possibly to his cyclothymic temperament which led to swings of mood at monthly intervals.

"When he was on the upcast of the curve he was full of energy and optimism, but in the troughs he tended to be without buoyancy and depressed in outlook."[1]

There are those who maintain that four years in supreme power are as much as mind and body can stand and it is true that, while the first term passed without any apparent adverse effect on his health, there were ugly whisperings in 1937 at the beginning of his second term. His Secretary of the Interior, Harold Ickes, whose comments about his own health and that of his colleagues reflect an innate clinical acumen, noted in the summer of 1937:

"He (Roosevelt) has paid a heavy toll during these past four years. His face is heavily lined and inclined to be gaunt . . . and he is distinctly more nervous".[2a]

He made further observations in November of that year:

"There isn't any doubt that the President is showing the strain he had been through. He looks all of fifteen years older since he was inaugurated in 1933."[2b]

At the same time, Jim Farley, the Chairman of the Democratic National Committee, naturally sensitive to Washington gossip, learned that there was worry over the state of Roosevelt's heart, and that Admiral Cary Grayson, who had been Wilson's physician, had heard a similar story. Rumours continued to spread, inspired, no doubt, by the bitter hatred of Roosevelt that was present in certain sections of the American community. Some said that Roosevelt had a fatal illness, that his mind was affected and even that he had died on his yacht. At this time Roosevelt had remarkable powers of recuperation which later in his career gave his supporters a misplaced feeling of confidence. Ickes noted that Roosevelt looked unusually well in September 1938 and after a holiday in the Caribbean in March 1939. He added a warning on this last occasion:

"However, I could not but notice at (the) Cabinet meeting that his face showed, perhaps more than ever, the terrific strain under which he has been working."[2c]

It is a matter for regret that, although Ickes lived until 1952, his published diaries contain no entries after 1940. In order to study Roosevelt's health after 1940 one must turn to observers who are more circumscribed, more discreet and less inquisitive. In November 1940 the controversial third term campaign led to Roosevelt's re-election. Apart from an episode in May 1941, diagnosed by Roosevelt himself as "intestinal 'flu", there is no mention of other illness in that year which ended with the Japanese assault on Pearl Harbor, or in the early part of 1942 as the American nation girded itself for war.

In January 1943 Roosevelt flew in a Pan-American Boeing to Casablanca to confer with Churchill and the allied political and service chiefs. He was accompanied amongst others by his personal physician, Admiral Ross T. McIntire, who was later to publish a book entitled *Twelve years with Roosevelt*. He was an eye and ear, nose and throat surgeon and was originally introduced to Roosevelt, a victim of chronic sinusitis, by Admiral Cary Grayson. As well as the daily supervision of his extremely important patient, he held an exacting post as Chief of the Navy's Bureau of Medicine and Surgery. He recorded that, as far as flying was concerned, Roosevelt had an "excellent ceiling"[3a] prior to Casablanca but does not explain why he was so anxious about Roosevelt's heart during this trip. Hopkins describes McIntire's anxiety, the latter's objection to the aircraft flying at 13,000 ft, and how Roosevelt looked pale at an altitude of 9,000 ft. The return trip to America began on 25 January 1943, and the plane avoided the Atlas Mountains because of McIntire's objection to altitude.

Roosevelt went abroad again in November 1943, travelling by sea to Oran, and flying to Cairo for meetings with Churchill. Subsequently the two allied leaders flew to Teheran for the first of the "Big Three" meetings with Stalin. Elliott Roosevelt asked McIntire, with reference to the Cairo-Teheran flight, the height at which his Father could fly safely and quoted the reply: "Nothing over 7,500 – and that's tops".[4] On the night of 28/29 November, Roosevelt had "an acute digestive" attack and there were ill-founded fears that he had been poisoned. It was he who had been the host at dinner that night and the meal had been prepared by his own Filipino mess staff. There are further reminders of McIntire's anxiety about Roosevelt's heart. During the flight from Tunis to Dakar on 9 December 1943, he did not consider that the plane should fly above the clouds and an altitude of 8,000 ft was selected.

Teheran was but a brief honeymoon for the Big Three. The hopes of a lasting relationship that would win the war and secure the peace were dimmed at Yalta in February 1945 and stilled by the end of that year. Teheran was the high tide of Roosevelt's presidency. Thereafter, slowly and at first imperceptibly, his physical and mental state deteriorated relentlessly. Early in 1944 Admiral William D. Leahy, his Chief of Staff, commented on Roosevelt's inability to throw off the effects of colds and bronchitis and to regain his normal state of health. Despite a week's rest at Hyde Park, in January, February and March 1944, he still had bronchitis at the end of March. Early in April he left for a month's holiday in South Carolina and during this time his son, Franklin, expressed concern about his health.

McIntire was also anxious about the so-called influenza and persistent bronchitis, for the constant coughing interfered with Roosevelt's sleep. In addition his patient had short attacks of abdominal pain and distension accompanied by sweating. Two consultants were called in and McIntire later recorded that they found arteriosclerosis, "bronchial irritation" and certain changes in the electrocardiogram. Roosevelt returned to Washington on 7 May 1944 and Hassett, a member of his personal staff, was certain that he had not thrown off the effects of influenza and bronchitis. Roosevelt had a further medical examination on 10 May and, although no mention was made of the blood pressure reading, the chest X-ray was reported as normal. At this critical moment in American history his work schedule was reorganized and virtually confined him to a four hour day. In July 1944, James Roosevelt witnessed one of the attacks of abdominal pain that McIntire had noted earlier in the year. Roosevelt writhed with pain and his face was white and agonized. By the autumn of 1944 McIntire told Roosevelt that he did not look well. His neck was scrawny, his face was lined and, presumably because of loss of weight, his shirt collar looked too big and his coat jacket hung on his shoulders like a bag.

McIntire gives certain details of medical examinations conducted on Roosevelt between 20 September and 1 November 1944. The systolic blood pressure varied between 165 and 180 mm. Hg. and the diastolic pressure lay between 85 and 100 mm. Hg. The electrocardiogram was unchanged but there is no mention of a further chest X-ray. Before the end of 1944 Roosevelt was examined by Dr Bruenn, a cardiologist, and Dr Robert Duncan, a chest physician. McIntire insists that Roosevelt was at his worst between his election for the fourth time in November 1944, and the fourth inauguration in January 1945. The systolic blood pressure varied from 170 to 188 mm. Hg. and the "heart reserve had to be watched". Roosevelt lost his appetite and his weight fell to 170 lbs. McIntire records deep concern for the first time in March 1945, because Roosevelt was at least 15 lbs below his normal weight. It was during this month that Roosevelt told a State Department official that he had lost 35 lbs in weight.

At the end of March 1945, as Roosevelt went to Warm Springs for the last time, Hassett told Bruenn that he (Roosevelt) "is slipping away from us".[6a] Bruenn admitted there was cause for alarm and later disclosed that he had found that Roosevelt had a systolic blood pressure of 210 mm. Hg. and even 300 mm. Hg. He said that Roosevelt had lost 25 lbs in weight, had no appetite and tired easily. McIntire had not come to Warm Springs but, after Roosevelt's fatal seizure on 12 April 1945, there was little that Dr Bruenn, or Dr Paullin, who drove frantically from Atlanta, could do.

Death was assumed to be due to cerebral haemorrhage, but in the absence of an autopsy or of a more detailed statement, there was, and still is, speculation about underlying pathological lesions. Roosevelt presents a fascinating diagnostic problem and McIntire's book stimulates further inquiry rather than satisfies curiosity. He limits Roosevelt's deterioration to the last six weeks of his life and, referring to the adverse comments about Roosevelt's health at Yalta, there is a suggestion of personal involvement and responsibility in his statement:

> "Had he been dying on his feet at Yalta, I, as one bound by his professional oath, could not and would not have permitted the President to have poured out his energy in day and night sessions."[3b]

He has grounds for denying that Roosevelt had any previous history of a stroke but less for stating that he "never had any serious heart condition".[3c] Roosevelt may not have had a myocardial infarction but McIntire had to admit that, "His heart, quite naturally, was our principal concern."[3d] A verdict that is reinforced by the fact that Bruenn, a cardiologist, went with Roosevelt to Yalta and on the last trip to Warm Springs. In fact there were considerable grounds for concern in 1944 for Moran has disclosed the contents of a letter, from Dr Robert Lee of Boston, that he received prior to the Yalta conference. Roosevelt had heart failure eight months before with hepatic enlargement and oedema. Coming events cast their shadows before and the blood pressure recordings and electrocardiographic changes indicated as early as 1931 that his cardiovascular system may have been vulnerable. Pathological changes in his arteries were responsible for his death but not for other symptoms and signs that had been present for over a year.

Loss of weight, loss of appetite and cachexia, were noticed by his associates and is now permanently recorded in the photographs that were taken at Yalta and long suppressed. Neoplastic disease is an obvious diagnosis, particularly in view of the history of "bronchitis". The negative chest X-rays, would not necessarily exclude a carcinoma of the lung. Furthermore Roosevelt was a heavy smoker, although the association between cigarette smoking and lung cancer was not appreciated at the time. McIntire said of Roosevelt that "cigarettes were his weakness",[3e] although in a letter to Hopkins on 18 May 1944, Roosevelt wrote that he had reduced his cigarette smoking from 20–30 a day to 5–6 a day. In view of the colicky abdominal pain a neoplasm of the gastro-intestinal tract or of one of the abdominal viscera cannot be excluded, but McIntire makes no mention of barium studies.

Great men should have an autopsy, and the findings made public, so that natural curiosity or unwarranted speculation may be dispelled. In the absence of authoritative information, private inquiries inevitably disclose facts that have been hitherto unexplained and which become the basis of mystery and legend. Further inquiries of this nature have even led to the suggestion that Roosevelt had an autopsy though the findings were not disclosed.

An American physician noticed that a pigmented naevus, above Roosevelt's left eyebrow, did not appear in photographs after 1943. He concluded that it had been removed surgically and suggested that Roosevelt's terminal illness was due to malignant deposits from a pigmented growth.[7] He supports his theory with additional evidence which, in default of information from the Roosevelt family, cannot be dismissed. Surgeons from the Walter Reed Hospital, Washington, D.C., presented a paper on the treatment of malignant melanoma at a meeting in St Louis, Missouri, in 1949. All the slides and specimens shown had a serial number with one exception. This was a section of brain with a large metastatic melanoma in the right hemisphere. It merely bore a date: 14 April 1945. The fact that this was the day on which Roosevelt's body arrived in Washington from Warm Springs makes this observation rather more than a mere coincidence.

Grave charges have been levelled against Roosevelt and his advisers by critics who insist that he was manifestly unfit to accept the democratic nomination in 1944 and to take the oath of office for the fourth time in January 1945. They contend that it was irresponsible and dangerous to allow an invalid, possibly a dying man, to engage in negotiations with Stalin and Churchill at Yalta that would virtually recast the maps of Europe and Asia and influence the lives of millions of people.

Only the doctors can proffer an opinion about Roosevelt's competence to discharge his obligations and, apart from McIntire, they have remained silent. After more than twenty years they are still bound by professional secrecy and by loyalty to the dead President. Their prime duty was to their patient and to the fulfilment of his wishes and ambitions. It was no part of their responsibility or function to tell Roosevelt what he could or should not do. Had the doctors possessed these powers, they could not have secured the President's compliance for he was also their Commander-in-Chief. Eleanor Roosevelt observed that her husband was determined to go to Yalta despite illness "and when he made up his mind that he wanted to do something he rarely gave up the idea".[8]

McIntire expressed no particular concern until after the 1944 election had been decided in Roosevelt's favour. Dr Howard Bruenn, the cardiologist, apparently only disclosed his anxiety within a few days of Roosevelt's death. The doctors may have laboured under the disadvantage of daily contact with the patient and their clinical senses, deadened by familiarity, may no longer have detected insidious and subtle deterioration. The experienced practitioner may, for the same reason, have the mortification of finding that a newly qualified locum tenens, seeing a patient for the first time, makes the diagnosis that has long eluded him.

The doctors may have kept silent for other reasons. They were not judges and many patients have survived fatal prognoses that have been given with every justification and in good faith. Despite their acceptance of valid pathological data, doctors are not alone in appreciating that where there is life there is hope. Death is inevitable sooner or later and reasonable optimism, or the avoidance of pessimism, should be condoned rather than condemned. However, James Roosevelt does not absolve the doctors from responsibility and said with reference to the fourth-term race in 1944:

"I never have been reconciled to the fact that Father's physicians did not flatly forbid him to run."[9a]

Members of Roosevelt's Cabinet and personal staff were in no better position than the doctors to offer advice about his conduct and had less reason to do so. They were serving a great President in the greatest war in history and had gained unprecedented power, privilege and influence. Moments of doubt and the promptings of conscience may have been resolved by the rationalization that they and Roosevelt were as expendable as a soldier in a foxhole or a pilot in a B.17.

It is easy to sit in judgement nearly a quarter of a century later and say that Roosevelt was failing. The bulk of the evidence is retrospective and tainted by the fact that contemporary witnesses might have subsequently painted what they should or might have seen rather than what they did see. Evidence from the Roosevelt family is of singular value for the members might be expected to protect his reputation. It is significant that Franklin Jun. told Leahy in April 1944 that he was concerned about his Father. James was the horrified witness of his Father's agonized writhings in July 1944 and has said:

"The fourth-term race in 1944 was Father's death warrant. I saw him only twice in that period – once just before the campaign and again on Inauguration Day. Each time I realized with awful irrevocable certainty that we were going to lose him."[9b]

The fact that he was failing before the election is confirmed by Robert Sherwood, one of his speech writers, and a long standing and ardent supporter. In September 1944 he met Roosevelt for the first time in eight months:

"I was shocked by his appearance. I had heard that he had lost a lot of weight, but I was unprepared for the almost ravaged appearance of his face. He had his coat off and his shirt collar seemed several sizes too large for his emaciated neck."[10a]

Moran saw Roosevelt at this time, during the second Quebec

conference, and has stated that "you could have put your fist between his neck and his collar."[11]

Once re-elected as President only death could stop the inauguration on 20 January 1945. The clinical picture had darkened for the blurred impressions of vague ill-health had hardened into the deep edged lines of overt disease. John Gunter wrote, "I was terrified when I saw his face. I felt certain that he was going to die."[12] Frances Perkins, the Secretary of Labour, describes his appearance at a Cabinet meeting just before the inauguration:

"When he came in I thought he looked bad and this was the first time I had ever thought so. His clothes looked much too big for him. His face looked thin, his colour was grey, and his eyes were dull."

After two hours in session she records further impressions:

"As I sat down beside him I had a sense of his enormous fatigue. He had the pallor, the deep grey colour of a man who had been long ill. He supported his head with his hand as though it were too much to hold it up. His lips were blue. His hand shook."[13]

Bernard Baruch commented on the trembling of his hands and Stettinius, the recently appointed Secretary of State, had noticed that Roosevelt's hands and body had trembled during the inauguration address. The significance of this tremor is uncertain for it seems that it had been present for years and was a family trait.

During the voyage to Yalta, Roosevelt made little preparation for the conference, and James F. Byrnes, the Director of War Mobilization and Reconversion, was disturbed by his appearance. A meeting was held at Malta on 2 February and Eden recorded that Roosevelt "gives the impression of failing powers".[14]

On 7 February 1945 Moran recognized that he had advanced signs and symptoms of hardening of the cerebral arteries. Roosevelt's colleagues, his daughter and his doctor would not admit that the outlook was hopeless. Churchill paints the most vivid picture of all:

"But at Yalta I noticed that the President was ailing. His captivating smile, his gay and charming manner, had not deserted him, but his face had a transparency, an air of purification, and often there was a far-away look in his eyes."[15]

Admiral Leahy, Roosevelt's Chief of Staff, though admitting that the President's health was a cause for concern, saw no signs of weakness. Roosevelt appeared ill in one photograph taken at Yalta and Leahy attributed this to a bad print. He said that Roosevelt looked tired after the conference but "so did we all".[5b] Roosevelt wrote to his wife on 12 February after the conference, "I am a bit exhausted but really all right"; and again on 18 February, "All well, but still need a little sleep."[16]

Sherwood, seeking to explain an unnecessary concession that Roosevelt made to the Russians over China, allows that there may have been incapacity:

"It is my belief that Roosevelt would not have agreed to that final firm commitment had it not been that the Yalta Conference was almost at an end and he was tired and anxious to avoid further argument."[10b]

The sea voyage from Yalta seemingly worked wonders for, on 28 February 1945, Hassett recorded that Roosevelt "hasn't looked better in a year."[6b] and Frances Perkins, who had been so gloomy in January, wrote that his face was gay, his eyes were bright and his skin was a good colour again. He sat for his report to Congress on 1 March 1945 and for the first time made public reference to his disability. Later in March a State Department official noted that Roosevelt was "unable to discuss serious matters", and that he "was in no condition to offer balanced judgements upon the great questions of war and peace which had concerned him for so long".[17] Mackenzie King, the Canadian Prime Minister, was distressed at Roosevelt's appearance:

"My old friend looked so badly, so haggard and worn, that I almost sobbed. I went up to him and kissed him on both cheeks . . ."[18]

His old friends at Warm Springs were equally disturbed when Roosevelt arrived at the end of March. His hand shook so much when he greeted the Mayor that he dislodged his own spectacles. There was a similar occurrence in church a few days later. In the morning of 12 April, Hassett was shocked at Roosevelt's appearance. The stroke occurred at 1.15 p.m. and life was extinct at 3.35 p.m., Central Time.

No part of the twelve years that Roosevelt spent as President has been more bitterly criticized than the seven days at Yalta. Here it is alleged, between 3 and 10 February 1945, Stalin dominated the dying Roosevelt and an unbelievably and uncharacteristically compliant Churchill. The ills of the post-war world have been laid at Roosevelt's grave.

These critics maintain that the Russians would inevitably have entered the war against Japan at a time and place to suit their own convenience. They insist that the concessions, made to Stalin by Roosevelt, were therefore unnecessary and merely enabled the Communists to dominate Manchuria and, later, the whole Chinese mainland. Sumner Welles and Robert Sherwood, two of Roosevelt's most ardent supporters, criticize the bargaining over China's future that was made moreover in the absence of Chiang Kai-shek and with the proviso that America and Britain would ensure his acceptance when finally he was informed.

Judgements of his political decisions, like the judgements about his clinical condition, are necessarily retrospective. Now that we can study the cards that were held by the Big Three at Yalta, we realize that Roosevelt did not have the strongest of hands though he might have played it better. His Chiefs of Staff were pressing for Russian support in the war against Japan. Roosevelt knew of a destructive projectile that might be ready in August but the atomic bomb had not been completed and none could predict its military and political potential. The Russians were negotiating from strength, they were within fifty miles of Berlin, whereas the allied advance had only recovered its momentum after the set-back in the Ardennes.

Political bargaining at the summit bears no relation to conventional morality, justice or ethics. There are those who maintain that the Roosevelt of the palmy days would have made a shrewder assessment of Stalin and have concluded that the short-term saving of allied lives did not compensate for the long-term losses entailed by Communist domination of the Far East and Europe. One piece of evidence suggests, however, that, well or ill, Roosevelt was already a committed man long before he went to Yalta. In an oft quoted talk with William Bullitt he had said:

"Bill, I don't dispute your facts, they are accurate. I don't dispute the logic of your reasoning. I just have a hunch that Stalin is not that kind of man. Harry (Hopkins) says he's not and that he doesn't want anything but security for his country, and I think that if I give him everything I possibly can and ask nothing from him in return, *noblesse oblige*, he won't try to annex anything and will work with me for a world of democracy and peace."[19]

References

1. Lord Casey. *Personal Experience, 1939–46,* p. 18. Constable.
2a. Harold Ickes. *The Secret Diary,* vol. II, p. 182.
2b. Vol. II, p. 246. Weidenfeld & Nicolson.
2c. Vol. II, p. 590. Weidenfeld & Nicolson.
3a. Ross T. McIntire. *Twelve Years with Roosevelt,* p. 19.
3b. p. 24. Putnam.
3c. p. 15. Putnam.
3d. p. 239. Putnam.
3e. p. 76. Putnam.
4. Elliott Roosevelt, *As He Saw It,* p. 146. Duell, Sloane & Pearce.
5a. William D. Leahy, *I Was There,* p. 244.
5b. p. 377. Gollancz.
6a. William D. Hassett. *Off The Record With F.D.R.,* p. 327.
6b. p. 318. Allen & Unwin.
7. F. M. Massie. *Modern Medicine,* March 6, 1961, p. 211.
8. Eleanor Roosevelt. *The Autobiography,* p. 273. Hutchinson.
9a. James Roosevelt and Sidney Shallett. *Affectionately, F.D.R.,* p. 313. Harrap.
9b. p. 311. Harrap.
10a. R. E. Sherwood. *The White House Papers of Harry L. Hopkins,* vol. II, p. 812. Eyre & Spottiswoode.

10b. Vol. II, p. 856. Eyre & Spottiswoode.
11. Lord Moran. *Winston Churchill: The Struggle for Survival*, p. 179. Constable.
12. John Gunther. *Roosevelt in Retrospect*, p. 31. Hamish Hamilton.
13. Frances Perkins. *The Roosevelt I Knew*, p. 312. Viking Press.
14. Earl of Avon. *The Reckoning*, p. 512. Cassell.
15. Winston S. Churchill. *The Second World War*, vol. VI, p. 416. Cassell.
16. Elliott Roosevelt. *The Roosevelt Letters*, vol. 3, p. 526. Harrap.
17. Robert Murphy. *Diplomat Among Warriors*, p. 303. Collins.
18. Francis Biddle. *In Brief Authority*, p. 376. Doubleday.
19. William Bullitt *Life Magazine*, 30 August 1948.

CHAPTER 8

The invalids who worked with Roosevelt:
Choice or chance?

Julius Caesar liked men about him who were fat, while Stalin preferred men who were under five foot six inches in height. Roosevelt had men about him who were infirm although the high proportion of valetudinarians in his Cabinets seems to have aroused little comment. His own rehabilitation may have persuaded him that strength of will can overcome physical weakness and that infirmity may act as a spur. It is unlikely that his personal experience led him to ignore sickness for many of his letters express genuine concern about the health of others. Perhaps he felt more secure in the company of the disabled and they in turn could have been attracted to him for a similar reason. It is possible that the distinguished invalids who were his Cabinet officers and intimates between 1933 and 1945 were assembled by chance or coincidence. Any rigorous inquiry about the health of senior officials in any country might reveal an equally large number of physical and mental abnormalities but allowance must be made for special circumstances during Roosevelt's first two terms. The diaries of Harold Ickes, the Secretary of the Interior, are a unique source and the profusion of clinical detail may give a distorted impression about the incidence of disease. No other country seems to have had an Ickes so it cannot be determined if other cabinets had as many geriatric patients as did the American.

Not only did Roosevelt come to be surrounded by invalids but it was an invalid who worked and schemed to make him President. Louis MacHenry Howe gave up his job as a political reporter to manage Roosevelt's second campaign for the State Senate in 1912. He moved with Roosevelt to Washington and served as his Secretary and Special Assistant in the war years. It

was Howe, as much as Eleanor Roosevelt, who fanned the
dimmed embers of his political ambition when he lay paralysed
in 1921. Howe had been handicapped since childhood by
respiratory disorders. He outlived a gloomy prognosis that had
been given in 1908 but had a serious collapse in 1913. Attacks of
"asthma" and "bronchitis" occurred in childhood and his heart
was also affected.

He established himself in the Roosevelt household after 1921
and Eleanor must have had mixed feelings about his presence.
Self-medication for asthma with a pungent incense made the
atmosphere of his room intolerable to others. Had he ceased to
smoke it would have been better both for his lungs and also for
Eleanor Roosevelt's cushions and carpets which were be-
spattered with cigarette ash. As Roosevelt overcame the
stigma of paralysis Howe became more incapacitated and by
1929 he could not climb a flight of stairs without discomfort.
From the year 1933 he had a suite in the White House though
exacerbations of respiratory disease required treatment in an
oxygen tent at the Naval Hospital. Howe was virtually acting
as a Minister without Portfolio and the strange association did
not escape notice:

> "It is a curious twist of fate which has placed the affairs of the
> world's wealthiest country in this crisis in the hands of two
> men, one of whom walks with difficulty and the other of
> whom has rotten internal workings . . ."[1]

Between 1934 and his death in April 1936 he was so short of
breath that dressing became a burden. Despite his condition he
still proferred political advice to his beloved Franklin. The
devotion was mutual for, despite the rarity of genuine friendship in political life, Howe's death left Roosevelt with a sense of
personal loss.

Early in 1933 Robert Sherwood, later to become a speech
writer for Roosevelt and the biographer of Harry Hopkins,
waxed lyrical about the triumph of the Democratic Party:

> "Blare of bugles
> Din-din
> The New Deal is moving in"[2]

This mood was not matched by the mobility of the Cabinet members. Thomas J. Walsh had been chosen as Attorney-General but, returning from a Florida honeymoon with his younger bride, died in a pullman car on his way to Washington before he could be sworn. The Treasury was first offered to Carter Glass who declined for reasons of health and then to William H. Woodin who, after little more than one year's service, died in May 1934. On 19 June 1936 Ickes noted that George H. Dern, the Secretary of War, had not attended the last few Cabinet meetings. Ickes learned from Farley in July that Dern had little idea of what was happening in the War Department, and from Roosevelt in August, that he might die shortly because of poisoning from bladder and kidney trouble. This prophesy was fulfilled on 24 August.

The Navy Department

Ickes devotes many entries to the appalling saga of Claude Augustus Swanson who had been made Secretary of the Navy in 1933, as much for the fact that his appointment would create a seat in the Senate, as for his interest in the Navy. Swanson was admitted to hospital with high blood pressure in December 1933 and, during his next appearance at the Cabinet in March 1934, had difficulty in holding a cigarette. In July 1936 Ickes had another gossip with Farley who said that Swanson might die at any moment. Swanson fainted at a White House reception in January 1937 but his wife explained that he had a long history of similar attacks. In 1937 Swanson, manifestly a sick man, was strongly urging war with Japan over the bombing of the gun-boat, U.S.S. *Panay*. He had to be lead in and out of the Cabinet, could not stand without support, and could hardly be understood because his voice was indistinct. In September 1938 McIntire indiscreetly disclosed to Ickes his doubts about Swanson's future which were refuted when the latter attended the Cabinet again in March 1939. By this time he was virtually speechless but he remained "in office" and died in harness, after a final stroke, on 7 July 1939.

Other officials, whom Roosevelt sent to the Navy Department, were dogged by misfortune and ill-health. Henry Roosevelt, a distant cousin, served as Assistant Secretary until his

death in 1936. He was replaced by Charles Edison who eventually succeeded Swanson in January 1940. Edison was "frail in
health and insufficiently enthusiastic about his job"³ᵃ and, as
the war clouds banked over the Atlantic, he made way for
Frank Knox, a Republican, in July 1940. Knox has been criticized for lack of energy and initiative but these defects can
fairly be attributed to failing health. One account states that he
had several heart attacks before the final, fatal seizure on 28
April 1944; however, Roosevelt's personal secretary wrote that
Knox was told by the doctors at the Naval Hospital that he was
in excellent condition only a few weeks before his death.

Roosevelt's next appointment lead to one of the greatest
tragedies in American public life and, though the sad climax
occurred four years after his own death, the seed was sown in his
lifetime. James Vincent Forrestal, an investment banker who
had become Under-Secretary of the Navy in August 1940,
succeeded Knox in May 1944. A successful but unhappy man,
driven and torn by buried tensions and compulsions, he discharged his duties in Washington with the same determination,
dedication and desire for perfection that he had shown in Wall
Street. During the next three years he became an uncompromis-
ing and militant anti-Communist at a time when the euphoria
about Russia, generated in the war years, had not been finally
dissipated. He was outspoken in his opposition to Jewish immi-
gration to Palestine, and the establishment of Israel, on the
grounds that the hostility of the Arab world would stem the vital
flow of oil to the Western Alliance. For this sincere opinion he
was accused not only of anti-Semitism but also of being unduly
influenced by the oil lobby. During these years as Secretary of
the Navy, he was engaged in bitter struggles with the War
Department over the unification of the armed forces and then,
manifestly aware that the task was well-nigh impossible,
accepted the appointment as the first Secretary of Defense in
July 1947. His worst fears were realized and in 1948 he was
embroiled in battles over the budget allocations with the
Secretaries of the three services.

He had spent eight consecutive years in Washington, five in
the hot war and three in the cold war, and his appearance and
manner began to alarm his intimates. He had lost weight, could

PLATE 5

Hoare, 13th September, 1935 "in August he was crippled by an attack of arthritis in one foot"
(Reproduced by permission of Radio Times and Hulton Picture Library)

Forrestal, 10th May, 1944
(Reproduced by permission of Keystone Press Agency Ltd.)

PLATE 6

Dalton, 12th November, 1947; a few minutes before the fatal indiscretion
(Reproduced by permission of Radio Times and Hulton Picture Library)

Ataturk
(Reproduced by permission of Radio Times and Hulton Picture Library)

PLATE 7

Stanley Baldwin, 10th December, 1936; The Abdication Crisis
(Reproduced by permission of Radio Times and Hulton Picture Library)

Bonar Law, April, 1923 "attended Parliament although he was unable to speak"
(Reproduced by permission of Radio Times and Hulton Picture Library)

PLATE 8

Curzon, Lloyd George and Briand, January, 1922
(Reproduced by permission of Radio Times and Hulton Picture Library)

Mussolini and Chamberlain, January, 1939
(Reproduced by permission of Radio Times and Hulton Picture Library)

not sleep and was continually tired. Worse still his mental resilience and acuity were failing:

"As his fatigue increased some associates felt that he became less and less willing to make decisions. Even after the decisions were made he frequently wanted to re-open them. . . . Indecisiveness increased the always heavy load of unfinished business . . ., an accumulation that worried both Forrestal and his staff, driving him to adopt a still more exhausting time-table."[4]

Early in 1949 a friend, who had lunch with Forrestal, was appalled by an unfinished portrait of his host and later wrote that "the artist had caught an expression almost of despair".[5]

There were also more serious causes for concern. Forrestal believed that he was being followed and that his telephone was tapped. President Truman asked the head of the Secret Service to investigate these charges and the latter reported that Forrestal had a psychosis with suicidal features. He had become so suspicious that, when the door bell rang, he would run to the area and peer furtively at the visitor.

At the end of January 1949 Truman apparently gave Forrestal the impression that Louis Johnson would succeed him in May. For this reason Forrestal was gravely disturbed by a summons to the White House on 1 March and a demand for his immediate resignation. At the end of March, following farewell ceremonies at the White House, the Pentagon and House of Representatives, he was agitated and depressed and attempted suicide. On 2 April he was admitted to the Bethesda Naval Hospital where his illness was diagnosed as involutional melancholia. He appeared to respond to narcosis and insulin shock therapy, but in the early hours of 22 May 1949, he fell to his death from a suite on the 16th floor of the hospital.

The naval psychiatrist who treated Forrestal died in September 1959 and left no records of the case and speculation may be unwise but not unprofitable. Forrestal had many of the manifestations of depression. His physical symptoms and signs were characterized by fatigue, insomnia, digestive disturbances, loss of appetite and loss of weight. Emotional symptoms such as anxiety, obsession, phobia and guilt were present. Psychic symptoms were represented by impaired memory and concentration, indecision, illusions and misrepresentation, and delusions of unworthiness and failure. Paranoid delusions of persecution may form part of a depressive illness although Forrestal's behaviour was sufficiently bizarre to suggest a schizophrenic psychosis. The head of the Secret Service, who had special means of garnering information, said Forrestal had "terrifying hallucinations and torturing delusions".[6] On vacation after his resignation he was convinced that the metal stands for beach umbrellas were listening devices. He had a gross failure of perception and failed to recognize people whom he had known for years. After a meeting with President Truman he was certain that he would remain in office until May 1949. Truman insists that Forrestal not only asked to resign but actually named Louis Johnson as his successor. Grotesque mannerisms, such as dipping his fingers in water and moistening his lips, were noticed. An episode in which he sat rigidly in his office, wearing a hat, could be descriptive of catatonia.

In this era of discovery and development in psychopharmacology, when drugs are available that may influence mind and behaviour for good or evil, the implications of the illness of James Forrestal should be remembered and debated. Had it occurred ten years later he might have been treated with a psychotropic drug and might have achieved a complete recovery. A potentially dangerous situation could have arisen if he had regained reasonable intellectual and social adjustment while retaining perceptual disorders and paranoid delusions about foreign, or even friendly, governments.

The Old Guard

Cordell Hull and Henry Stimson were old in years when Roosevelt appointed them to high office and older than their years in temperament and attitude. Common to both was a tendency to wilt under the strain of war and, like their President, to absent themselves from their departments. Common to both were entanglements in the relations between America and Japan which influenced the Japanese attack in December 1941 and their final surrender in August 1945.

Hull was sixty-one years old when he went to the State

Department in 1933 and he remained in office until his seventy-third birthday on 2 October 1944. Roosevelt may have wanted only a figurehead because he ignored Hull and, when he wanted departmental advice, often made a direct approach to Hull's juniors. The delicate and dangerous negotiations with the Japanese representatives in Washington before Pearl Harbor proved such a strain that Hull had to rest from 5 February until 20 April 1942. His debility must have been profound for he could no longer play the gentle game of croquet.

"But in my last several years at the State Department, as the work taxed my strength more and more, my doctor required me to taper off on the game . . ."[7a]

In September 1944 he told Roosevelt that:

". . . I had been over exerting myself for some time and now found myself in such physical condition that I should have to resign."[7b]

He was admitted to the Bethesda Naval Hospital and, during his stay of seven months, his condition was serious. He lived another eleven years and death was attributed to arteriosclerosis and diabetes. His peculiar susceptibility to cold is unexplained. Lord Halifax, the British Ambassador in Washington, said that Hull kept his room at the temperature of a greenhouse which made "every vein in his head seem like bursting".[8] Eden also remarked on the high temperature at which Hull worked and complained that at a meeting of Foreign Ministers in Moscow he nearly fainted. Undue sensitivity to cold can occur in the elderly, in those with little subcutaneous fat and in subjects with hypofunction of the thyroid gland. The changes of senescence were a possible cause and the likelihood of this diagnosis is enhanced by reports of difficulty with speech, and of fatigue, which was excessive even for a man in his seventies. Churchill, only three years his junior, reproved Hull for retiring to bed at midnight with the words: "Why, Man, we are at war!"[9]

The dates of onset of arteriosclerosis and diabetes are not readily available. Both conditions can be associated with narrowing of the arterial lumen and impairment of the circulation.

The extremities became unduly susceptible to cold which may also explain why Hull went to great trouble to ensure a high environmental temperature.

When Roosevelt appointed Frank Knox in the summer of 1940 he invited another Republican, Henry L. Stimson, to be Secretary of War. Stimson, both in appearance and as a result of distinguished service, would now be called a member of the establishment. Educated at Yale and the Harvard Law School, he had been Secretary of War in 1911. He was Governor-General of the Phillipines in 1928 and President Hoover's Secretary of State from 1929 to 1933. Unfortunately he was now in his seventy-third year and was described as "a very tired decayed old man".[10] He had attacks of insomnia, which slowed his mental reactions, and a medical examination was made a condition of employment. Far from welcoming such an innovation Stimson's private doctor reluctantly gave an opinion merely because he could detect no abnormality. In his view Stimson was just tired because of frustration. Ickes did not share this opinion and noted on 17 October 1940:

"... I had the impression that Stimson wasn't working out any too well on account of his age. Frank (Knox) said that he was terribly slow, and he corroborated what I had heard from other persons, namely, that Stimson is good for only about three or four hours a day."[11a]

and again on 14 November 1941:

"I was surprised and discouraged not only by Stimson's attitude but by his slowness in grasping what the President had in mind. His mind seemed to be far from alert."[11b]

Bundy who collaborated with Stimson, in preparing an account of his service, admitted that:

"Stimson's mind was so constructed that it could only hold one major problem at a time. He disliked interruptions; he liked thoroughness."[12a]

By July 1944 Stimson was in poor condition and Lord Alanbrooke, who rivalled Ickes in his clinical interest, noted:

"Stimson quite finished and hardly able to take notice of what is going on round him."[13]

There was concern about his cardiovascular system and, like Roosevelt, his working day was reduced and his week-ends lengthened. After April 1945 he had to restrict his activities further in order to conserve his failing strength.

"More and more he was forced to limit his effort, concentrating after April (1945) mainly on the policy questions presented by the atomic bomb."[12b]

The first bomb was dropped on 6 August 1945 and two days later, on medical advice, he proferred his resignation. He left the War Department on 21 September, had a myocardial infarction in October, but lived for another five years.

One biographer of Stimson emphasizes certain traits of character and behaviour that probably became more dominant with advancing age. Motivated by moral principles rather than practicalities, his approach to situations and problems was unyielding rather than flexible. In his rejection of compromise his attitude and actions are reminiscent of Woodrow Wilson. It may have been these traits which led him as early as 1931, when Secretary of State, to apply pressure on Japan at the time of the Manchurian incident. He was certain that Japan would only respond to a show of force and apparently ignored the fact that Presidents, as diverse in thought and action as Theodore Roosevelt and Woodrow Wilson, had realized that certain areas of North China must inevitably be regarded as Japanese spheres of influence. When Japan felt compelled to leave the League of Nations in March 1933, Roosevelt and Cordell Hull adopted Stimson's policy and incidentally were curiously silent about Russian encroachment in Outer Mongolia. Cordell Hull was also a man with a rigid outlook and "his all or nothing attitude constituted one of his major shortcomings as a diplomat".[14]

The preservation of peace between America and Japan was by no means impossible in 1941. Joseph C. Grew, the American Ambassador in Tokyo, argued that, with patient diplomacy and concessions on both sides, conflict might be averted.

If the inflexible and ingrained attitude of Roosevelt, Hull and

Stimson militated against any rapprochement, the personalities
on the Japanese side were, if anything, more unfortunate. Prince
Konoye, the Japanese Prime Minister, whom Grew regarded "as
a man of weak physique, poor health and weak will . . ."[15] took a
disastrous step when he appointed Yosuke Matsuoka, as
Minister of Foreign Affairs, in the summer of 1940.

Matsuoka signed the triple alliance between Germany, Italy
and Japan on 27 September 1940 and used this as a threat to
deter America from rendering aid to Britain in Europe. In 1941
Matsuoka was labelled as mentally deranged by his colleagues
and the Navy Minister flippantly remarked "The foreign
minister is crazy, isn't he?"[16]

When Prince Konoye formed his third Cabinet in July 1941,
he excluded Matsuoka whose presence was making, and would
have made, any understanding with America quite impossible.
Matsuoka was in a pitiful state and Shigemitsu, a diplomat and
official of wide experience, "could not help wondering whether
his wild speech was not the talk of a madman" and noted that
"his face was ashen and he seemed to have lost his vitality".[17a]

Neither America nor Japan emerge with great credit from
their diplomatic negotiations in 1941 for the statesmen concerned, in the words of the editorial writer in 1912, had become
"so enmeshed in the formulas and the jargon of diplomacy".
Only the most bitter protagonist would contest Shigemitsu's
calm and judicial statement:

> "The Americans played for time to complete their prepara-
> tions against attack. The Japanese Army and Navy bided
> their time to resort to direct action. From start to finish the
> negotiations were cumbered with contradictions and cross-
> purposes."[17b]

Cordell Hull had striven early on for conciliation and had
warned Henry Morgenthau, the Secretary of the Treasury, that
denial of raw materials might merely force Japan to gain their
ends by war. Hull was confused by Matsuoka's histrionic
behaviour and concluded that he was "as crooked as a basket of
fishhooks".[18a] Unfortunately Hull was away sick in July 1941
when signal intercepts were decoded in Washington which
revealed Japanese plans for a breakout to the south:

"Hull, ill and discouraged, remained at White Sulphur Springs, from where he sent advice in equal parts of fire and foam. With him away, the advocates of action had easier going."[18b]

He returned to Washington on 1 August 1941, "still having trouble with his throat".[18c] He had permitted the economic containment of Japan but hoped to avoid a fatal confrontation. Prince Konoye, who remained as Prime Minister until 16 October 1941, also continued to pursue a conciliatory policy despite the aggressive attitude of Tojo, the Army Minister, and the fact that the Japanese Navy followed the wishes of the Army. Any hopes of an understanding foundered over the Japanese occupation of Chinese territory. The Japanese would not, indeed could not, withdraw and perhaps should not have been asked or have been expected to withdraw. On 6 November 1941 Roosevelt discussed the possibility of a truce with Japan but Stimson objected to the suggestion. The Japanese put forward further proposals on 5 and 20 November and the last of these (Proposal B) was regarded by Hull as "clearly unacceptable".[18d] Feis, having analysed the Japanese records, casts doubt on Hull's judgement.

"It is not certain that the meaning which Hull attached to some of the points in Proposal B is the necessary meaning; or that his total estimate of the Japanese offer to begin to retreat was just. Perhaps so, probably so, but not surely so."[18e]

Hull having taken his decision "after tormenting uncertainty",[18f] merely sent the Japanese a comprehensive basic proposal which they regarded as an ultimatum. Hull's biographer, Professor Julius W. Pratt, wrote that this action "was a petulant one by a tired and angry old man".[19] Next day, with regard to the situation, he told Stimson "I have washed my hands of it, and it is now in the hands of you and Knox, the Army and Navy".[18g] Thereafter Hull exerted a baleful influence. Roosevelt considered an offer of help to the British and Dutch if they were attacked by the Japanese; a warning to Japan; or a statement to Congress. Largely due to Hull he did nothing. Roosevelt thought that he might send a personal message and a warning to the Emperor: Hull found reasons, "unconvincing and mixed up",[18h] to dissuade Roosevelt who eventually sent the message on the eve of the Japanese attack.

Roosevelt, or one of his speech writers, coined the emotive words, "a date that will live in infamy" for 7 December 1941. The attack on Pearl Harbor and other installations in the Pacific struck the American people as a sudden treacherous and unexpected blow. It was no surprise to Roosevelt, his Cabinet and his service chiefs who, through signal and cable intercepts, had long been able to decode Japanese messages. After the breakdown in negotiations the attack was inevitable rather than infamous.

Stimson may have had his hours of work reduced in April 1945 but his responsibilities, as onerous and fearful as any one man has borne, progressively increased. As Chairman of the Interim Committee he was responsible, more than anybody else, for advising President Truman about the final stages in the development of the atomic bomb. History is full of grotesque drolleries as is exemplified by the inappropriate appointment of George L. Harrison as Stimson's deputy on the Committee; he was President of the New York Life Insurance Company. Stimson agreed independently with the Committee's recommendation that the atomic bomb should be employed against Japan and, as Truman's main adviser on its use, accordingly reported to the President on 1 June 1945. In those shortened days, Stimson crammed weeks of anxious study and thought. This tired, elderly man had to weigh in the balance a number of imponderables. A seaborne invasion of the Japanese islands might decimate American youth, particularly if the war lasted until 1946. Russian co-operation, although it would ease the strain, would have inconvenient and imponderable political and military repercussions. The most unpredictable item was the bomb itself or, more precisely, the three bombs that existed. Even Admiral Leahy doubted if they would work.

Stimson's memorandum to Truman on 2 July 1945 was decisive. He made no mention of the atomic bomb but the select few knew that this was the weapon that would bring Japan to heel. He argued that the Japanese must be given an opportunity to surrender before the seaborne invasion was mounted and before her armed forces were embroiled in last ditch, last round and last man struggles on their own islands. They should be warned of the terrors that lay ahead but should be made to realize that surrender would give them hope of a national life in the future. He was in favour of announcing that the Japanese could retain the Emperor but Cordell Hull, hearing of this during his convalescence, objected to this reasonable concession as appeasement of the ruling class. The Potsdam Conference started on 17 July 1945 and the American delegation immediately learned of the successful detonation in New Mexico of the first atomic bomb on the previous day. Truman at once consulted Byrnes, Stimson and his military advisers, who agreed that atomic bombs should be used against Japan. Stimson was in such poor health at the time that Truman had not at first asked him to come to Potsdam.

Two bombs were dropped on 6 and 9 August. Russia declared war against Japan on 9 August, and Japan surrendered on 14 August. The Russian entry was as big a blow as the bomb. Despite ethical and humanistic consideration the bomb, once made, was there to be used. The main motive, almost certainly, was to save American and allied casualties. Its power was so devastating that it even gave the military clique in Japan a convincing reason to surrender. Whether it should have been used has tortured the civilized conscience ever since. The American Navy considered that they had almost starved Japan into submission by August 1945. The American Air Force maintained that they had already destroyed Japanese resistance. If the bomb had not been dropped the American ground forces would have been the guinea-pigs to test these hypotheses. Truman, Stimson, Leahy and the other service chiefs perhaps had no choice but to preserve, as well as they could, the youth of their generation without too much speculation about the morrow. Decisions of such enormity should not, however, be influenced by an elderly gentleman of seventy-eight years.

Stimson had second thoughts and in 1947 he wondered if a different approach to Japan, in May and June 1945, might have led to an earlier surrender before the bomb was ready for use. Conciliatory moves foundered for two main reasons; reluctance to hint about the potentiality of an untried weapon and objection to any concession about the retention of the Emperor.

Admittedly Stimson's interim committee had set the ball rolling on 31 May when it agreed that the bomb should be used without warning. Perhaps the die was not finally cast on 18 June when President Truman met the Joint Chiefs of Staff but Stimson, rising from a sickbed to attend, curiously made no mention of the use of the bomb or the subject of unconditional surrender. He retired forthwith to his house on Long Island for rest and reflection and missed the last meeting of his interim committee on 21 June. On this occasion members listened to the views of the scientific committee and reaffirmed their decision to use the bomb.

Stimson scrupulously recorded his subsequent doubts about his own conduct and it is difficult to escape the feeling that this ailing man may have abdicated his responsibility and lost his influence at the eleventh hour. When he emerged from his period of retreat on Long Island the initiative had passed to others and he had merely to follow their instructions as to where and when the bomb should be dropped.

Harry the Hop

The ubiquitous Ickes, meticulous as always, recorded a talk at lunch on 17 September 1941:

> "Bill Bullitt ruefully remarked to me that it seems that the President had to have someone near him who was dependent upon him and who was pale and sick and gaunt. He had had such a person in Louis Howe and now another in Harry Hopkins. Bill insisted that the two resembled each other physically, being cadaverous and bent and thin."[11c]

There was more than a physical resemblance. Both chain-smoked and had raffish habits. Howe was said to have doped racehorses in his youth while Hopkins, in the midst of his relief or Government activities, would sneak away for a day at the races. Both, however, were absolutely and utterly dedicated to Roosevelt and seemingly lived through him.

Many of the photographs taken at Yalta were long suppressed because of Roosevelt's appearance but two give a measure of

Hopkins's acceptance and influence. One was taken of a family party on the U.S.S. *Quincy* and shows Roosevelt and Churchill with Anna and Sarah, their respective daughters. Hopkins, slumped limply in a wicker chair, is the only outsider present. A second is a scene at the conference table. Roosevelt is flanked by his official advisers; Stettinius, who had replaced Cordell Hull, Leahy, his Chief of Staff, and James F. Byrnes. Behind him sits the ever faithful Hopkins who, though he attended these sessions, spent the rest of the time at Yalta in bed. There was every reason to conceal the photographs for the limits of their life-span were painfully obvious. Roosevelt was dead in two months and Hopkins within twelve months.

Harry Lloyd Hopkins was born in 1890 and, after leaving Grinnell College, Iowa, he undertook social work in New York. A sensitive appreciation of the sordid effects of poverty and genuine concern for the underprivileged did not deter his personal ambitions and, after service in various welfare organizations, he became executive director of the New York Tuberculosis Association in 1924. In the course of the next seven years, while Hopkins absorbed the Heart Association and other health agencies, Roosevelt had been elected Governor of New York State and the Wall Street financial collapse of September 1929 heralded the great depression. Roosevelt became aware of the successful way in which Hopkins had organized Relief Administration in the State and, after his own move from the Governor's Mansion in Albany to the White House in 1933, invited him to Washington. It was only to be expected that Hopkins would play a prominent part in furthering the relief measures of the New Deal. In 1938 Roosevelt began to groom a number of candidates for the Presidential election of 1940 and, presumably as a part of this process, he nominated Hopkins as Secretary of Commerce in 1938. It was an extraordinary appointment for Hopkins had infuriated the business community by his apparently uncontrolled and lavish expenditure of welfare funds. It was even more extraordinary for medical reasons. Hopkins had been treated for a peptic ulcer in 1936 but, when a gastrectomy was performed in the following year, the pathologists found evidence of cancer. Throughout 1939 he was ill and the details that he gave to his brother in September suggest a malabsorbtion syndrome. He had lost thirty pounds in weight and had oedema of the ankles, while laboratory tests revealed low plasma proteins and steatorrhoea. David Hopkins was told in September that his father had only four weeks to live. According to Ickes the Mayo brothers said that Hopkins had cancer of the stomach "and would not live till Thanksgiving"[11d] but that the Naval doctors thought that he had some tropical disease. Presumably the fatty diarrhoea puzzled Admiral E. R. Stitt, an expert in tropical medicine, who was now in charge. The diagnosis of cancer of the stomach was hushed up as much as possible but his absence from Cabinet and office must have been hard to explain. From March 1939 until his resignation in August 1940 he spent no more than thirty days in his office. He was now out of the running for the Presidency and was free to devote himself to ensuring that Roosevelt was nominated for an unprecedented third term in July 1940. Next month he maintained that he was no longer able to meet the physical demands of high office but Roosevelt was to make use of this "half-man" as his eyes and ears. As Special Adviser and Assistant to the President, Member of the War Production Board and Chairman of the Munitions Assignment Board, he flitted from country to country and continent to continent and became the intimate and the confidant of Presidents, Prime Ministers, Statesmen and Soldiers.

He was hardly well enough to go to Russia in July 1941, for conversations with Stalin, and had such a severe relapse that it was thought that he would not live to report the details of the conference. In November 1941 and again in January 1942 he was readmitted to the Naval Hospital in Washington.

Hopkins at times was so prostrated that he could hardly crawl upstairs. Two pathological conditions may have contributed to this weakness. Muscular disorders have recently been reported in patients with fatty diarrhoea. Furthermore, the protein malnutrition that may follow even a partial gastrectomy can cause a variety of signs and symptoms; emaciation, mental changes characterized by an irritable apathy, and difficulty in walking due to profound weakness.

He was back in hospital again in the autumn of 1943, after the first Quebec Conference, and for a much longer stay after the

Teheran Conference. During this last admission between January and July 1944, when Roosevelt himself was either away or on reduced hours, he had a further operation at the Mayo Clinic. Recalled to service by Roosevelt for Yalta, Hopkins was not without influence. When the British delegation raised objections to the astronomical and economically ridiculous reparations that were demanded by Russia, Hopkins slipped a note to Roosevelt:

"The Russians have given in so much at this conference that I don't think we should let them down. Let the British disagree if they want to – and continue their disagreement at Moscow. Simply say it is all referred to the Reparations Commission with the minutes to show the British disagree about any mention of the 10 billion."[3b]

Immediately after Yalta, Hopkins had to return to the Mayo Clinic although, looking like a walking ghost, he managed to attend Roosevelt's funeral. Early in May 1945 a summons by Truman to visit Stalin seemed to give him a new lease of life. Despite the fact that the Russians had shown no indication of honouring any of the obligations they had contracted at Yalta, Hopkins was still an enthusiastic and uncritical supporter. As he said on his return:

"We can do business with Stalin. He will co-operate".[20]

This was his last mission and the remaining months of his life were a sad contrast to those twelve stimulating years of power and influence. On 22 January 1946 he wrote the last letter of his life to Winston Churchill and he died a week later. Without Roosevelt life had no meaning or purpose for Hopkins. Both have been accused, not only of betraying the Western Alliance at Yalta, but also of advancing the Communist cause with deliberate intent. Such condemnation is unjust and absurd for, despite mental and physical weakness, their behaviour was an expression of a long standing attitude. Both reacted with exceptional urgency to German and Japanese aggression but were apparently blind to Russian aggression. Both thought that Russia, if treated with generosity and humanity, would gladly find a place with the more enlightened democracies. Neither appreciated that Communism was intent on world domination. Stalin had the sense to rely on medical advice and refused to travel beyond the boundaries of Russia. Roosevelt and Hopkins had to play the fixture away from home after a long and exhausting journey by sea and air. Their capacity was impaired, their interest narrowed, and there was only time to meet the more urgent demands of the day. There was no time for reflection, analysis, judgement, initiative or change. It is difficult at any age to alter fixed habits of thought and action but Roosevelt and his half-man, had they been less ill, might have looked beyond the immediate defeat of Germany and Japan to the potential menace of Communist Russia.

Hopkins wrote in the last letter to Churchill that he had cirrhosis of the liver but dismissed the influence of alcohol as an aetiological factor. The subsequent autopsy produced no evidence of cirrhosis of the liver or cancer. According to his biographer, "He was killed by a disease known as haemochromatosis, the result of his inadequate digestive equipment."[3c] Here we enter a terminological jungle which pathologists and research workers have done much to clear since 1946. Haemochromatosis is a rare disorder, probably due to an inherited or innate inability to transport and metabolize iron; cirrhosis of the liver occurs and iron is deposited in the liver, pancreas and other organs. There is another condition, associated with a disturbance in iron storage, called haemosiderosis in which iron is deposited in the liver though true cirrhosis is not present. It is known to occur after repeated blood transfusions or excessive iron therapy for resistant anaemia. An editorial in the *Richmond News Leader* in April 1942 mentioned that Hopkins frequently had blood transfusions and he may have had many more during his subsequent absences. It is difficult to decide whether Hopkins had haemosiderosis or haemochromatosis.

Advances in medicine, surgery and therapeutics have done much to improve health and prolong useful life. Occasionally the patient may be relieved of one disorder but left with another. Nothing less than an extensive gastrectomy was indicated when Hopkins was found to have a cancer of the stomach. The malabsorbtion of protein, fat, iron and minerals was not too high a price for him to pay. Gastrectomy could have left another legacy which was wrongly attributed to self-indulgence. Though the mechanism is obscure the operation can induce a craving for alcohol and drugs of addiction. The structural and mechanical changes of gastrectomy may be followed by the "dumping syndrome" and its unpleasant manifestations, sweating, palpitation, nausea and giddiness, are relieved by alcohol which is more rapidly absorbed in these subjects. Lord Chandos was perhaps more perceptive than he realized when he said of Hopkins:

"For a sick man, or perhaps because he was a sick man, he liked to drink more whisky when the sun went down than was good for his health. It probably kept him alive, but it also impelled him to sit up very late and make a round of the night clubs in Washington."[21]

Alcohol in its turn may have added to the iron overload in his organs. One-third of the patients with haemochromatosis have a history of alcoholism, and alcohol, in the form of whisky or brandy, increases the absorption of ferric iron.

The clinico-pathological conference originated in America and is a fruitful method of instruction. A physician is given the clinical history of a patient who has died. Laboratory data and the results of special investigations are available to him. In front of a critical audience he then attempts to make a diagnosis which is confirmed or refuted by the pathologist who follows him with detailed reports of the autopsy. Hopkins would have made a most interesting subject for a "C.P.C." He would have made an even better subject for a clinico-political conference; the influence that a sick man has on world history.

References

1. Alfred B. Rollins, Jun. *Roosevelt and Howe*, p. 432. Knopf.
2. Arthur M. Schlesinger, Jun. *The Crisis of the Old Order*, p. 498. Heinemann.
3a. R. E. Sherwood. *The White House Papers of Harry L. Hopkins*, vol. I, p. 137. Eyre & Spottiswoode.
3b. Vol. II, p. 851. Eyre & Spottiswoode.
3c. Vol. II, p. 920. Eyre & Spottiswoode.

4.   Walter Millis. *The Forrestal Diaries*, p. 509. Cassell.
5.   Lewis L. Strauss. *Men and Decisions*. Macmillan.
6.   U. E. Baughman. *Secret Service Chief*, p. 91. Heinemann.
7a. Cordell Hull. *The Memoirs*, vol. I, p. 179.
7b. Vol. II, p. 1715. Hodder & Stoughton.
8.   Earl of Halifax. *Fullness of Days*, p. 256. Collins.
9.   Earl of Avon. *Memoirs: The Reckoning*, p. 402. Cassell.
10. Elting E. Morison. *Turmoil and Tradition*, p. 481. Houghton Mifflin.
11a. Harold L. Ickes. *Secret Diaries*, vol. 3, p. 353.
11b. Vol. III, p. 642. Weidenfeld & Nicolson.
11c. Vol. III, p. 616. Weidenfeld & Nicolson.
11d. Vol. III, p. 82. Weidenfeld & Nicolson.
12a. Henry L. Stimson, and McGeorge Bundy. *On Active Service in Peace and War*, p. 209. Hutchinson.
12b. p. 392. Hutchinson.
13. Arthur Bryant. *Triumph in the West*, p. 233. Collins.
14. George M. Waller. (Ed.). *Pearl Harbor: Roosevelt and the Coming of War*, p. 102. D. C. Heath & Co.
15. Joseph C. Grew. *Ten Years in Japan*, p. 285. Hammond & Hammond.
16. Robert J. C. Butow. *Tojo and the Coming of War*, p. 208. Princeton University Press.
17a. Mamoru Shigemitsu. *Japan and her Destiny*, p. 238.
17b. p. 265. Hutchinson.
18a. Herbert Feis. *The Road to Pearl Harbor*, p. 115.
18b. p. 227. Princeton University Press.
18c. p. 248. Princeton University Press.
18d. p. 309. Princeton University Press.
18e. p. 309. Princeton University Press.
18f. p. 318. Princeton University Press.
18g. p. 321. Princeton University Press.
18h. p. 335. Princeton University Press.
19. Forrest Pogue. *George C. Marshall: Ordeal and Hope*, p. 207. Macgibbon & Kee.
20. Robert Murphy. *Diplomat among Warriors*, p. 320. Collins.
21. Lord Chandos. *The Memoirs*, p. 312. Bodley Head.

CHAPTER 9

Ill health in senior officers, 1939–45: An unexplored influence on command decisions

Fatigue is difficult to define and difficult to measure, which may account for the fact that its victims receive scant sympathy. Up to a certain point hard mental or physical effort can produce an almost languorous satisfaction. Beyond this point lies fatigue which has been described as a weariness resulting from bodily or mental exertion. This is as good a definition as any although others mention a decrement or disintegration of performance.

Fatigue is invariably experienced by the fighting man. He is called upon to perform arduous mental and physical tasks in climatic extremes, with broken sleep and irregular meals, and under conditions that cause anxiety, frustration, and boredom. Senior officers are not immune from fatigue and, because of this, some are removed from command, often for ever, with an unjustified slur on their names. In the recent past a discussion of this problem was resented on the grounds that such comment was in bad taste. That investigation was not designed to denigrate or criticize certain senior officers but merely to ventilate the problem.

Although many studies have been made on the bodily effects of fatigue surprisingly little has been written about the mental effects. There can be no doubt that excessive fatigue has an adverse effect upon judgement, and this may be illustrated by a wartime experience. A surgeon, who served on the Western Front during the First World War, later said that he could operate for hours on end. After a few hours, however, although surgical dexterity was retained, judgement was lost. He would continue to operate, but he would first ask a less tired colleague to examine the patient and advise on the nature and extent of the operation.

Complaints of fatigue might be expected at the beginning of a war when senior officers, possibly near the age limit, are subjected to unaccustomed stress after years of peacetime routine.

The lessons of the First World War were learned too late by the British Army and it was not until July 1938 that the age limit for generals and lieutenant-generals was reduced from 65 to 60 years. The age limit for major-generals was set at 57 years and that for colonels at 55. These modest changes had not come in time to bring younger men into the principal commands by September 1939, though it must be admitted that the average age of divisional commanders who went to France in September was about three and a half years younger than their counterparts in August 1914. However, it must also be recorded that it was one of the two younger divisional commanders who broke down after the advance into Belgium on 10–11 May 1940.

The commander of I Corps was another casualty. Left in charge at Dunkirk he was fearful of the responsibility and later had to be replaced.

The twists and turns of the Norwegian Campaign after the German invasion on 6 April 1940 ruthlessly exposed physical imperfections. General Hotblack was appointed Military Commander in Norway and briefed by Churchill on the night of 17 April. In the early hours of the following day he was found unconscious on the Duke of York's steps, the victim presumably of a circulatory lesion. The G.O.C. of the 49th Division who had to co-ordinate operations around Narvik was in no better shape. He was ill during the campaign and failed to attend an important conference on 13 May. He was removed from the command on the next day.

THE BATTLE OF FRANCE, 1940

In January 1940, General Gamelin, the Commander-in-Chief, then aged sixty-seven years, placed the Allied forces in north-eastern France, including the British Expeditionary Force, under the operational control of General Georges. This latter officer was sixty-five years old and had had traumatic experiences in peace and war. After being wounded in 1914 he was out of action for two years. In 1934 he was wounded in the chest and hand when King Alexander of Yugoslavia and Barthou, the French Foreign Minister, were assassinated in Marseilles. He was again away for a long period. He had neuritis in the injured arm and wore a woollen glove over the affected hand. The chest injury prevented him from flying. In August 1939 Spears, who knew him well, thought that although he had aged he was as alert as ever.

On 10 May 1940, Georges was suddenly confronted by a German Army using methods which, owing to lack of time, money, equipment and training, could not be matched by the Allied forces. When he heard on the night of 13 May, that the Germans had broken through at Sedan, he burst into tears. By 18 May he was in a state of physical collapse which Gamelin attributed to the wounds received in 1934 and from which he thought that the victim had never sufficiently recovered. On 19 May General Weygand, himself aged seventy-three years, arrived from the Middle East to replace Gamelin. He thought that the latter was fatigued and anxious, and formed an unfavourable impression of Georges: "I was painfully struck by the change in his appearance. He said to me, indeed, at once, that he could no longer sleep, and he did not hide from me his extreme fatigue."[1]

It is tempting to speculate whether at this stage a well coordinated and vigorous counter-attack might have delayed the German armoured thrust, or whether it was already too late for remedial action. Georges remained in command and his physical condition worsened. On 11 June 1940 Spears noted that Georges looked ghastly and on 14 June Alanbrooke observed that he was tired and haggard.

THE WAR AT SEA, 1939-43

On 15 July 1939 Sir Dudley Pound, then aged sixty-two years, became First Sea Lord in rather inauspicious circumstances. His predecessor, Sir Roger Backhouse, had died in office of a cerebral disorder which was generally attributed to overwork. He had driven himself too hard and, as he never relaxed, he was always tired and nervous. Pound had little chance to remedy this situation, even had he so desired, for on the outbreak of war in September 1939 his responsibilities became even greater than those of the other Chiefs of Staff. Not only was he the professional adviser to the War Cabinet but he was also in operational command of the the Royal Navy.

At the end of 1941 Alanbrooke became Chief of the Imperial General Staff, and he formed an unfavourable impression of Pound. On 17 February 1942 he recorded in his diary: "Am getting more and more worried by old Dudley Pound as First Sea Lord. With him it is impossible for Chiefs of Staffs to perform functions it should in the biggest Imperial war we are ever likely to be engaged in. He is asleep 75 per cent of the time he should be working."[2]

This was not surprising in view of the fact that Pound never allowed himself more than four hours' sleep each night. He probably would not have got more sleep if he had tried for arthritis of the hip prevented him from lying down in comfort. Increasing deafness was a more serious impairment, although Churchill made use of it. On occasions Pound did not like to admit that he had not heard Churchill's arguments and therefore was compelled to agree.

Continued contact with Pound must have blurred Alanbrooke's first and most keen impression. Writing after the war he recalled that it was on 12 August 1943 that he and his colleagues first noticed signs of serious failing. On a fishing trip, during the Quadrant Conference in Quebec, Pound lost his balance and nearly fell into a ravine. He was helped into a car with difficulty and he seemed completely exhausted. Churchill remarked on the subdued part that Pound played at this conference, and commented on a meeting with Roosevelt early in September 1943 at which Pound appeared to have lost his precision in answering questions. Next day Pound resigned, telling Churchill that he had a stroke and that his right side was paralysed. This paralysis grew worse and he died on Trafalgar Day, 1943. He was found to have a tumour of the brain but it is not known whether this was the cause of the paralysis or whether there was a cerebrovascular lesion in addition. It is only natural to wonder over what period of time, and to what degree, the brain tumour may have been responsible for the fatigue and drowsiness which were noticed by lay observers.

On 4 July 1942 his decision to scatter PQ17, a convoy to

Russia, had disastrous and tragic consequences. The circumstances of the meeting were etched in the memory of one officer whose description is almost clinical in its penetration.

> ". . . a very tired-looking Dudley Pound sitting gazing in a mesmerised fashion at a small-scale chart of the Barents Sea area, calculating with a pair of dividers where the *Tirpitz* could be at that time."[3]

Indecision, possibly; fatigue, certainly; but in view of his death eighteen months later a sinister factor should also be considered. Depending on its position in the brain, and the pressure it exerts on different areas, a tumour could impair the appreciation and assessment of temporal and spatial relationships. A naval battle, whether followed from the bridge of a fighting ship or the operations room at the Admiralty, is an exercise in temporal and spatial relationships. This additional burden may have handicapped Pound more than the others that he bore so patiently and bravely.

Admiral Sir Tom Phillips, who had first been Deputy and then Vice-Chief of the Naval Staff at the Admiralty since July 1939, was an unfortunate by-product of Pound's Spartan régime. In May 1941 he was made C.-in-C. designate of the Eastern Fleet and he arrived at Singapore on 2 December 1941. Witnesses have stated that Admiral Phillips looked very fatigued before the last tragic action of *Prince of Wales* and *Repulse*. During his two years at the Admiralty, before he sailed for the East, his nights were invariably disturbed and he never had proper rest or sleep.

Even under favourable circumstances command is an exhausting task and the fate that befell two relatively young and successful commanders is worthy of consideration.

OPERATION "SHINGLE", ANZIO, 1944

The career of the American Corps Commander, John P. Lucas, illustrates that little mercy is shown to tired generals.

In December 1943 it had been decided that an assault at Anzio should be mounted by VI Corps irrespective of the position of 5th Army which was advancing northwards towards

Rome. The attack was intended to cut the enemy communications in the Alban Hills area, south-east of Rome, and would both threaten that city and the rear of the German 14th Corps.

The orders given to Lucas did not precisely state whether he was to advance to the Alban Hills or consolidate the beachhead. Lucas achieved a complete surprise in the landing on 22 January 1944, and chose the second course. On 27 January he was pressed to break out of the beachhead and, after a number of visits from his superiors, he was relieved on 22 February. The general opinion was that he was worn out and it seems that he was relieved for reasons of health rather than military incompetence. Certainly the previous North African campaign had tired him and it is a pity that remedial action could not have been taken before the battle. Lucas, who was fifty-four years old at Anzio, wrote in his diary: "I am afraid I feel every year of it."[4] He mentioned his burdens and anxieties and added plaintively: "Who the hell wants to be a general?"[5]

OPERATION "DRAGOON", SOUTH OF FRANCE, 1944

Rear-Admiral D. P. Moon, U.S. Navy, was the attack force commander on Utah Beach in Normandy on 6 June 1944. This operation had tired him considerably but he was transferred to the Mediterranean for the landings in the South of France in August 1944, which were finally given the code name "Dragoon". He worried excessively over the details of the plan and what he thought was the unpreparedness of his force. After a series of sleepless nights he asked if the date of the landing could be postponed. His superior, Admiral Hewitt, tried to reassure him and suggested that first they should watch the rehearsal and then consider any postponement. This appeared to satisfy Admiral Moon but during the night he took his own life.

Extreme mental and physical stress can cause a serious depression. Spears has described a conversation with General Maistre in 1914. This officer said that, thinking all was lost in the retreat, he contemplated suicide. In this same period a divisional commander of the French V Corps actually committed suicide.

·   ·   ·   ·   ·

Fatigue is a symptom of many illnesses when it may appear after relatively little exertion. In the examples that have been quoted, Pound alone was the victim of organic disease although his mode of life was at least as likely to cause fatigue as the brain tumour.

- "CRUSADER", "AIDA", "SUPERCHARGE" and "BARBAROSSA"

For three years, the issue in doubt until the final shot, the battle raged in the Western Desert. The terrain was ideal for a practical examination of the theoretical concepts of armoured warfare. The absence of fixed defences for much of the campaign created opportunities for manoeuvre, deception and surprise. Even without tracked and wheeled vehicles the desert would have induced mobility: the presence of these vehicles increased the scope and speed of mobility.

"Crusader" was the first major offensive by the newly formed 8th Army and the first occasion in the war in which a large British armoured force engaged a German armoured force. High hopes had been raised in political and military circles, but by 22 November 1941 the situation was so confused that the 8th Army Commander, General Sir Alan Cunningham, wished to withdraw and regroup his forces. The Commander-in-Chief relieved Cunningham of his command and ordered the 8th Army to stand and fight. Some interesting medical evidence has recently been revealed. A month before the offensive, Cunningham was found to have defective vision in one eye. It was the type of defect that may sometimes be due to excess of tobacco, and it was suggested that he should stop smoking. He carried out these instructions, but the effect on the nervous system of a heavy smoker can well be imagined. Indeed, an eye-witness describes him as being tense and agitated just before the attack.

By July 1942 Field-Marshal Erwin Rommel and his Afrika Korps were in the ascendant and "Operation Aida" was designed to drive the allies from Egypt. Despite the great victories that are described in history books or in the auto-biographies of commanders a mere grain can turn the scales to victory or defeat. Victory may stem from the mind or will of a commander and is often nothing more than an unwillingness to admit defeat. It was Auchinleck who defeated Rommel in the first, and forgotten, battle of Alamein in July 1942, and who was harshly and summarily dismissed by Churchill two weeks later. Rommel retained his command but he and his Korps were in far worse shape than the revivified 8th Army. On the eve of his disastrous attack on Alam Halfa which started on 30 August 1942, Rommel, though he was concerned about his blood pressure, thought that he was fit for battle. This view was not shared by his physician who stated:

> "Field-Marshal Rommel suffering from chronic stomach and intestinal catarrh, nasal diphtheria and considerable circulation trouble. He is not in a fit condition to command the forthcoming offensive."[6a]

Even Rommel had at last to admit that he was sick and he returned to Germany for treatment in September.

The statement that Montgomery defeated Rommel at the second battle of Alamein is generally accepted as a part of history. The fact that Rommel was still in Germany when Montgomery launched "Supercharge" on 23 October 1942 is forgotten. Rommel, though responsible for the German dispositions, had no influence on the immediate reaction of the German and Italian forces. He stated later that these forces, despite shortage of ammunition, made a grave mistake when they failed to shell the assembly areas of the 8th Army. When Rommel did arrive on 25 October the best chance of stopping the 8th Army had been lost. Confusion was worse confounded for General Stumme, Rommel's deputy, had died on the previous day. As he was hypertensive and unfit for tropical service, Rommel's assumption that his fall from a vehicle was due to a heart attack was reasonable.

In as far as Hitler would allow him Rommel conducted a masterly withdrawal to the west through Libya and denied the 8th Army the real fruits of victory. This was accomplished at the cost of his health and at the end of January 1943 he no longer concealed his condition from his wife:

> "Physically I am not well. Severe headaches and over-strained nerves, on top of the circulation trouble, allow

me no rest. Professor Horster is giving me sleeping draughts
. . ."[6b]

He and his forces were now in Tunisia and about to be pinned
down by the Americans and the British 1st Army in the west and
by the advancing 8th Army from the east. In an effort to prevent
the junction of these forces, and to gain time, he shattered the
Americans at the Kasserine Pass on 19 February. Here he
showed glimpses of his old form but on the 26th of the same
month his words gave cause for concern.

"Heart, nerves, and rheumatism are giving me a lot of
trouble, but I intend to stick it out as long as is humanly
possible."[6c]

It was not to be for long. On 6 March 1943 he had to take the
only opportunity that offered to delay Montgomery's deliberate
advance from the east. It was a disaster, for German tanks were
thrown against fixed defences at Medenine. He had punished
the British forces on many previous occasions when they had
broken this fundamental rule of tank tactics. Even the British
had at long last learned the rules of armoured warfare and
Rommel, showing uncharacteristic and incredible lack of judgement, was hoist with his own petard. This was not the end in
Africa but it was the end of Rommel's reign in Africa. He
returned to Germany on 9 March for a lengthy spell of treatment and convalescence.

Hitler started operation "Barbarossa" against Russia on 22
June 1941. For many weeks spectacular advances were made,
and great victories were won, under blue skies and blazing sun.
But winter came to the aid of Russia as it had during previous
invasions, and the German advance slowed as dust on the
primitive tracks became first a sea of mud and then a sheet of
snow and ice. Men from temperate zones apparently have the
ability to adapt physiologically to hot conditions; the response
to cold, if it can be acquired, is less comprehensive. The desert
may have been, as General Freyberg told Montgomery, the
grave of lieutenant-generals; "General Winter" decimated the
German Army and did not spare the senior officers in the process. Even a fanatical devotee of physical fitness, Field-Marshal

von Reichenau, had to be evacuated in January 1942. During the attack on Poland in September 1939 he swam a river during the advance and in Russia his physician tried to deter him from cross-country runs at temperatures of 20° below zero. As commander of Army Group South and 6th Army his task was too heavy for one man. A second stroke lead to his evacuation and he was killed in an aeroplane crash while returning to Germany. Field-Marshal von Bock was compelled to relinquish the command of Army Group North because of stomach trouble in December 1941. After a period of convalescence he was offered another Army Group but was dismissed in June 1942. Field-Marshall von Brauchitsch, the Commander-in-Chief, who had advised against the winter offensive was dismissed by Hitler. He had a heart attack but went to the front after he had recovered. A second heart attack and a nervous breakdown compelled him to go sick again. General Heinz Guderian was also dismissed by Hitler despite his brilliant leadership of Panzer Group II in 1941. He was later told he had a weak heart and in November 1942 had a complete collapse and was unconscious for several days. He enjoyed a degree of military rehabilitation for Hitler appointed him Inspector-General of the Armoured Corps in February 1943 and Chief of the General Staff in July 1944.

The strain that a commander must bear is inevitably severe and every endeavour must be made to ease this burden. In most situations his position may be likened to that of a surgeon who, after performing minor operations for twenty years, is suddenly expected to operate on the chest or abdomen; and probably in an ill-lit theatre and under shell fire.

The British are empiricists by nature and it must be admitted that the training of officers during their formative years has been in most cases an adequate preparation for the rigours of command. This method might be criticized on the grounds that, while every effort was made to train the officers to resist bodily stress and fatigue, little was done to train them to resist mental stress and fatigue. As only a minority of commanders are overburdened by their responsibilities in war there would be a natural reluctance to alter a well-accepted routine.

It is doubtful whether stricter medical examination would be helpful since the present method is extremely thorough. Routine examinations have their limitations for, even with modern techniques, they are still not delicate enough for slight deterioration in fitness to be detected. Even supposing that Pound had been willing to submit himself to routine examinations the tumour might not have been diagnosed in the early stages. Nor is the rigid application of an age limit satisfactory for the exact period when mental and physical qualities begin to fail is not known with any certainty and is subject to individual variation.

Routine examinations, if rigidly observed, may even be unhelpful. The results can lead to the exclusion of officers who had a slight change in blood pressure or an abnormality in a chest X-ray but whose mental powers are unimpaired. Lord Montgomery was taken ill in Palestine in May 1939, and, as tuberculosis was suspected, he was returned to England as a stretcher case. On arrival he walked off the ship and in a few weeks he was importuning the War Office for employment with the B.E.F. Admiral Somerville was less fortunate for he was actually invalided with tuberculosis and was retired in July 1939. A few weeks later he returned to active and distinguished war service. General H. H. Arnold had a heart attack in 1943 but continued his successful command of the United States Army Air Force. General Matthew B. Ridgway had a severe blackout in September 1945 and was advised to retire. He insisted on returning to duty which eventually included appointments as Supreme Allied Commander in the Far East and Europe, and Chief of Staff, United States Army.

More might be attempted in special training, and innovations in this field could be rewarding. Individuals vary in their susceptibility to mental and bodily fatigue and this individual susceptibility is not even constant for in its turn it may be influenced by such variables as the state of body and mind, climatic conditions and diet. One psychiatrist has suggested that potential commanders should be subjected to severe mental and physical stress in situations that produce fear, tension and frustration. Tests would be conducted in extremes of temperature and if necessary the subjects could be deprived of appropriate amounts of food, drink and sleep. Any failings or errors in the making of decisions could be determined by special tests under statistical control. This scheme is not designed to find the minority who thrive under such conditions or the few who fail. It would give the majority an insight into the development of fatigue, the frequency and types of error in decision making that may result and, most important, the means of adjustment.

In the days before mechanization it was a tradition in the British Army that the horses were fed before the men and the men before the officers. Indeed so little attention was paid to the well-being of the officers that they seemed at times a readily expendable item. One sees the counterpart of this in industry. In the past 100 years increasing attention has been paid to the welfare of the manual worker. He is protected from noxious fumes, vapours and dusts, the temperature of his environment is controlled, and his hours of work are restricted. Only recently has any attention been paid to the health of the senior executive or manager.

Perhaps senior officers and senior executives have only themselves to blame for this lack of care. They are the survivors of a hard struggle for promotion. They are men with unusual mental and physical qualities who have won battles in the field and in the board room. They must continue to assert their superiority over their business rivals, their nations' enemies, and, at times, their own colleagues. If fatigue or illness obtrudes their instinct is to conceal it for the penalty of revelation is the same as that which follows defeat in battle or factory; banishment from office and command.

Fatigue tends to be the fate of the ambitious, the conscientious, or the idealistic. It is rarely experienced by the astute, the lazy or the clever, who may in fact go to considerable trouble to avoid the condition. In our national game no reproach is levelled at the bowler who is rested after a long spell. In American football the whole team may be changed during a game depending on whether the situation is one of offence or defence. Such substitution of commanders and forces would be difficult, but not always impossible, in war. It is neither efficient nor economic to run the human mind and body to avoidable and irremediable destruction. The loss of talented leaders of the type that have been described, often after they have gained priceless experience, cannot and should not be tolerated.

References

1. Maxime Weygand. *Recalled to Service*, p. 48. Heinemann.
2. Arthur Bryant. *The Turn of the Tide*, p. 308. Collins.
3. Donald McLachlan. *Room 39*, p. 287. Weidenfeld & Nicolson.
4. Wynford Vaughan-Thomas. *Anzio*, p. 28. Longmans Green.
5. Martin Blumenson. *Command Decisions*, p. 263. Methuen.
6a. B. H. Liddell Hart. *The Rommel Papers*, p. 271.
6b. p. 391. Collins.
6c. p. 410. Collins.

CHAPTER 10

The Labour ministers wilt under
the strain, 1945–51

The Labour Government was exalted by the results of the General Election in July 1945. For the first time the Socialists had a clear majority over other parties and Hartley Shawcross's words, "we are the masters now", set the tone of the administration. Unfortunately the Cabinet members were not eager, energetic men whose drive had been frustrated by years in opposition. Truculence and arrogance concealed the weariness that many of them felt after five years hard labour in the war-time Coalition.

Miss Ellen Wilkinson was the first to go. She had become Parliamentary Secretary to the Minister of Home Security in 1940 and Minister of Education in 1945. She died on 6 February 1947 and, during the afternoon of the same day, Hugh Dalton visited Herbert Morrison, Lord President of the Council and Leader of the House, who was warded in the Postgraduate Hospital, Hammersmith. Earlier in the year a sharp pain in his calf heralded a venous thrombosis which was followed by pulmonary complications. Morrison later realized the extreme severity of his illness which explained why political affairs and interests became for a time remote. He had insight into his temporary limitations and firmly declined to advise Emmanuel Shinwell who was distraught with anxiety over the fuel crisis. Morrison was over-anxious to return to duty and, though he did not appear in the House until July, his speech on the 7th of that month showed that "he has not yet regained his mental or physical stature". He merely read "without much animation and, at some points, without too deep an understanding, a long typewritten essay".[1a]

The pace was too hot to last. No doubt the Labour Government had to seize the opportunity that had been so long denied. Bills for national and social reform had to be enacted while supreme power was still unchallengeable. At the end of the 1945–6 session Acts of Parliament had been passed to nationalize the Bank of England, the Coal Industry, Civil Aviation and Cable and Wireless, while other enactments dealt with National Insurance, Industrial Injuries, the National Health Service, New Towns and Trade Disputes and Trade Unions.

Herbert Morrison had been the first to break down under the strain and it is ironical that the ebullient and apparently tireless Dalton was the first to be broken. The fuel crisis and the food shortage made 1947 a bad year for everybody and Hugh Dalton, Chancellor of the Exchequer, since 1945, had a personal and particular involvement in the financial difficulties that arose. Problems followed his cheap money policy while the public for the first time were made aware of terms that they have never been allowed to forget: unbalanced external payments, exhaustion of American and Canadian loans and drain on gold and dollar reserves.

Dalton records that the seven months, from April to November 1947, were the most unhappy in his life. The mental arithmetic that racked his brain at night could only be stilled by sleeping tablets. The free convertibility of sterling, instituted on 15 July 1947, had to be suspended and when Dalton spoke in Parliament on 7 August he was "sustained by Benzedrine".[1b] He later admitted that he might have resigned at any time, on grounds of ill health, before the tragic incident in November 1947 that lead to his resignation. "Though depressed and conscious of the strain" it was pride that kept him in office: pride in his accomplishments and above all "passionate pride in my own physical fitness".[1c]

Before he opened his fourth Budget on 12 November 1947 he spoke to a correspondent in the lobby. Next day he was informed that these confidences had been leaked to the Press. He made a frank and full admission of his lapse of judgement and tendered his apologies to the House and his resignation to the Prime Minister. The lobby correspondent was one he had known for years and, though he could not recall any conditions, he had every reason to suppose that his words would be treated as

confidential. Dalton's manners, gloating and almost boastful, had
made enemies in all three parties and his departure was not
widely mourned. Had a combination of mental arithmetic and
sleeping tablets on the previous night blunted his acumen? Had
he repeated his medicine of 7 August and could benzedrine have
caused undesirable stimulation as he walked to the Chamber on
that fateful November afternoon? His colleague had noticed a
change in him for some months and to quote the words of
Aneurin Bevan:

> "Anyone could see for some time that Dalton was under such
> strain that something was bound to happen. There is no
> immaculate conception of disaster."[2]

Richard Stafford Cripps, though only two years younger than
Dalton, had certain characteristics that made him a suitable
replacement for the times. Dedicated to high thinking and plain
living he is the only man who has ever convinced the British
electorate of the virtues of austerity. Churchill, looking over the
sand and rock of the Western Desert is said to have exlaimed:
"how Cripps would love it". His career in the public service
began in the First World War when he served as an assistant
superintendent of a munition factory. He became a Labour
Member in 1931 and was made Solicitor-General by Ramsay
MacDonald. His activities on the extreme left wing of the
Labour Party, which lead to his expulsion in 1939, contrasted
strangely with a wealthy and successful practice at the Bar.
Stranger still in restrospect was his appointment as British
Ambassador to Moscow in 1940 which gained him unjustified
credit when Russia was forced to go to war in the face of the
German invasion. He served Churchill, briefly as Lord Privy
Seal and Leader of the House, and from 1942 to 1945 as
Minister of Aircraft Production. His experience as President of
the Board of Trade from 1945, and his admittedly brief spell as
Minister of Economic Affairs, were an excellent introduction to
his responsibilities as Chancellor of the Exchequer.

His medical history is long and obscure. He was rejected for
military service in 1914 and, after a serious illness of some
months duration, he was invalided from the Ministry of
Munitions. After the First World War he remained unfit and

had trouble with his digestion and insomnia. There is no record of any illness while he was in Russia but he collapsed on a Cabinet Mission to India in May 1946. The altitude of Simla may have accounted for a fainting attack after a call on Gandhi and he was treated at Willingdon Hospital. He was greatly troubled by insomnia and in August 1946, after his return, he recuperated in Switzerland. He was to receive treatment there on subsequent occasions: steps that lead to criticism at a period when currency restrictions, applied by his own Ministry, prevented patients with tuberculosis from receiving in Switzerland what was thought to be the best treatment then available.

In June 1949 there was a fresh financial crisis conditioned by those factors that are now all too familiar: widening of the dollar gap and pressure on sterling. On 14 July he spoke in the House and his biographer records:

"His speech on this occasion was as lucid as ever but there was a weariness about it . . . he was not able to sleep and suffering from digestive trouble. He could not go on, he had forthwith to abandon the Treasury for six weeks of rest and recuperation in a Swiss Clinic . . ."[3]

On his return in August the controversial decision was taken to devalue the pound and he and Bevin sailed for the United States on 31 August. Rest and freedom from responsibility had restored his health and strength and a story is told that he amazed the members of our Washington Embassy by running round the garden at 5 a.m. in the nude. Devaluation of the pound was announced by Cripps in a broadcast on 18 September and he was confident that this step would provide a breathing space in which he could increase production and improve exports. The acceptance of his Budget in 1950 led to stormy debates and, though the Finance Bill finally was passed on 10 July, the burden was too much for Cripps. Once more he returned to Switzerland but treatment on this occasion was of no avail. He was forced to resign the Chancellorship in October and further reports from Switzerland mentioned the diagnosis of a spinal infection. He lay in a plaster cast for several months and by October 1951 his doctors were confident that the infection had been controlled. The optimism was ill-founded for symptoms recurred in October 1952 and he died in the same year. The available evidence suggested a tuberculous infection of the spinal vertebrae though myelomatosis has been mentioned as a possible diagnosis. The obscurity of his illness, and the treatment in Switzerland, inevitably led to rumours of mental disturbance; a diagnosis that is readily attached to distinguished personalities. Research work, begun just before his death, suggests that we might now consider the possibility of yet another condition before making a final diagnosis.

It may have been his digestive troubles as much as his austere temperament that prompted Cripps to become a strict vegetarian. Ivan Maisky, the Soviet Ambassador in London from 1932 to 1943, remembers a dinner party when Cripps only ate certain vegetables and nuts. "Chips" Channon recalls another dinner at which Cripps ate mashed carrots and drank orange juice. At one time he allowed himself the luxury of eggs and ice-cream but latterly he confined himself more and more to grated vegetables. It is now realized that some of the most dedicated vegetarians, the vegans, present a clinical picture that is related to their low intake of cyanocobalamin, classified as Vitamin B_{12}, which is present in liver, kidney, milk, eggs and muscle tissue. Low intake of Vitamin B_{12} is not necessarily related to low levels in a vegetarian's blood nor are low blood levels necessarily associated with signs and symptoms of B_{12} deficiency. In some cases the B_{12} that is present in the blood may be unavailable for use. In 1951 Dr A. G. Badenoch of Edinburgh studied two vegans who had noticed increasing mental incapacity.[4] They had pains in the back and limbs which members of this strict sect referred to as the "vegan back". They commented on the occurrence of a number of sudden and unexplained deaths in their group. Both subjects had X-ray appearances in their spine which suggested ankylosing spondylitis and one had signs and symptoms of subacute combined degeneration of the spinal cord. Both improved on a vegetarian diet fortified with eggs, milk and butter. Green vegetables, fruits and nuts contain large amounts of folic acid which can precipitate degeneration of the spinal cord in patients with pernicious anaemia. The relative sufficiency of folic acid in their diet could have comparable ill-effects in vegans who are already deficient in Vitamin B_{12}.

Another factor may have affected Cripps. As might be expected from their personality vegans rarely smoke or drink. Their limited levels of Vitamin B_{12}, mainly in the form of hydroxycobalamin, is probably enough in most cases to protect their nervous system; and this is the reason why low levels of Vitamin B_{12} may be found in vegans who have no signs or symptoms.

Dr A. D. M. Smith studied two vegans with subacute combined degeneration of the cord, both of whom smoked, and suggested that their hydroxycobalamin, or precursor of Vitamin B_{12}, was exhausted during the detoxification of the cyanide in tobacco smoke.[5] Cripps, oddly enough, was a heavy smoker and during an evening he would ring the changes on cigarettes, cigars and pipe tobacco. At conferences he was a chain smoker.

Two questions, though provocative, must be left unanswered. Should Cripps have been advised to eat a more varied diet and smoke less? Were any of the signs of physical and mental deterioration in his years as Chancellor related to dietary insufficiency?; the reverse of the more usual dietary indulgence but an indiscretion all the same.

Ernest Bevin, the Secretary of State for Foreign Affairs from 1945 until 1951, was formidable in stature and in manner but his massive frame was deceptive for it cloaked severe disability. In 1937, at the age of fifty-six years, he had the first manifestations of cardiac trouble which were associated with a noticeable alteration in his appearance. He joined the wartime Coalition in 1940, as Minister of Labour and National Service, and by 1943 his colleagues were anxious about the state of his health. In April 1945 a severe degree of heart block led to episodes of loss of consciousness. In July 1946 he collapsed on the eve of the Peace Conference which was to convene in Paris and had a similar attack in his room at the House of Commons.

He desperately hoped that he would recover in time to go to Paris and with great secrecy took a short holiday. These hopes were dashed and he could not return to the Foreign Office until 8 August. After a conference' lasting about two hours he complained of pain and constriction in the chest. He half agreed to a second opinion and his private secretary informed the Prime Minister's private secretary who in turn contacted the secretary of the British Medical Association; an interesting sidelight on the method of selecting a consultant in the corridors of power. Bevin's own doctor was then informed of the appointment that he could have arranged himself more expeditiously. Bevin had a slight heart attack, while walking in New York, on 20 November 1946, and from then on his increasing disability, if not quite as alarming as that of Claude Swanson, was sufficiently disturbing. It was noticeable at Cabinet Meetings but was attributed to "tummy trouble" and "flatulence". Early in 1947 Attlee noticed that Bevin gasped for breath to such an extent that he was speechless. When Shinwell had to restrict electricity, because of the fuel crisis in February, Bevin was an unfortunate victim. The mounting of two flights of stairs at Great George Street caused complete prostration. There were grave misgivings about his ability to withstand the demands of the Moscow Conference; particularly as he seemed unable to husband his waning energies and even pottered ineffectually about the Foreign Office on a Saturday morning to the chagrin of the officials who could not tidy up the week's work. He had a heart attack in Moscow but followed his doctor's instructions with regard to diet, regular hours and sleep, so returned to England in May in good shape. In March 1948 he signed the Treaty of Brussels but observers noticed the difficulty he experienced in climbing the grand staircase of the Belgian Academy. On 5 April he was taken ill during a reception at the American Embassy.

In the Autumn of 1949 Bevin was in New York for the General Assembly of the United Nations and collapsed in the aisle after a performance of "South Pacific". Nitroglycerine was given but Bevin expressed preference for a strong drink. On his way to the Colombo Conference in January 1950 he was optimistic but he was taken ill again and had to be carried in a special chair up the two flights of stairs to the Council Chamber. On 21 April 1950, he submitted a progress report to the Prime Minister. Apparently there was less concern about the angina pectoris but "fibrillations, or something of that kind"[6a] made him breathless. Swelling of his legs had responded to some new treatment which would take the place of injections. In addition to the assessment and treatment of these cardiovascular disorders he underwent some surgical operation which caused considerable pain and discomfort.

In May 1950 Bevin collapsed in his own office and Dean Acheson, the American Secretary of State who had witnessed the attack in the previous autumn, attributed this fresh episode to a combination of exhaustion and sedatives. He thought Bevin looked better in the autumn at the NATO meeting and United Nations General Assembly in New York. Bevin stayed to the bitter end and went to the lengths of spending each week-end in hospital. Attlee commented on the last phase:

> "He clung on. The doctors were often really quite hopeful and he hung on as long as he could but he was suffering intensely. I don't think it affected his judgement, although some of the newspapers tried to say it did. . . ."[6b]

His displacement on 10 March 1951, and appointment as Lord Privy Seal, was a bitter blow to his pride and ambition for, according to a member of his staff, "he wanted to die in the Foreign Office".[1d] His wish was likely to be fulfilled for on 20 March he appeared in the House, "sallow and shrunken (and), looked as if he had been kissed by death".[7a] Death came all too soon. He appeared for the last time in the House of Commons on 10 April when "clearly he was in great physical distress and short of breath, for he kept on panting heavily";[1e] in addition he "had the parchment pallor one associates with death".[7b] Four days later he died of a heart attack. His cardiologist later stated that Bevin had had two "coronaries" at least and the "distressing pain and disability"[8] to which he also referred were no doubt due to angina pectoris and loss of consciousness. One Member of Parliament thought that Bevin was enabled to carry on with "the assistance of a very big ration of alcohol".[9] Nitrites were introduced for the treatment of angina pectoris in 1867 but the value of alcohol in this condition had been realized one hundred years before that date. Indeed alcohol is a valuable prophylactic in angina pectoris and only its propensity for addiction leads to the nitrites being preferred. The large whiskies that Bevin drank may have been rather more an essential medication than an indulgence, though those around him experienced its side effects: "whisky improved his temper and caused him to tell endless stories about drunkards and churchmen".[10]

Less was known in Bevin's time of the ill-effects that may accrue when nitroglycerine, for the relief of anginal pain, and alcohol are given together. Such a combination may lead to an undesirable drop in blood pressure and the subsequent collapse may be attributed to myocardial infarction.[11]

Clement Attlee, the Prime Minister since 1945, was the last to go and, forced no doubt to ignore socialist doctrines of equality, he went to the private wing of St Mary's Hospital. A previous illness had also occurred at a time of great drama. When Chamberlain teetered on the brink of war in the first days of September 1939, it was Arthur Greenwood and Dalton who harried him unmercifully about our pledges to Poland. Attlee was in hospital undergoing a prostatectomy. The symptoms of duodenal ulcer, which necessitated rest in April 1951, could not have occurred at a more difficult time for the Labour Party. The National Health Service has always excited passionate feelings that might well be devoted to the more vital aspects of national life. The storm that followed the budget proposals in April 1951 proved no exception. Taking his political courage in his hands, the Chancellor of the Exchequer, Hugh Gaitskell, had proposed charges for spectacles and false teeth, articles that apparently had become a necessity of life, to offset an increase in defence costs. Aneurin Bevan, the Minister of Health, and Harold Wilson, then President of the Board of Trade, bitterly opposed these charges and, though Attlee tried to settle the differences from his hospital bed, they resigned on the eve of the Budget. What had started as a party difference over a domestic matter became internecine strife over rearmament which was a national matter with serious international implications. The Government had gained a narrow majority of 10 seats early in 1950 and its precarious grip was loosened further by the resurgence of Persian nationalism in May 1951, which resulted in the humiliating loss of our oil installations at Abadan. Apart from the loss of prestige and authority in the Middle East the Government was also faced with an ugly run on the gold and dollar reserves. Attlee had no choice but to go to the country again but the loss of 19 seats gave the Conservatives in their turn a narrow majority. Attlee lead his party once more in the General Election of 1955 but, divided as the Socialists were by warring factions, it is not surprising in retrospect that the Conservatives increased their majority to 60. Attlee was then seventy-two years old, and a minor stroke in August, put paid to any hopes he may have had of welding together the disparate Labour elements. On 6 December 1955, quietly and unobtrusively, he terminated his twenty-year leadership of the Labour Party.

References

1a. Hugh Dalton. *High Tide and After*, p. 256.
1b. p. 260. Muller.
1c. p. 6. Muller.
1d. p. 359. Muller.
1e. p. 359. Muller.
2.   Francis Williams. *The Triple Challenge*, p. 50. Heinemann.
3.   Colin Cooke. *The Life of Richard Stafford Cripps*, p. 389. Hodder & Stoughton.
4.   A. G. Badenoch. *British Medical Journal*, 1952, 2, 668.
5.   A. D. M. Smith. *British Medical Journal*, 1962, 1, 1665.
6a. Francis Williams. *A Prime Minister Remembers*, p. 242.
6b. pp. 242–3. Heinemann.
7a. Robert Rhodes James. *Chips*, p. 457.
7b. p. 458. Weidenfeld & Nicolson.
8.   Geoffrey Bourne. *St Bartholomew's Hospital Journal*, 1958, 62. 271.
9.   Sir John Smyth. *The Only Enemy*, p. 238. Hutchinson.
10. Jacques Dumaine. *Quai D'Orsay*, 1945–51, p. 58. Chapman & Hall.
11. N. Shafer. *New England Journal of Medicine*, 1965, 273. 1169.

CHAPTER 11

Winston Churchill: A medical text book in himself

For the first forty-six years of his life Winston Churchill believed he was under sentence of death for he was convinced that he would die at the same age as his father. The inevitability of death is not usually realized until middle age and the effect on Churchill of this premature awareness, though unfounded and even ridiculous, is impossible to determine. It is tempting to suggest that he was driven by an irrational acceptance of a suspended sentence to cram three score years and ten into forty-six years. This theory in no way diminishes those unique qualities which would have made him a world figure in any sphere of activity that he cared to choose. It may explain the burning ambition, the frenetic activity, the self-absorption and the obsessional drive which distinguished him from his contemporaries and brought him to Cabinet Office at the early age of thirty-three years. His brashness and assertiveness made him that much more conspicuous than the angry young men of his day. As a subaltern he talked to Generals and as a fledgling Member of Parliament he attacked Cabinet Ministers. His young contemporaries were not cursed by any foreknowledge of mortality and could bide their time. Churchill lived on borrowed time and had to reach his goals ten or fifteen years earlier.

This shadow that clouded the first half of his life may have led to preoccupation with his health and a tendency to self-medication and unorthodox remedies. In his early years he travelled with cylinders of oxygen and had inhalations before a major speech. Towards the end of his life he was one of the many distinguished patients of Stephen Ward, the notorious osteopath, whose activities indirectly lead to the disintegration of a Conservative Government. Long convinced that the expert is not invariably correct, and should always be challenged,

Churchill was a doctor to himself and to friends with results that were at times bizarre and usually farcical.

Soon after the First World War he seriously advised Lord Curzon to consult a hypnotist for insomnia and gave Lord Beaverbrook attentions which might have been disastrous. Churchill and Beaverbrook were staying at Deauville in 1921 and the latter was taken ill on the night of 5 August. The hotel doctor prescribed two remedies: one to be taken by mouth and the other, as is the Continental fashion, per rectum. Beaverbrook could not read French so Churchill was called to translate and in effect to administer the treatment. An unfortunate misunderstanding lead to each medication being given by the wrong route; such confusion must happen more often than doctors realize but the result on this occasion was a remarkable recovery. A similar incident occurred early in the Second World War when Churchill and his staff were travelling to Scotland by train on a visit to the Fleet. Churchill insisted that Sir Dudley Pound, the first Sea Lord, and Air Marshal Sir Richard Peirse tried a new sleeping tablet. Reluctant as they may have been to take part in such a primitive clinical trial the unquenchable insistence of the enthusiastic "doctor" compelled compliance. No sooner had they dutifully swallowed their medicine when an agitated detective informed them that they had been given tablets from the wrong box; a box containing a new type of laxative tablet for the treatment of constipation.

When Harry Hopkins came to Britain in February 1941 Churchill was concerned about his health and insisted that he took some new "pink pills" which were in current favour. These pills were passed to President Roosevelt and Admiral McIntire who arranged for them to be analysed. The best that could be said about them was that they would do no harm.

The furore that was created by the publication of Moran's diaries obscured the fact that many details of Churchill's medical history were already known. Indeed, for the years 1940–45, Moran does not add a great deal to what has already been published by Churchill himself and Lord Alanbrooke. The main contribution that he makes is the description and assessment of Churchill's medical history from 1945–55, during the years of so-called peace and cold war.

Churchill was sixty-five years old when he became Prime Minister in May 1940 at a most critical period in English history. Judged by conventional standards he had already reached the age of retirement but there was an unusual and mitigating factor. He had bemoaned his years in the wilderness from 1929 to 1939 but they may have been a blessing in disguise. Although he had been actively involved in Parliamentary duties and literary and country pursuits, with which he filled every moment of the day, he was spared the enervating demands and responsibilities of the highest office. Frustrating and even exhausting as it must have been to sit on the side lines, he was probably fitter in mind and body than his colleagues when he took office again at the Admiralty in September 1939. Nevertheless there was concern about his health which led to Moran's appointment and to his first call on a most reluctant and unco-operative patient on 24 May 1940. The misgivings about his health may have been groundless but they were widespread for Mackenzie King, the Canadian Prime Minister, said in June: "Churchill was under a terrific strain, that the possibility of his having a haemorrhage of the brain at some stage was not to be overlooked."[1] Despite this gloomy prognosis his health was well sustained until 1943 when the tide had begun to turn for the Allies. In February he had the first of what was to prove a series of attacks of pneumonia. On 14 November 1943 he left for the first meeting of the big three, Roosevelt, Stalin and himself, at Teheran. En route he developed a heavy cold and was upset by the inoculations which he had received. On arrival at Cairo he ate little and, since he advised others to take Moran's pills to prevent "The Egyptian Stomach", he may have fallen a victim to a bowel infection. He had a severe sore throat during the conference at Teheran and the sound of Churchillian oratory was muffled by laryngitis. Back in Cairo Smuts was alarmed by Churchill's appearance and in the early hours of 12 December Alanbrooke was woken by Churchill demanding medical attention. This second attack of pneumonia was complicated by an irregularity of the heart beat which was diagnosed as auricular flutter. A third attack of pneumonia began on his return from Italy on 30 August 1944, but responded to treatment quickly enough to enable him to attend

the second Quebec Conference. Further bouts of fever, without
pneumonic complications, occurred during meetings with
Stalin in October 1944 and on the way to Yalta in January
1945. Dramatic as these incidents were the infections responded
rapidly to sulphonamides. What gave grounds for concern was
the fact that his mind and body no longer responded to the
abnormal demands that he made.

Moran was later to name 1944 as the year in which Churchill's
mental and physical powers began to decline. Supporters of
Churchill and critics of Moran, have cast doubt on this judgement by insisting that the physician saw less of Churchill
between illnesses and therefore of necessity had a biased view of
his capacity. The same charge cannot be levelled at Alanbrooke,
the Chief of the Imperial General Staff, who saw Churchill
daily and, to his increasing horror, nightly; and if the soldier
was not a physician he was a shrewd observer as might be
expected of a keen naturalist. During the spring and summer
of 1944 as the allied armies poised for the invasion of Europe,
Alanbrooke makes a number of references to Churchill's
exhaustion and deterioration. On 28 March 1944 he noted:
"He seems quite incapable of concentrating for a few minutes
on end, and keeps wandering continuously." On 4 May he
complained that a meeting with Churchill after dinner "mean-
dered on" and on 7 May quoted Churchill as saying that "he
felt as if he would be quite content to spend the whole day in
bed".[2a]

When his diaries were being prepared for publication Alanbrooke tended to modify, excuse and tone down many of his
original observations about Churchill on the grounds that they
were written in the heat of the moment and at the end of a long
and exhausting day.

> "Winston had been a very sick man with repeated attacks of
> pneumonia and frequent bouts of temperature; this physical
> condition together with his mental fatigue accounted for
> many of the difficulties I had with him, a fact for which I
> failed to make adequate allowance."[2b]

Moran saw at first hand the hostile reaction of the Churchill
family to Alanbrooke's revelations; a reaction that was mild in

comparison to the storm that was to fall on him seven years later.

Nor is Alanbrooke the only source. The Polish Ambassador in London, Count Edward Raczynski, recorded on 31 May 1944:

"This was the first of our meetings at which I began to wonder whether Churchill was overtired, or whether he really grasped all that was going on."

"Perhaps, however, he has his own reasons for repeating certain things to us over and over again."[3]

In the spring of 1944 Lord Tedder, General Eisenhower's deputy, remarked on Churchill's fatigue and how the burden of events since 1940 had sapped his vitality. It may be, as his supporters insist, that everyone else was exhausted but it was noticeable at the Potsdam Conference in July 1945 that for the first time he was too tired to read his briefs. If they still persist in denying that a man in his seventy-first year was not worn out after five years of supreme command during the greatest war in history they should turn to his own account. He tells of his fatigue, indeed of his feebleness, in May 1945 and describes how he had to be carried in a chair from Cabinet meetings which were held in a specially constructed underground head-quarters. Despite the weakness he felt constrained to insist that ". . . I had the world position as a whole in my mind. . . ."[4]

A dramatic change in political fortune ensured that Churchill had another long period, as unexpected as it was unwelcome, in the hated backwaters of the wilderness. The landslide in July 1945 brought a Labour Government into power with a crushing majority and Churchill did not return to Downing Street for his second administration until October 1951.

Rumours have always spread, or been spread, about the onset of degenerative diseases in those who hold high office. Although Churchill was a legend in his own lifetime, both at home and in particular abroad, the allegations that were made about several strokes which impaired him were no exception to the rule. On 10 April 1966, one week before publication of the first instal-ment of Moran's diary, an extract from the Churchill-Beaver-brook letters, later to appear as a book, gave details of the cerebro-vascular accidents from which Churchill had suffered.

Degenerative changes in the arteries are an inevitable concomitant of the ageing process and obstruction of circulation to
the brain, described by the alarming word "stroke", does not
necessarily carry a gloomy prognosis. In the early hours of 24
August 1949, after a long session of gin rummy, Churchill
noticed weakness in his right hand. He realized full well the
implications of the incident but optimistically hoped that it was
nothing more than a warning. His expectations were fulfilled
and, though Moran who flew out to examine him confirmed the
diagnosis, he made a satisfactory recovery. At Beaverbrook's
insistence the public were informed that Churchill had a chill
which necessitated rest and quiet. In the same extract Kenneth
Young, who had prepared the Churchill–Beaverbrook letters for
publication, gave details of a second stroke on 23 June 1953,
after Churchill had returned to office. This episode occurred
after an official dinner and the full facts again were kept from
the public. Further light on this incident may have been cast as
early as February 1965, over a year before the revelations of
Kenneth Young and Moran, by a senior Civil Servant who
witnessed the consequences. Sir George Mallaby, a former
Under-Secretary in the Cabinet Office, described vividly the
painful embarrassment of the Cabinet although he gives no
date. Churchill, virtually speechless, rambling and palpably
lacking comprehension; members of the Cabinet, puzzled, un-
comfortable, disturbed and finally determined to bring the
ghastly charade to an end.

We owe a great debt to these lay observers, and of course to
the patient himself, for their clinical vignettes, and although
parts of the jigsaw are missing we can form a reasonable picture
of the Churchill puzzle. It is Moran who gives us the balanced
story in the longest and most detailed medical history on record.
Here is the model for the aspiring medical student: history of
present complaint, past history, family history, examination,
diagnosis and treatment. Distinguished patients are notoriously
fickle and, as succeeding illnesses are treated by the fashionable
physician of the moment, the historian may have to garner
medical details from a number of different sources. Perhaps
Moran is unique and that never again will one distinguished
physician have the opportunity and privilege of being in

sole medical charge of one historical figure for twenty-four years.

Moran fills in some gaps in the story of the war years. He confirms that the disturbance of heart rhythm which followed Churchill's pneumonia at Carthage was auricular fibrillation and not auricular flutter as he had told Alanbrooke at the time. Presumably the diagnosis was confirmed by the distinguished cardiologist who was called into consultation by Moran and was bullied later for his pains by Churchill who objected to his opinion. Moran records interesting observations about Churchill's reaction to drugs and, though he makes no particular comment, leads one to speculate on the effect that standard treatments may have had on him. He did not escape the fever and discomfort of T.A.B. (Typhoid-Paratyphoid) vaccine. When Churchill had pneumonia, before the second Quebec Conference in September 1943, Moran stopped the mepacrine tablets which had been administered to suppress malaria during the Italian visit in the previous month. Apart from a yellow discoloration of the skin mepacrine can cause gastro-intestinal symptoms and even mental disturbance. His indisposition on the way to Yalta in January 1945 was blamed on sulphaguanidine tablets which had presumably been given to ward off gastro-intestinal infections. Their therapeutic value apart, side effects of these tablets include nausea, vomiting and fever. Students of decision making processes must appreciate that the untoward action of a widely used drug could affect both the analysis of information and final judgement. The examination of State papers, documents or Cabinet minutes should ideally be accompanied by a simultaneous inspection of the medical records of the participants. Much might be explained and even more might be excused if that measure of attention was paid to the contemporaneous mental and physical state of ministers as is paid to what the existing, and often exiguous, State papers tell us of their thoughts, motives, decisions and mistakes.

If Moran can merely throw an extra glimmer of light on the Churchill of the war years he turns a vivid and penetrating beam on the Churchill who still dominated the international scene, in opposition and in power, from 1945 until 1955. In 1948, apparently for the first time, he observed degenerative

changes in Churchill's arterial system. The blood vessels of the
retina are readily available for inspection with an ophthalmo-
scope. A similar examination by de Schweinitz showed that
Woodrow Wilson had such changes at the early age of forty
nine. Churchill was seventy-three years old when changes of
this type were noted and, though they could be regarded as a
natural process of senescence, their prognostic significance
could not be ignored. The first stroke in August 1949 was
followed by a minor arterial spasm in January 1950 and a more
serious attack in February 1952, early in his second administration, when his speech was affected. Moran was really concerned
by now and approached John Colville, one of Churchill's
principal Private Secretaries, for an opinion. Colville announced
that Churchill was not working efficiently and his insistence that
five-page documents had to be compressed into a single para-
graph limited the proper consideration and solution of problems.
The Private Secretary to the Queen confirmed that Churchill
often could not follow the trend of a discussion and Moran, on
the strength of these opinions, felt bound to warn Churchill
about his condition. A plan to persuade Churchill that a move
to the House of Lords might provide a solution met with no
more success than had a similar attempt with Campbell-
Bannerman.

These ranging shots across his bows did not deter Churchill
but the menacing threat of the stroke on 23 June 1953 could not
be ignored. It occurred after a dinner to the Italian Prime
Minister and Churchill's condition, since he could neither
speak nor move from the table, suggested intemperance to those
unfamiliar with his medical history. The gravity of the situation
was soon realized for, in contrast to the stroke in 1949, the left
side of the body was now affected which indicated the widespread involvement of his arterial system by pathological
change. The consultants whom Moran called were gloomy. Sir
Russell (later Lord) Brain, the neurologist, doubted whether
Churchill would live a year although he agreed that death
might be hastened by immediate retirement. He was not sure
whether Churchill would be able to make speeches or answer
questions in the House and whether he could seriously expect
to remain in politics. Late in August 1953 Sir John Parkinson,

the cardiologist, who had not seen Churchill for four years was shocked by the way he had aged and was emphatic that he could no longer act as Prime Minister.

Churchill had already ignored and defied these opinions for he had presided at a Cabinet Meeting on 18 August. For the next few months, with the help of special pills that were prescribed by Moran, Churchill overcame a series of hurdles. Whereas early in September he was exhausted by a game of croquet he made an impressive showing during the Conservative Party Conference at Margate on 10 October. Ten days later he reappeared in the House of Commons and answered questions. On 3 November he made a speech in the House and, early in December, he was able to attend the Bermuda Conference with President Eisenhower and the French Prime Minister. He had to steel himself for these ordeals with the same determination that he had shown as a neophyte in politics over fifty years before; but now he was creating a façade, and putting on an act, for selected audiences on special occasions. The public could see and worship their respected and beloved idol but behind the mask lay shadow rather than substance. Churchill no longer studied State papers but avidly read novels and interminably played bezique.

In July 1954 the Lord Chancellor told Moran that Churchill could no longer follow discussion in Cabinet. His striking performance at the Conservative Party Conference in 1953 was not to be repeated for his speech in 1954 was poorly delivered and marred by mistakes and mispronunciation. On 23 November 1954, during a speech in his constituency, he said that he had sent a telegram to Field-Marshal Montgomery in the summer of 1945 ordering him to collect discarded German weapons which could be reissued if the Russians menaced the Western part of the alliance. This statement was embarrassing to the Government, since talks with the Russians were contemplated, and proved even more embarrassing for Churchill when no trace of the telegram could be found. In the evening of his unique Parliamentary career he had to undergo the humiliation of apologizing to the House of Commons on 1 December 1954.

Early in February 1955 the meeting of Commonwealth Prime

Ministers gave him the last opportunity to preside over a big
international conference. Fortified by Moran's pills he
weathered the storm and it was he who caught a fainting
Attlee, a mere stripling of seventy-two years, when he collapsed
during a reception at Buckingham Palace. The end could no
longer be delayed for, even if he had not entirely outlived his
usefulness, the Conservative Party as a whole and certain
members in particular wished to be rid of him. By the time
that Churchill relinquished the Premiership on 6 April 1955, he
was spending most of the day in bed. Unless there was a Cabinet
meeting he did not get up until lunch-time. If there were no
questions in the House he remained at the table until late
afternoon, returned to bed in the early evening, and only roused
himself again for dinner.

Churchill's fitness to take up office again in October 1951 is
perhaps a matter for debate. According to Moran, "The old
capacity for work had gone, and with it much of his self-
confidence. He forgot figures. Everything had become an
effort." "Physically, too, he was changed; he walked like an old
man." His retention of office after his second serious stroke in
February 1952 is a matter for concern: "After this it was
noticed in the office that he was not doing his work. He did not
want to be bothered by anything"; his struggle to retain
personal power after the stroke in June 1953 may regrettably be
a matter for censure: "The year that followed was rather a sad
affair for Winston's friends. It had become plain to the Party
that he was no longer fit to carry out his duties as Prime
Minister."[5]

The mental and physical imperfections that dragged
Churchill down were not merely pulmonary infections or the
progressive paralysis of cerebral degeneration. According to
one writer "Fate is temperament" and, though retrospective
psychological studies may be as inaccurate as they are fashionable, basic traits of character and personality cannot be ignored.
Moran provides a vital clue, perhaps the key to Churchill's
behaviour, when he reveals that his patient had spells of severe
depression. Churchill called this state "Black Dog" in contrast
to Ernest Hemingway who called his depressions "Black Ass".
As early as May 1915, when Churchill was facing the most

disastrous set-back to his career over the Dardanelles fiasco, Lord Beaverbrook wrote: "What a creature of strange moods he is – always at the top of the wheel of confidence or at the bottom of an intense depression."[6] His position as First Lord of the Admiralty hovered in the balance and the unexpected news of German fleet movements in the North Sea gave grounds for hope that a dramatic victory might restore his stock at the eleventh hour. The German fleet did not oblige and there was no reprieve for Churchill who dissolved into tears. There is on record a portrait of Churchill in this mood of profound depression for he sat for William Orpen after he left the Admiralty.

When Ironside was Chief of the Imperial General Staff in 1940, and in close contact with Churchill, he felt the same:

> "He is a curious creature of ups and downs. Very difficult to deal with when in his downs."
>
> "He is so like a child in many ways. He tires of a thing, and then wants to hear no more of it."[7]

Two years later General Ismay, Churchill's Military Assistant, made a shrewd assessment of his master in a letter to Auchinleck, then C-in-C Middle East.

> "You cannot judge the P.M. by ordinary standards: he is not in the least like anyone that you or I have ever met. He is a mass of contradictions. He is either on the crest of the wave, or in the trough, either highly laudatory or bitterly condemnatory: either in an angelic temper, or a hell of a rage: when he isn't fast asleep he's a volcano. There are no half-measures in his make-up. He is a child of nature with moods as variable as an April day."[8]

Swings of mood characterize the cyclothymic temperament which is often present in the more accomplished and successful members of the community. Relatively barren periods of depression may be more than offset by the creative productivity of the opposite state which, at its extreme limits, merges into hypomania. What they lose on the swings of despondency they gain on the roundabouts of elation and their periods in high gear allow them to outstrip the more "normal" members of the community who, if not incidentally handicapped by other psychological traits, give a modest but sustained performance in low gear.

In 1960 a group of American psychiatrists and psychologists concluded that Nikita Khruschev, the Russian Premier, "was a stable hypomanic character".[9] One amateur psychiatrist has been quoted as saying: "Lyndon Johnson is a manic-depressive in a mild sort of way. Hubert (Humphrey) is just plain manic – he's almost always on an up."[10]

Dr Macnamara may have been describing the psychopathology of hypomania but his words conjure up a picture which has many of the characteristics of those who dominate their respective walks of life:

"Imagination is very active. Business, social, scientific or political projects are rapidly developed, much talked of and occur in swift succession. The schemes are of a sweeping character, of large scope and often clever, though generally vitiated by some absurd impracticability which escapes the notice of the patient. His conversation has often a certain brilliance, in part due to the exuberance of his reproductive memory, whereby all sorts of matters long forgotten surge into consciousness, and in part to the absence of that restraint which normally checks the expression of a large proportion of a conversationalist's ideas. Egotism is accentuated."[11]

From all accounts, and they are numerous, Churchill had certain of these characteristics but at a level that was psychologically normal and socially acceptable; moreover he displayed the distinctive diurnal rhythm which characterizes the cyclothyme. The sluggish start to the day and the late rising; the leisurely lunch and the afternoon nap which was taken whenever possible, whatever the crisis, in peace and war. In the evening as his colleagues wilted, after more conventional hours of work, Churchill began to bloom. The flow of his talk at the dinner table quickened and his weary staff and colleagues had to sit into the small hours as he held the stage. Between film sessions he talked, argued and poured forth ideas; the brilliance of the talk, the flight of the ideas and the fantastic feats of memory owed nothing to champagne and brandy. After the novelty had worn off the habitué's longed for sleep and must have regarded these extraordinary activities with a mixture of awe and dread. On Churchill's part it was not a conscious conquest or suppression of mental and physical fatigue but rather a conscious, and generally profitable, adaptation to the dictates of his inborn temperament.

The historians of the first half of the twentieth century plotted new territory as they put Churchill under the microscope. The historians of the second half of the century can explore a new dimension if they use a high power lens and simultaneously chart Churchill's decisions and actions with his mental and physical state. Could it be that the magnificent failure at the Dardanelles in 1915 was conceived in elation and executed in depression or conceived in depression and executed in elation? Was the tempo of Government slowed or altered when he was afflicted by Black Dog? Can changes of mood explain the enthusiastic appointment of Auchinleck in 1941 and the ungenerous dismissal in 1942; or account for the optimism about the Anzio landing and the pessimism about the Normandy landing in 1944? Was the exuberance of elation cancelled out by the lethargy of depression or did neither of these extremes have any noticeable effect on those devoted servants who control the elaborate machinery of the ship of State? One day we may know how many vital decisions were taken by Churchill in an hour, in a day, in a week and in a month; and how these decisions were influenced by sickness and health, M and B and mepacrine, boredom and excitement, austerity or indulgence, frustration or fulfilment, and envy or contentment. The questions are not idle ones and the gaps in our knowledge call for serious study rather than academic speculation. Drugs are now available that can stimulate those who are depressed and quieten those who are elated. Drugs are available that can alter perception and distort the patterns of thought and reason. Nor must one forget the everyday drugs that are used for trivial illness which can have unexpected and untoward effects on the mind. The task of a future Moran is a daunting one for he will need to know as much about the machinery of government and international relations as he knows about the machinery of mind and body if he is to discharge properly his crushing obligations.

References

1. Laurence Thompson. 1940, p. 178. Collins.
2a. Arthur Bryant. *Triumph in the West,* pp. 175, 186, 187.
2b. p. 481. Collins.
3. Edward Raczynski. *In Allied London,* p. 218. Weidenfeld & Nicolson.
4. Winston Churchill. *The Second World War,* vol. VI, p. 512. Cassell.
5. Lord Moran. *Winston Churchill: The Struggle for Survival,* p. 787. Constable.
6. Lord Beaverbrook. *Politicians and the War,* p. 118. Oldbourne Books.
7. R. Macleod and Denis Kelly. *The Ironside Diaries,* pp. 263, 278. Constable.
8. John Connell. *Auchinleck,* p. 472. Cassell.
9. Bryant Wedge. *Washington Post,* 27 October 1968.
10. Stewart Alsop. *Sunday Telegraph,* 1 September 1968.
11. F. W. Price. *Textbook of Medicine,* 1922, p. 1605.

CHAPTER 12

Anthony Eden and Harold Macmillan:
From Suez to Blackpool

It would be difficult to find any person over the age of fifty years who is free from some physical or mental imperfection. Fortunately most of the departures from the norm are no more indicative of serious change than the weathering of bricks in a building. Furthermore even more marked abnormalities do not necessarily preclude intense mental and physical effort over a long period. Nature has set the standards for the constructional engineer who allows for several multiples of the amount of stress that he anticipates; although resilience and resistance is impaired by advancing years and disease, the human body has considerable, and often untapped, reserves of vitality.

Since some of the business of government has been adequately discharged by statesmen with obvious deficits in mental and physical efficiency, a rigorous analysis might show that it is only a certain type of illness in a certain type of situation that leads to inefficiency and incompetence. If moments of crisis often seem to be associated with illness in the protagonists, the association may merely be apparent because less attention is paid to politicians in uneventful periods. Yet the rush of events in an international crisis, with each incident causing a chain reaction of complications, may be beyond the power of any one man to control. In the decisive moments of history a statesman, whatever his mental and physical condition, may be the impotent victim of multifarious and irremediable circumstances.

Robert Anthony Eden succeeded Churchill as Prime Minister in April 1955 and is likely to be remembered for the abrupt ending of a short and unhappy tenure of office which was preceded by detailed and widespread rumours about his state of health. His departure for a holiday in Jamaica on 23 November 1956, soon after the premature conclusion of Operation "Musketeer" at Suez, gave further grounds for concern since it was announced that his doctors had ordered him to rest. Returning to London three weeks later to face an embarrassed party, a hostile opposition and a divided country, it was apparent that any improvement in health was as superficial as his suntan. A recurrence of his illness at the end of the month must have have contributed to his decision to resign on 9 January 1957. Twelve years after Suez it is difficult to disentangle cause from effect or even to define cause and effect with accuracy.

Eden entered public life as the Conservative member for Warwick and Leamington in 1923. He was made Lord Privy Seal in 1934 and Minister for the League of Nations Affairs in the following year. He came under medical supervision in 1935 and, from his autobiography and the accounts of others, the details of the illness can be pieced together. Early in 1935 the long journeys, the broken sleep, the interminable discussions and the irregular meals, which constitute the normally-accepted hazards facing a senior official, were wearing him out. An extended trip to the capitals of Eastern Europe, ending in an appalling flight between Leipzig and Cologne, was the last straw. The unpressurized aircraft of the day could not operate above turbulent conditions and Eden's plane was the only one flying in Europe.

He was violently airsick and came off the aircraft in a state of collapse. His pulse rate was 45 and there was talk of a strained heart. Eden returned to England by train and boat where, on King George V's recommendation, he saw a distinguished consultant who confirmed the diagnosis and advised convalescence. It should be noted that some of the younger cardiologists, following the teaching of the great Sir James Mackenzie, were then propounding his opinion that the normal heart could not be strained; and that aspiring young athletes and tired business men could thus be spared lives of invalidism. The man on the spot is the best umpire but it is possible that the slow pulse rate was the natural consequence of an alarming flight; the nervous impulses to the heart, rather than the heart muscle itself, may have been the site of the disorder and the cause of the slow pulse.

In February 1938, Eden felt compelled to resign. He strongly disapproved of Chamberlain's attempts to conciliate Mussolini without any assurance of Italian good faith; and he felt resentful and humiliated by the clandestine negotiations conducted behind his back. Meantime ugly rumours were being spread about his health. Sir John Simon, the Chancellor of the Exchequer, was the instigator of this whispering campaign which was intended to show that mental and physical ill-health, rather than political disagreement, was the main cause of Eden's resignation from the Government. On this occasion there was nothing amiss with Eden's health and his parliamentary private secretary, J. P. L. Thomas, vigorously refuted Simon's sly innuendoes.

After the declaration of war in 1939, Eden returned to the Government as Dominions Secretary and, on Churchill's accession to power in May 1940, took over the War Office. The same year saw his re-appointment to the Foreign Office where he remained until the fall of Churchill's ministry in July 1945. His arduous departmental duties, together with the leadership of the House, which he assumed in 1942, were competently discharged and he escaped with nothing worse than a duodenal ulcer which incapacitated him in May and June 1945. The years as Deputy Leader of the Opposition between 1945 and 1951 were relatively healthy except for an attack of appendicitis in March 1948 and an episode at a meeting in June 1949 when he collapsed. It was between 1951 and 1955, as Foreign Secretary again and Deputy Prime Minister, that the seeds of an illness were sown that had such disastrous consequences during his Premiership.

In June 1952 he had an attack of jaundice but it was not until April 1953 that a diagnosis of chronic cholecystitis indicated that an inflamed gall bladder, presumably with gall stones, was the cause. He had been in poor health for some weeks and had taken a rest in January 1953. On 12 April 1953 he had an operation, at which the gall bladder was removed, and a second on the 29th of the month. By this time it was apparent that the original operation had not been a complete success and must have been complicated by stricture of the bile ducts and consequent obstruction of the free flow of bile. In June 1953 a third operation on the biliary tract was performed in America during which a reconstructive procedure ensured an adequate flow of bile. Unfortunately the bile passages still became blocked at intervals leading to the condition of acute obstructive cholangitis. Such episodes may be accompanied by high fever, rigors and sweating together with pain and jaundice. Charcot's intermittent biliary fever is another name for this condition and is an apt description that we owe to that distinguished French physician. These episodes may have more serious consequences than an ordinary bout of fever and Professor Sheila Sherlock, who has made a special study of this disorder, states that some patients become introspective, querulous and suspicious. Fever may have incapacitated Eden on three occasions in 1955: he had to cancel visits to Turkey and Scotland and he was away in December with "a chill". A dramatic attack, vividly described by Eden himself, occurred on 5 October 1956 as the Suez crisis was approaching its climax. On a visit to Lady Eden in University College Hospital he was prostrated by a fever of 106° F. and forthwith had to be admitted as a patient. Three days later he was fit for discharge but Eden admits that the improvement was only temporary: "it is a common feature of these fevers and is apt to be followed by recurrent bouts of weakness."[1a] By early November, as the Suez adventure ended in disaster, Eden was certain that the attack had weakened him but, as unprecedented pressures might also have led to fatigue, his physicians advised a holiday as a therapeutic test. He left for Jamaica on 23 November but a recurrence of fever, after his return on 14 December, made him realize that he could no longer discharge the duties of Prime Minister. He wrote later of "fever attacks so weakening that nobody could suffer from them and do a good day's work" and of the claims of his office: "There is no possibility of carrying through with work of this responsibility under any recurring disability."[1b]

Others bear witness to his condition. On 25 October, Sir Walter Monckton, still a member of the Cabinet, confirmed the rumours of Eden's illness. He added that Eden had always been excitable and temperamental and that he had been on the verge of a breakdown for some months. Robert Murphy, an official from the American State Department, thought that Eden lost his nerve; ". . . perhaps his lowered physical stamina did affect his judgement when quick decisions became necessary later."[2] Lord Rothermere considered that Eden's calmness and resolution varied with the bouts of fever. A Labour member described the scene in the House in early November:

> "The Prime Minister sprawled on the front bench, head thrown back and mouth agape. His eyes, inflamed with sleeplessness, stared into vacancies beyond the roof except when they switched with meaningless intensity to the face of the clock, probed it for a few seconds, then rose again into vacancy. His hands twitched at his horn-rimmed spectacles or mopped themselves in a white handkerchief, but were never still. The face was grey except when black-ringed caverns surrounded the dying embers of his eyes. The whole personality, if not prostrated, seemed completely withdrawn."[3]

The nature of Eden's illness differs from those that finally handicapped his predecessors. MacDonald, Baldwin, Chamberlain and Churchill were afflicted in the end by the diseases and degenerations of senescence. Although their interest, initiative, energy and output waned they remained true to type. Even if they were no longer the great figures of their prime their attitudes and reactions were substantially the same. Even if they had still possessed enough physical energy to dominate events their minds were too set in the past to contemplate any fresh change in a long established routine. They were guilty of sins of omission rather than sins of commission but, in the balance sheet of history, the man who does nothing is often spared the criticism that is levelled at the man who tries to influence events. Eden courageously inspired a riposte to a new dictator and only the perverse malignity of fate rendered his initiative so unrewarding and self-destructive.

Fever at irregular intervals is not necessarily or completely incapacitating although frequent absences from the scene may be a handicap if attendance at Cabinet meetings, conferences or in Parliament is uncertain. The effects of drugs administered for the relief of symptoms must be weighed against the effects of the symptoms themselves. Professor Hugh Thomas, who now holds the chair of history at the University of Reading, mentions certain drugs that were given to Eden.[4] As early as July 1956, according to Thomas, Eden told an adviser that he was living on benzedrine and in September the Israeli Ambassador noted that Eden talked incessantly at a luncheon. After his discharge from University College Hospital in October an "official adviser" is quoted as saying that Eden was "in a state of acute intoxication in the technical sense of the word". Depending on the dose, and on the reaction of the individual patient, the benzedrine group of drugs may cause excitement, euphoria, irritation, restlessness, tenseness and insomnia. Large doses in susceptible patients may lead paradoxically to depression or fatigue and even to delusions and feelings of suspicion.

Seldom has a Prime Minister been so completely misunderstood and so vindictively denigrated. In August 1956 he was sure that the country realized the potential danger of Nasser and the risk of instability in the Middle East and Africa. The apparently solid front was a façade that soon cracked. Without a declaration of war he was forced to prepare for war. Without the complete understanding of the Leader of the Opposition he could not withstand the attacks of the extreme left. Without wartime measures of control he could not contain the unbridled comments of Press and radio. Without elaborate and lengthy preparations and plans the armed forces could not mount with sufficient speed the complicated amphibious operation against Egypt. Without American understanding and tacit support the Egyptians realized that their position was strengthened. A British operation would have been sufficiently complicated but, because of French involvement in the Suez Canal, an Anglo-French plan was proposed on 14 August. Further warnings from Eisenhower led to postponement of the assault a few days before the intended date of 15 September. A month later the Anglo-French plan had become an Anglo-French-Israeli plan for the French, aware that the Israelis were contemplating an assault on Egypt, suggested that collaboration would allow all interested parties to have a stake in any military operation verging on the Suez Canal. The Israeli attack on Egypt began on 29 October and, next day, the British Cabinet sent an ultimatum to both the parties demanding a cease fire. The air bombardment began as early as 31 October but for administrative reasons the parachute troops and the seaborne tail could not land until 5 and 6 November. As the Israelis had already reached their objectives by 4 November and had suggested a cease fire, the Anglo-French cover story about separating the combatants was disingenuous to say the least. Professor Finer maintains that when Eden was berated by Eisenhower over the transatlantic telephone on 31 October, he burst into tears. A combination of irresistible pressures, national, international, political, military and economic, compelled Eden to order a cease fire on 6 November; at which Mollet, the French Prime Minister, wept in his turn. The tears were flowing as freely as they had in July and August 1914.

At periods of crisis, when the spotlight is focused on the comings and goings in Downing Street and Westminster, it is inevitable that the activities and the whereabouts of ministers are more carefully recorded. Eden was by no means the only member of the government who was ill between July and December 1956, although it is impossible to say whether the sickness rate was any higher than might be expected in more tranquil times. Furthermore, if allowance is not also made for diplomatic chills and absences, a false impression of the incidence of genuine sickness can easily be given.

On the 27 July, the day after Nasser had nationalized the canal, R. A. Butler, the Lord Privy Seal and Leader of the House, went sick. Anthony Nutting, the Minister of State for Foreign Affairs, who strongly disapproved of the Suez adventure, was away because of illness in the first half of August; for some days, before the public announcement of his subsequent resignation on 4 November, curious reporters were told he had asthma. The show goes on and a politician must step into any role like a good trouper. When the Marquess of Salisbury, the Leader in the House of Lords, had a heart attack in October it was Nutting of all people who had to read the jingoistic address that had been prepared by the invalid for the Conservative Party Conference. The motives for the resignation in October of Walter Monckton, the Minister of Defence, were mixed. His views, which he gave at a cocktail party, were promptly relayed to President Eisenhower on 24 October. Physical exhaustion was the main cause although disapproval of the Government's policy played a part; holding such opinions only loyalty to his party could have persuaded Monckton to accept the appointment of Paymaster-General and remain in the Government.

Even the robust Selwyn Lloyd, the Foreign Secretary, began to wilt under the strain. Over in New York he and his fellow Foreign Ministers, Pineau of France and Fawzi of Egypt, had been persuaded by Dag Hammarskjoeld, Secretary-General of the United Nations, to propose six principles as a basis for an agreement on the Suez Canal. However, on 14 October, when the Security Council approved the principles, representatives of the French Government were meeting Eden and Nutting at Chequers in great secrecy and hinting at the possibility of a combined Anglo-French-Israeli operation against Nasser. Eden summoned Lloyd back from New York and, dismissing any debate of other proposals, whirled him off to more secret discussions in Paris a few hours after his return on 16 October. On 22 October Lloyd went to yet another secret meeting in Paris, attended by the Israeli Prime Minister, though his absence from his office was attributed to sickness. When pressed by a colleague for his opinion on a situation that was rapidly deteriorating, Lloyd could only say: "I really don't know. I am so confused and exhausted that I honestly have no advice to offer any more."[5]

Malcolm Muggeridge was not entirely facetious when he later wrote that Eden was prostrated "by excessive doses of sedatives, pep-pills and John Foster Dulles".[6] Eden's tragedy cannot be considered without Dulles who gave him the final push on 2 November 1956 when his resolution at the United Nations, condemning aggression and calling on the combatants to cease fire in the Middle East, was carried by 64 votes to 5.

In the early hours of the following morning Dulles was seized by a sudden attack of abdominal pain, and a surgical operation revealed a cancer of the bowel. Even then he would not lie still and within three days he was sending orders from his bed to the Acting Secretary of State.

Although it has been suggested by one biographer it is unlikely that the antecedent strain and anxiety caused cancer; however the progress of the disease, not necessarily unheralded, may have imperceptibly sapped his energy and efficiency. Dulles was already sixty-eight years old at the time of the Suez crisis and had overcome a series of grave illnesses. Gangrene of the foot in 1944 due to thrombo-phlebitis required an operation to improve the circulation and a caution against smoking. Spinal injuries had lead to a prolapsed intervertebral disc which was treated surgically. Tension may have exacerbated a liability to gout but facial twitching, eye blinking and sucking movements of the lips were more obvious signs of nervous instability. A drooping of the right side of his mouth has been attributed to a stroke, though such asymmetry is not necessarily of serious significance. Similarly the squint in one eye has been attributed to nothing more weighty than an overdose of quinine in 1911.

It was unfortunate that Dulles came to the crisis, marked by the scars of old disease, and under attack by another which, apart from local signs and symptoms, may have unpredictable and unmeasurable effects on the rest of the body as well as the mind. His main objective in the second half of 1956 was to avoid a war in an election year when President Eisenhower was standing as an apostle of peace. If one concedes that was his duty one can only remark that his least attractive characteristics were appallingly conspicuous; in particular his equivocation and the use and misuse of ambiguous phrases couched in sanctimonious and self-righteous tones.

Even if allowance is made for an innate clumsiness and crudity in diplomatic affairs his behaviour during the crisis towards Britain and France, a combination of hostility and bullying, was possibly influenced by an adverse change in personality. Dulles precipitated the crisis on 19 July 1956 when he abruptly withdrew the American offer of financial help to Egypt over the Aswan dam. Then he encouraged the international users of the canal to take joint action but later, when he saw that America might be embarrassed, discouraged Britain and France from appealing to the United Nations. Later he proposed a Suez Canal Users Association (SCUA) but soon sabotaged it by saying that America would not contemplate the use of force. His extraordinary Press conferences gave comfort to Nasser and depressed and unsettled England and France. A former British Cabinet Minister vividly described a diabolical expression on Dulles's face as he was interviewed on television about Suez. With all his faults Dulles was not an evil man and, if he disliked British mannerisms, and British food in particular, he was an admirer of the French and their way of life; and as Suez was an Anglo-French combined operation he could hardly condemn one partner and ignore the other. Perhaps the clue to his behaviour lies in his extraordinary volte-face at the end of November when he flabbergasted Selwyn Lloyd, the Foreign Secretary, by asking why the British and French had stopped their advance down the Canal. It could be argued that removal of the growth and rest brought about a temporary improvement and change of heart; though little is known of the systemic effects of a growing cancer in the latent period before it produces localizing signs and symptoms. It may have been past experience rather than rational anticipation that, two years later, led him to talk ". . . about the possibility that either persistent pain or a recurrence of cancer might lead to a blurring of his judgement, a state of mind that would render the execution of his job difficult".[7]

His sister was in no doubt "that his mood and even his condition changed from time to time from the end of October (1958) on".[7] On 5 December 1958 he was found to have a hernia and an "inflamed colon". A week later, at the meeting of NATO Foreign Ministers in Paris, he could neither sleep nor eat. On 30 January 1959 he left for his last European trip. Even on a diet of raw eggs and gruel he vomited persistently and could neither bathe nor dress himself alone. He refused to take sedatives during the day in case his judgement was affected and he later told the Vice-President that concentration on controversial subjects made him forget the pain. On 14 February it was announced that the cancer had recurred and deep X-ray therapy and radioactive gold was started on the 20th. There was no response to treatment and evidence of cancerous deposits in the neck vertebrae indicated a rapid spread of disease. His resignation, delayed as long as possible, was not announced until 15 April and he died on 24 May 1959 at the age of seventy-one years. Many in Great Britain and France ignore the long struggle that Dulles waged against Communism and only remember his anti-colonial tendencies and his sabotage of the Suez operation. If they cannot yet forgive him they should not forget that at the height of the crisis he was handicapped by the immensurable effects of a carcinoma of the bowel.

There is another figure who must be woven into the Suez tapestry, whose apparent remoteness from the drama should not mask his involvement. Harold Macmillan had been Chancellor of the Exchequer since December 1955 and, though this office seemed far removed from military plans and secret alliances, he gave Eden every support and encouragement. It must have been with a feeling of mortification that, on 6 November 1956, he was forced to draw attention to the imminence of national bankruptcy.

Macmillan was within a month of his sixty-third birthday when he succeeded Eden as Prime Minister in January 1957. He had been luckier than Eden in other respects for an operation for gall-stones, also performed in 1953, had been successful. Macmillan was reputed to enjoy the political game and to face the machinations and manœuvres with every sign of enjoyment. He revivified the Conservative Party and its electoral triumph in 1959, when there was a further increase in the majority, exceeded the wildest dreams of the supporters. The giddy hopes of five more years in office were soon dispelled for in July 1961 yet another financial crisis brought the electors of the new "Affluent Society" face to face with economic reality. A series of security scandals increased the Government's unpopularity and the time seemed ripe for the usual expedient of an embarrassed government; a discreet reshuffle of portfolios, creating the impression of improvement and efficiency while in practice effecting little change. Macmillan was a professed devotee of the works of Trollope and his actions on 12 July 1962 would have provided that author with material for several books though he might have regarded them as too sensational and incredible for fiction. In a lightning stroke Macmillan dismissed seven Cabinet Ministers and nine Junior Ministers with a speed and ruthlessness that earned him the nickname of "Mac the Knife". The purge did not distract attention from a government that soon lost the confidence of its supporters, incurred the hostility of the Press and was humiliated by its mishandling of a scandal involving a senior minister. Macmillan survived some searing debates in the summer of 1963 and by the autumn it appeared that he might even remain in office. A sudden illness in October, just before the Party Conference, put paid to his hopes and he resigned later in the month.

It had been known for more than a year that Macmillan's prostate was enlarged and the emergency in October could not have been a complete surprise to his advisers. In August 1963 he had discussed the possibility of his resignation in October and the advisability of leading the party in the next election. Lord Swinton, his confidant, noted the talk:

"In the latter event, win or lose, he would probably retire in a year or eighteen months, for he was very tired and in poor health. There were already some alarming symptoms."[8]

The gravity of his physical condition at this time is confirmed by Reginald Bevins, the Postmaster-General, who served in his Cabinet and was in close contact:

"Due either to illness, age, or sheer fatigue he was only the shadow of the man I had known so well and admired so much for most of his long and distinguished career."[9]

The natural history of his illness followed the textbook description almost to the letter and Randolph Churchill who wrote *The Fight for the Tory Leadership* has charted it with an almost clinical precision.

In the morning of Tuesday, 8 October, retention of urine, due to an enlarged prostate, was temporarily relieved by his son's general practitioner. Later he held a Cabinet meeting but, after a further consultation with his medical advisers, it was agreed that an immediate operation was indicated and admission to the King Edward VII Hospital for Officers was arranged. On Wednesday, 9 October, preparation for the operation included prescription of sedatives, for he was in considerable pain. During the course of the day he saw only two members of the

Cabinet and he hinted to Lord Home, the Foreign Secretary, that he might have to renounce his peerage and lead the party: despite the fact that a few days before the illness he had made a similar suggestion to Lord Hailsham. Later in the day, still presumably under mild sedatives, Macmillan apparently-decided that he should resign. A major operation for the removal of his prostate had been planned for 10 a.m. on Thursday, 10 October. Pre-operative sedatives must have been given as a routine but he had a busy morning and took some vital decisions before he was wheeled to the theatre. First he sent Home a letter which he had drafted on the previous evening. This was to be read at the Party Conference then assembling at Blackpool, and announced that since he could neither lead the party at the next election nor perform his duties as premier his successor must be chosen. Only an hour before the operation his son-in-law, Julian Amery, telephoned from Blackpool and received the impression from Macmillan that Hailsham should be backed for the leadership.

It is a tribute to the remarkable advances in surgical technique, anaesthesia and resuscitation that Macmillan was able to conduct business from his hospital bed once more on Monday, 14 October. Thirty years before, even twenty years before, the immediate sequelae were not so easily overcome. Yet the ability to sit up in bed and converse gives little idea of the true state of a patient. A prostatectomy is a major operation and, although surgical trauma and shock is reduced by modern techniques, the patient is of necessity given pre-operative sedatives and narcotics, a general anaesthetic, and post-operative sedatives, narcotics and analgesics. It is a combination of these factors, together with fluid imbalance and general metabolic changes and adjustments, that can lead to a stormy convalescence in elderly patients. Indeed there must be few patients, even in the younger age groups, who can honestly claim to be mentally alert in the first few days after a major operation. However, on 14 October, he initiated the necessary inquiries so that his successor, acceptable to all the different factions in the Conservative Party, could be selected. On Thursday, 17 October, he was moved into the Matron's sitting-room and learned that Lord Home was the most acceptable candidate.

Thereupon Macmillan resigned and when the Queen, putting aside precedence, called on him next day and sought his advice, it is clear that he was still incapacitated.

> "Macmillan explained that he did not feel well enough to speak to her spontaneously and asked permission to read her the memorandum he had prepared the night before."[10]

His decision to resign, taken before the operation when he was understandably anxious and in pain, may have been premature. Even on 17 October, when it was still too early to assess the outcome of the operation, his act of resignation can with the help of hindsight be regarded as hasty.

Simple enlargement of the prostate is often present in men over the age of fifty years, although only about one third of them have symptoms. Mechanical disturbance causes increased frequency of micturition and difficulty in starting and finishing the act. Far more serious than this inconvenience is impairment of kidney function caused by obstruction to the flow of urine which results in back pressure on these organs. Loss of appetite, loss of weight, constipation and digestive disturbances may ensue. In addition the increased frequency of micturition and the interrupted nights may cause nervousness, irritability and impairment of concentration.

Sudden and complete retention of urine can occur without any apparent reason or may be related to the consumption of alcohol, undue postponement of the act of micturition, cold weather or confinement to bed for another reason.

Neither the presence of prostatic enlargement, the size of the organ or the presence of symptoms are sufficient indications for immediate surgery. Supervision for some months is preferable. Even after acute retention a régime of expectant treatment is advised. After the passage of a catheter the normal flow of urine may be re-established and surgery is only indicated if retention is still present after forty-eight hours. One of the most experienced surgeons in this field has written:

> "Many patients by the time they reach hospital are apprehensive, worn-out, dehydrated old men, and twenty-four to forty-eight hours spent in making them comfortable, assessing

their renal function and preparing them for operation are
usually well worth while."[11]

1963 was the Year of Profumo and the revelations about his
War Minister did more to unseat Macmillan than the Government failures in more weighty affairs of State. The peccadillos
of John Dennis Profumo brought to a head the festering dis-
content about the Conservative administration and it was one
incident, with medical and therapeutic implications, that forced
the War Minister to confess his involvement. On 21 March 1963
rumour had almost been replaced by accusation, and in view of
a menacing debate in the House, the Conservative Chief Whip
took action. He called an immediate meeting of the Leader
of the House, the two Law Officers, another junior
minister and Profumo. In the early hours of 22 March a statement was drafted, repeated by Profumo in the House later that
morning, in which he denied any impropriety with Christine
Keeler. It was a gratuitous, unnecessary and irrelevant admission and one that sealed his fate. The opposition and the Press,
now openly hostile, scented blood and by 4 June Profumo,
forced to admit that on this trivial matter he had misled the
House, tendered his resignation.

The meeting of Ministers, convened in haste and panic, was a
disaster. Profumo was in no state to take part in discussions
which would obviously have far-reaching consequences. He and
his wife had arrived home after midnight and had taken sleeping
pills. At about 2.45 a.m. they were woken by the arrival of the
Chief Whip's assistant, and Mrs Profumo later recalled "we
were so groggy".[12] Extreme states of sleep deprivation can cause
disturbances in understanding, perception, attention and
awareness, which in turn lead to incoherence, confusion and a
failure to recognize and correct errors in thought. Force of cir-
cumstance rather than deliberate intent dictated the nocturnal
summons but it must be noted that this is standard procedure in
police states for interrogation at this time of night may lead to
unfounded confessions and revelations. It is the circumstances
under which they are taken, rather than the problems themselves, which create such difficulties for those who are forced to
take decisions. Statesmen and officials are rarely allowed the

luxury of quiet reflection and adequate time in order to weigh the pros and cons in moments of crisis. Profumo and his colleagues who composed the statement may have wished to sleep on the problem; but repose, which brings so many answers through resting the mind, was denied them. Long past the normal hour for retiring these officials, in varying stages of exhaustion, irritation and exasperation, were compelled to draft the fatal speech that cooler heads and clearer minds might have made less incriminating for the unlucky Minister.

References

1a. Earl of Avon. *Full Circle*, p. 568.
1b. p. 581. Cassell.
2. Robert Murphy. *Diplomat among Warriors*, p. 465. Collins.
3. *New Statesman.* 10 November 1956, p. 576.
4. Hugh Thomas. *The Suez Affair*, pp. 35, 99, 100. Weidenfeld & Nicolson.
5. Anthony Nutting. "No End of a Lesson" (Extract in *The Times*, 3 May 1967).
6. Malcolm Muggeridge. *New Statesman*, 16 October 1964, p. 57.
7. Eleanor Lansing Dulles. *John Foster Dulles; The Last Year*, p. 222. Harcourt Brace & World.
8. Earl of Swinton. *Sixty Years of Power*, p. 188. Hutchinson.
9. Reginald Bevins. *The Sunday Express*, 24 January 1965.
10. Randolph S. Churchill. *The Fight for the Tory Leadership*, p. 138. Heinemann.
11. Alec W. Badenoch. *Manual of Urology*. Heinemann.
12. *The Denning Report*. Paragraphs 173, 175.

CHAPTER 13

Ike, Jack and L.B.J.: Old diseases
and new treatments

On Saturday, 2 July 1955, Lyndon Baines Johnson, then Senate Majority leader, was clearing his desk before taking a much needed week-end in the country. Next he summoned the representatives of the Press in order to review his party's record but shortly the proceedings became as sultry and heated as the Washington weather. Under mild questioning he lost his temper and the interview was abruptly ended. After six months of eighteen-hour days, Johnson was at the end of his tether and the drive through the Virginia countryside brought neither refreshment nor ease; only an attack of nausea, heaviness in the arms and a constricting sensation in the chest. A fellow guest, a Senator from New Mexico, who had been a victim of a coronary attack in the past, shrewdly diagnosed this condition and returned an unwilling Johnson by ambulance to Washington where he was lodged in the Bethesda Naval Hospital.

President Eisenhower courteously visited the patient and within three months, exposed to similar stress, joined the coronary club. On Friday, 23 September 1955, he had interrupted his holiday in Colorado to deal with urgent business. Late in the morning he arrived at the Cherry Hills golf club to be told that the Secretary of State wished to speak on the telephone. By the time Eisenhower was connected he was told that Dulles had to fulfil another engagement but would call in an hour. Punctually Eisenhower returned to the club-house but there was considerable delay and difficulty in arranging the call. The morning game had been disorganized but Eisenhower, fortified by a large hamburger and slices of raw onion, hopefully started another round. After one hole there was a further summons from the State Department and an understandably exasperated President drove back once more to the club-house in his golf cart, only to find that this call was a false alarm. This was too much for Eisenhower who, like Johnson, lost his temper though he described his feelings more delicately:

> "My disposition deteriorated rapidly. I was made the more unhappy by an uneasiness that was developing in my stomach, due no doubt to my injudicious luncheon menu."[1a]

Shortly after midnight, on 23 September, he woke with a severe pain in the chest and a myocardial infarction was soon diagnosed.

Empirical observations have long been made about the relation between emotional stress and heart disease. Nearly 200 years ago John Hunter, the celebrated surgeon and biologist, realized that his heart attacks were provoked by tension or ill temper and observed that "My life is at the mercy of any rascal who cares to take it". It is tragic to recall that he died in 1793 a few hours after a bitter argument in the board room at St George's Hospital, where he was a member of the surgical staff. In 1964 the possible relation between stress and heart disease was widely discussed in New Zealand after six members of parliament had suffered myocardial infarctions; the deputy Prime Minister, the Minister of Finance, the Minister of Education, the Leader of the Opposition, the Senior Opposition Whip, and a Government back-bencher. During the course of an interview with newspaper and broadcasting reporters, Dr J. D. Hunter, Professor of Medicine at the University of Otago, suggested that these parliamentarians were members of a group which faced special risks in this connection for they were middle-aged men from a particular socio-economic background who were living in a prosperous welfare state. It is apparent from a number of studies that a failure to take regular exercise together with excessive eating, drinking and smoking are factors that may be associated with the development of coronary artery disease. It should be remarked that these influences are often present in subjects who are leading a stressful life and that so-called stress alone need not be considered the sole, or even the dominant, cause of myocardial infarction. All types of executives, because of their circumstances, are put in hazard and preliminary studies at the Institute of Directors in London has given Dr H. Beric Wright the impression that when accurate figures are available "we shall find that businessmen are more coronary prone, particularly at a younger age".[2]

Lyndon Johnson was certainly a victim of the unhealthy and abnormal features of executive life. He had been smoking in the region of 60 cigarettes a day at the time of his heart attack and was required to shed 40 pounds in weight during convalescence. In contrast Eisenhower had not smoked for six years and only had to be persuaded to lose a mere 6 pounds in weight.

When the ages of Presidents, at the beginning of the first term, are compared it is surprising to find that Eisenhower was one of the oldest, being sixty-two years and three months at the time of his first inauguration in January 1953. On historical grounds the precedents were unfortunate for two of the three Presidents who were older than Eisenhower on induction died in office. William Harrison may have wished to emphasize that his vigour was unimpaired at sixty-eight for, refusing to wear an overcoat or gloves, he made the longest speech on one of the coldest inauguration days. A severe infection followed and despite cupping, blistering, cathartics and native Indian remedies, treatment that must have been particularly agonizing to the President who had studied medicine briefly in his youth, he was dead in a month. Zachary Taylor was sixty-four years old at his inauguration and, after eighteen months in office, died of a gastro-intestinal infection seemingly provoked by a surfeit of cherries. However, the third President who was older than Eisenhower when he first took office, James Buchanan, served his term from 1857 until 1861 in good health and lived to the age of seventy-seven.

It was the advances in medical and surgical diagnosis and treatment, rather than immunity to disease or good fortune, that enabled Eisenhower to serve not merely one but two terms as President. Long aware of the manner in which the details of Woodrow Wilson's illness had been kept from the public, and of the absence of presidential authority and government due to incapacity, Eisenhower set a number of precedents. He authorized his Press secretary to issue all the clinical details though, when he read them later, he was embarrassed that the peoples of the world had been made aware of his bowel habits. Again, with the Wilson era in mind, he gave instructions that the Vice-President should take the chair at meetings of the Cabinet and National Security Council, although as early as 1 October he was able to discuss affairs with his personal assistant. At a Cabinet meeting on 29 September, Dulles, conscious no doubt that his uncle, Robert Lansing, had been dismissed by Wilson for holding unauthorized meetings, suggested that the position must be clarified. Channels of communication and delegations of authority were agreed and from 8 October, Eisenhower dealt with urgent business and saw leading members of the Government and administration. He left Denver for his farm at Gettysburg for a short holiday on 14 November and eight days later, just two months after the heart attack, signalled his return to full duties by presiding at a Cabinet meeting.

It was fortunate for Eisenhower that on this occasion his illness came at a quiet period in American affairs. Congress was not in session and consequently there were no bills to approve or veto. Finance and commerce were satisfactory and meetings with his economic advisers were unnecessary. Above all he was not required to take any decisions about the mobilization or operation of the armed forces. He realized later that he could not have resolved the dangerous situation that arose in the Lebanon in 1958 since "the concentration, the weighing of the pros and cons, and the final determination would have represented a burden, during the first week of my illness, which the doctors would likely have found unacceptable for a new cardiac patient to bear".

It is a matter for comment that, although the anxious and tedious processes of analysis and judgement were thus precluded, split second decisions were not. In the same reflective passage Eisenhower wrote:

"Certainly had there been an emergency such as the detection of incoming enemy bombers, on which I would have had to make a rapid decision regarding the use of United States retaliatory might, there could have been no question, after the first forty-eight hours of my heart attack, of my capacity to act according to my own judgement."[1b]

From his own account he was kept in an oxygen tent "for two or three days" so from the time of its removal, he was prepared to take action. For Eisenhower "the concentration, the weighing of the pros and cons" were less necessary apparently to evaluate the veracity of reports about the hypothetical bombers or to assess the risk of weapon escalation and spread of the conflict that might have stemmed from ill-judged or over hasty action.

The illness could have had a more serious effect on Eisenhower's temperament than he realized, although later he contested an assertion, made by the Chairman of the Republican National Committee on 28 November, that he was depressed. In the weeks at Denver he undoubtedly was depressed and lost hope in the future to such an extent that General Clay was concerned that he might prematurely announce his refusal of a second term. Just before Christmas, according to the Vice-President, Eisenhower was despondent and mentioned that his blood pressure increased after exertion. Uncertainty and despair may have been dissipated by urgent demands that he should run for a second term. On 19 January 1956, after his name had been entered in the New Hampshire primaries, he told his news conference that "My future life must be carefully regulated to avoid excessive fatigue".[1c] On 14 February, after extensive investigations at the Walter Reed Hospital, Dr Paul Dudley White, a renowned cardiologist, and his colleagues announced: "Medically the chances are that the President should be able to carry on an active life satisfactorily for another five to ten years."[1d]

Despite Eisenhower's statement that his future life must be "carefully regulated", and the studied vagueness of the medical bulletin, the party had decided that he was the only Republican who stood a chance of election in 1956. The old soldier was caught in the draft again and announced on 29 February that he was willing to be nominated as a Presidential candidate. There was a hitch before the nomination which must have scared his sponsors. For some years he had been seized by attacks of abdominal pain and, as far back as 1947, a diagnosis of "partial small bowel obstruction" had been entertained. During a speech on 16 April 1953, shortly after Stalin's death, he suggested to the Russians the possibility of disarmament and the control of atomic energy. The sweat on his brow and his evident concentration were not due to the terrifying issues at stake; as he spoke the pain in his abdomen was so severe that it could neither be eased by specific drugs or sedatives. Statesmen must be made of the sternest stuff for, immediately after this ordeal, he had to inaugurate the new season by pitching a baseball and then fly to North Carolina and deliver yet another speech. In May 1956 radiological studies had shown the presence of regional ileitis of the small bowel and consequently yet another attack of pain at 12.30 a.m. on 8 June 1956 was easily diagnosed. Conservative measures failed and the surgeons had to relieve the obstruction by a by-pass operation on 9 June. Absence of motility in the small bowel caused concern and a tube was inserted via the nostrils and throat into the stomach to aspirate the contents. His body fluids were controlled by intravenous transfusions. On the fifth post-operative day, not only was the nasogastric tube removed and food given by mouth for the first time, but official visitors in the shape of Chancellor Adenauer and John Foster Dulles were permitted. Eisenhower made a rapid recovery and was able to attend the meeting of American Presidents on 21 July; though for some days after the operation he was in great pain and looked more ill than he had after the heart attack.

Thus he survived a medical and a surgical emergency. Attention to his diet and the prescription of drugs that reduced the liability of blood clotting would do much to reduce the chance of another myocardial infarction. The surgical procedure, while relieving the immediate bowel obstruction, was likely to check the pathological process and its tendency to spread. Neither of these two incidents impaired his activity or capability for more than a few weeks but the next illness, although the shortest, had, because of its nature and site, the most grave and far reaching implications. As he sat at his desk after lunch on 25 November 1957, he felt a momentary giddiness. He could neither pick up a sheet of paper nor read the words and was unable to grip his pen which he had dropped on the floor. He was unsteady on his feet and, worse still, he could not find the correct words to express his thoughts and needs. His doctors concluded that a spasm in a blood vessel had affected the speech centre on the left side of his brain but gave a cheerful prognosis. Since he was showing improvement during the course of their examination they predicted that normal function would be restored in days or hours. So rapid was his own sense of recovery that it was difficult to dissuade him from attending a State banquet that same evening; only his inability next morning to describe the details of a favourite picture forced him to realize the gravity of the episode. Although he was able to attend a Thanksgiving Day service three days later he found that the doctors were in error when they assured him of a complete recovery. He continued to experience difficulty in enunciation and in selecting the correct word to use; and he was occasionally embarrassed when he found that he reversed the syllables in a long word. The resultant inability to express himself with precision, and the uncontrollable selection of the wrong word, irritated and angered him. It could not have been comforting to be told that, unless he calmed himself, suppressed rage might precipitate another vascular accident.

The rapid recovery and the accompanying diagnosis of "arterial spasm" made it easy to dismiss, if not to conceal, the underlying abnormality. To put the facts bluntly his speech defect was due to a stroke and there was no certainty that the "spasm" or thrombosis of the cerebral arteriole would not be repeated or would not occur in other blood vessels. Like Churchill he was not to be denied and, for his therapeutic test, he selected a NATO meeting in Paris, to which Heads of State had been invited, as his personal Margate. Despite the misgivings of his entourage he left by air on 13 December, less than three weeks after the onset of illness, and fulfilled his engagements to his complete and evident satisfaction.

Apart from the threat of two previous illnesses he had received yet another warning which could no longer be ignored. Early in 1958 he wrote a detailed though involved letter to the Vice-President, in which he stated that if in the future he was conscious of disability he would hand over to Nixon, but charged him with the responsibility of assuming Presidential authority if this could not be transferred formally. At the same time he arrogated to himself the right to decide when he was fit to take office once more. If the disability was permanent he would resign but, if he was incapable of taking this step, the Vice-President, after consulting certain political and medical authorities, was given the right to take the presidency. It was a move in the right direction but Eisenhower begged the question that had been asked 170 years before by the Delegate from Delaware when presidential incapacity was first discussed. "What is meant by the term disability, and who is to be the judge of it?"[4a]

Limited by the two-term rule Eisenhower made every effort, in the closing months of his presidency, to contribute to world peace and international friendship. In December 1959, he left on the first of a series of tours which on that occasion included visits to Italy, Turkey, India, Pakistan, Afghanistan, Iran, Greece, Spain and North Africa. The warmth of his reception from every race and creed was a testimony to his engaging personality and to the noble ideals which inspired him. Every precaution was taken to ensure his safety and comfort but the hazards of high altitudes, recently a matter of concern for athletes in Mexico City and for rugby players in Johannesburg, nearly proved his undoing. Kabul is 6,000 feet above sea level and, in the course of a ceremony, he collapsed after climbing twenty-four steps. Fortunately the Secret Service, in the Jeeves tradition, had even anticipated this emergency and produced oxygen cylinders and resuscitation apparatus.

The effects of high altitude are insidious and dangerous and the experience of Stafford Cripps at Simla in 1946 emphasizes the risks that accrue after middle age. Simla, with its altitude of 7,000 feet, nearly claimed another victim before the First World War; the Chief of the General Staff almost succumbed but he had added to the circulatory risks and embarrassment by cock-fighting in the mess after dinner.

Eisenhower enjoyed a further triumph in Latin America in February 1960 but the rest of his term was clouded by conflict and disappointment. In May the summit meeting in Paris coincided with the destruction of an American reconnaissance plane over Russia and the capture of its pilot. Khruschev exposed the American cover story and made such humiliating and unacceptable demands on Eisenhower that the long awaited discussions with Macmillan and De Gaulle were abandoned. As if this was not enough he received yet another bitter blow in June when communist demonstrations prevented his visit to Japan.

This was his swan-song though he threw himself, as far as the dignity of his office would allow, into the Presidential election campaign of 1960. By 9 November, profoundly depressed at Nixon's defeat by Kennedy, he had fought his last battle:

> "The doctors, I later learned, had been concerned in the last days that I had temporarily used up all my available cardiac reserves in the closing weeks of the campaign."[3]

He was a few months past his seventieth birthday and, had there been no limitation about a third term, this weary man might have been drafted again merely because he was the best hope for another Republican victory.

The Democratic National Convention had been held at Los Angeles in June 1960 and it is revealing to look beneath the skin-deep image that had been created by the supporters and public relations teams on behalf of the aspirants for the Presidential nomination. The frankness which Eisenhower had shown about his illnesses encouraged similar confidences by the candidates at the same time as it made the subject of health something of an issue at the convention.

Stuart Symington, the tall and handsome Senator for Missouri, had undergone a sympathectomy for the relief of high blood pressure in 1947: luckier than Sir Edward Grey, he had been spared the retinal degeneration which impaired the vision of his three brothers. Lyndon Johnson, as ebullient as ever, showed friends and rivals his most recent electrocardiograph. Hubert Humphrey, the Senator from Minnesota, was still trying to live down his rejection by the armed forces in the Second World War: certainly bilateral hernias and a calcified focus in the lung justified exclusion. John Fitzgerald Kennedy, eight years younger than Johnson and better looking than Symington, projected the attraction and vitality of youth. It must have appealed to his sense of humour that he, the candidate with the most precarious health, should have made a political issue of the subject. Shortly before the Convention his statement that the Presidency demanded "the strength and health and vigor of young men",[4b] was regarded as a pointed reference to Lyndon Johnson's heart attack. The "Citizens for Johnson" did more than refute this oblique insinuation; John B. Connally, later to be wounded in the Presidential car at Dallas, flatly stated that Kennedy had Addison's disease. This was a charge that could not be ignored but Kennedy's supporters and Press agents made clever use of the ambiguities of medical definition. In 1855 Thomas Addison of Guy's Hospital noted that tuberculosis, carcinomatosis or atrophy of the adrenal glands was associated with weakness, pigmentation of the skin and low blood pressure. The Clan denied that Kennedy had classical Addison's disease since he did not have pigmentation, low blood pressure or weakness; but the members conceded that he had "partial adrenal insufficiency" and had received replacement therapy, including cortisone and allied products, almost continuously since 1947.

Kennedy secured the nomination at Los Angeles and won the election in November 1960. From the millions of words written during his tragically foreshortened term, and from the massive volumes written by his intimates after his death, one learns a good deal about the injuries he sustained in his naval adventures and almost nothing about the adrenal disorder. Diseases of the adrenal glands, both before and as a result of modern treatment, may be associated with serious physical and mental disturbance. Eisenhower, as might be expected from a straight-backed old soldier, insisted on complete frankness about his health. Kennedy used a mixture of revelation and concealment, although the revelations were partly cloaked in double talk and partly obscured by the glittering image that the propaganda machine created and the Clan perpetuated.

The medical details that were disclosed in 1960 and 1961 emphasized the vigour of youth and the gallantry of early manhood. A recurrence of infectious hepatitis even explained why he left Princeton after one term and joined its ranks of celebrated "drop-outs" which includes James Forrestal and John Winant. A back injury in 1937, far from a sign of weakness, was sustained at Harvard during the gladiatorial clashes of American football. The sequelae led to rejection by the Army authorities in 1941 but the rebuff neither eased his conscience nor stifled his desire to serve. After a course of special exercises and rehabilitation, he was accepted for the Navy where his adventures in the Pacific were later recorded for posterity in book and film. His brave leadership in the Solomon Islands in 1943 ensured the survival and rescue of his crew; but his back injury was exacerbated when the P.T. boat was rammed by a Japanese destroyer while his convalescence was complicated by malaria. Recurrent pain and disability dogged him for the rest of his life. An operation in 1944, for removal of a prolapsed intervertebral disc which had now been diagnosed was successful though later some shortening of the left leg was found. Challenged to slide down the pole in a fire station during his Senate Campaign in 1952, he provoked the old symptoms again. On 21 October 1954 he underwent lumbo-sacral and sacro-iliac fusion and these procedures were complicated by a urinary tract infection, a transfusion reaction and a mild infection at the site of operation A metal plate that had been inserted was later removed uneventfully in February 1955. On his accession to the Presidency he appointed Professor Janet Travell as his personal doctor. She was an advocate of novocaine injections, for the relief of local muscle spasm and pain of neuromuscular origin, and with these, frequent hot baths and heat therapy, Kennedy's movements were relatively unimpaired. His left heel was built up and he was forced to rely on a corset-type brace. He had used crutches as early as 1952 and depended more on their support after 1961 when over-exertion while planting a tree at a ceremony in Canada, led to a recurrence of the lumbar pain. Kennedy, eschewing the feeble motions that are usually made at such events, swung his silver spade with exemplary zest. He had as much reason to regret this contact with Canada as had Franklin Roosevelt who contracted poliomyelitis on the Canadian island of Campobello.

Continual pain can be physically debilitating and mentally depressing but all the evidence suggests that Kennedy overcame its effects. Pain was the symptom that could be discussed in public for its defeat added lustre to the heroic image. The state of the adrenals should have been discussed as freely for however "partial" or "mild" was the insufficiency he had received replacement therapy ever since the condition was

first diagnosed in England soon after the end of the Second
World War.

Shortly before polling day in November 1960, Walter H.
Judd, a Republican Congressman and a former medical mis-
sionary, demanded that Kennedy should confirm or deny
whether he had Addison's disease as he had been identified as
the patient, with Addison's disease and spinal trouble, whose
case history appeared in a surgical journal in 1955.[5] Painstaking
research work in 1967 clearly identified Kennedy as this patient
and the article clearly defines the state of his adrenals and his
need for steroids such as cortisone.

At the time of the operation in 1954 Kennedy was receiving
25 mg. cortisone daily and one 150 mg. implant of desoxycor-
ticosterone acetate every three months. The dose of cortisone
was increased in 1961 and the White House correspondents,
soon aware that steroids can cause facial oedema, became
experts at assessing the puffiness of his cheeks. Even Kennedy
had to admit to Schlesinger "The doctors say I've got a sort of
slow-motion leukaemia, but they tell me I'll probably last until
I'm forty-five".[6]

Even with modern therapy, and possibly because of these
recent advances, a patient with Addison's disease must be
treated with delicate precision and watched with a penetrating
eye. If the condition is well advanced at the time of diagnosis,
debility and susceptibility to fatigue may be associated with
nervous irritability, emotional instability, periods of depression
and negativistic conduct. Cortisone, in the dose range administered to Kennedy in 1954, works wonders. Dr Leonard Simpson,
who has had considerable experience of this comparatively
rare disorder, describes how the patients regain their strength,
spirit and capacity for physical effort. He mentioned how "their
negative, apathetic and depressed Addisonian personality is
changed back into their normal positive, active, interested and
alert personality," but added that such remarkable improvement was associated "perhaps with some euphoria";[7] a term
that is used to describe an alteration in personality and mood
that is characterized by undue, and at times unfounded, friend-
liness, cheerfulness and optimism. Mild reactions of this type
may be socially acceptable but some patients on steroid therapy

can display gross disorders of mood or behaviour and even graver manifestations of mental disintegration.

The hectic whirl of his thousand days allowed little time for introspection or reflection. Changes in his mood, if they occurred, would have been attributed to pain rather than to steroids. Yet there were in his brief reign certain inconsistencies of behaviour that have not been admitted, investigated or explained. Defective judgement and poor leadership during the fiasco at the Bay of Pigs in 1961 is not necessarily attributable to his own inexperience and to the failures of his advisers. Nor is his brilliant statesmanship during the Cuban missile crisis one year later entirely explained by added experience and better advisers. The tragic pilgrimage to Texas in November 1963, taken against sober advice and in defiance of the openly expressed hatred in Dallas, should not be dismissed as the casual fatalism of a man who once admitted that an American President could be killed at any time; there could be elements of imprudent overconfidence and unfounded optimism that influenced the fatal decision. Dr Travell treated his back with novocaine injections but a separate team prescribed the steroids. If records have been kept a future Schlesinger may be able to compare Kennedy's moods and performance with the drugs that were administered; and to establish in particular whether steroids did more than merely replace the adrenal deficiency. The Kennedy era was a far cry from the early days of steroid therapy when heroic doses made patients feel ten feet tall and produced bizarre and alarming aberrations of conduct. It must be emphasized that steroids are but one of a long list of compounds, used in the treatment of somatic diseases, which may have untoward effects on the psyche. They range from the ubiquitous eye drops, cold cures and nasal sprays stored in the medicine chests of many households, to analgesics, old and new, anti-inflammatory drugs for the relief of joint diseases, and less commonly used compounds prescribed for the treatment of high blood pressure and malaria. The triumphs of therapeutic research have been reduced, in barely twenty years, to the humdrum status of simple, everyday drugs. Nevertheless, common usage must never still unremitting vigilance by physicians for the occasional untoward response in susceptible patients;

certainly not in the ranks of those who treat Prime Ministers and Presidents. These are the patients most likely to ignore drug reactions and conceal their consequences; these are the men in whom side effects, and those that involve the psyche in particular, are likely to be truly disastrous for the victim and his country.

It must have been with mixed feelings of surprise, horror, reluctance and eagerness that Lyndon Johnson took over the presidential torch at Dallas on 22 November 1963. The inevitability of Vice-Presidential succession dismissed any fears or considerations about his health. It was over eight years since his heart attack and legend may have exaggerated its gravity just as it magnified the L.B.J. image. So much about Johnson has been invested with drama. A combination of bronchial stenosis and infection in 1942 was called "a near fatal siege";[8] stones in the kidney are distressingly common but Johnson's are made to sound unique. Over the years Johnson's infarct enlarged like an angler's catch but it should be realized that, by the end of 1955, the outlook was as good as could ever have been hoped. His heart was not enlarged, his blood pressure was normal and, except for a knowledge of the attack, a slight abnormality of the Q wave in his electrocardiogram could have been passed as normal. His history exposes the limitations of regular examinations for the detection and, as some claim, the prevention of disease; only a day or two before the heart attack a routine electrocardiograph was normal.

If "stress" alone contributes to coronary artery disease, Johnson might have been expected to have another attack even before he assumed the Presidency. The smug statement that hard work never killed anybody applies more to physical effort than to the mental strains of crushing responsibility; even so men with vulnerable coronary arteries should be prevented from clearing snow too vigorously in cold weather. The physical accompaniments of the executive life that have a bearing on coronary disease have already been considered; excessive intake of food, alcohol and tobacco associated with insufficient exercise. Psychological factors may have as much influence; a frustrating inability to effect policy: humiliation by superiors and intrigue by juniors: insecurity in the present and fear of the future. When

Johnson became President the deleterious effect of many of these psychological factors were removed for at last he had won the race that he had been running since those early days in Texas. Indeed the threat and likelihood of coronary disease had passed to others than himself.

Nevertheless it was fear that he would not survive another term that led Lyndon Johnson to withdraw from the Presidential nomination and election in 1968. He was only too aware that he was in his sixtieth year and that many of the male members of his family had not survived their early sixties. He had planned to make the announcement during his State of the Union message in January but found, in the middle of the speech, that he had mislaid this part of his notes. He discovered later to his consternation that he had left them by the telephone in his bedroom. Psychologists would provide one obvious explanation for this error. Historians would recall a tragic analogy: on the eve of his major stroke Woodrow Wilson was disturbed that he had left his watch lying on a table.

References

1a. Dwight D. Eisenhower. *Mandate for Change,* p. 536.
1b. p. 545. Heinemann.
1c. p. 572. Heinemann.
1d. p. 572. Heinemann.
2. H. Beric Wright. *The Director,* February 1967, p. 225.
3. Dwight D. Eisenhower. *Waging Peace,* p. 602. Heinemann.
4a. *Time Magazine,* 9 December 1957.
4b. *Time Magazine,* 9 December 1957.
5. J. A. Nicholas, *et al. Archives of Surgery* (1955), 71, 737.
6. Arthur M. Schlesinger. *A Thousand Days,* p. 87. Deutsch.
7. S. Leonard Simpson. *Proc. Roy. Soc. Med.* (1953), 46, 566.
8. The President's Heart. *Esquire,* August 1964.

CHAPTER 14

The Dictators: The Devil is not as black as he is painted

Only the younger generation could possibly view with any detachment the Dictators who dominated Europe and the newspaper headlines during the brief interval between the first two world wars. Interested undergraduates might even see the Dictators in perspective but, as members of an age group that turns to the present and future rather than to the past, they would probably regard them as lifeless and incredible as figures in a waxworks.

Unfortunately it is nearly impossible for members of older generations, who lived and suffered in what one distinguished authoress has aptly called "The Europe of the Dictators", to regard them with any pretence of objectivity or dispassion. It would be necessary to shed the ingrained prejudices implanted by wartime propaganda and to forget the deep emotions that were stirred by the zealots of the left and the right. Those who were over the age of twenty years in 1939 might well now ask themselves if the dictators were as powerful, as sinister and as frightening as they undoubtedly appeared at the time. They may reproach themselves for a degree of *naïveté* and ignorance that lead them to be impressed by the meretricious façade of the elaborate and impressive stage effects that characterize and camouflage so many totalitarian regimes. The dictators were certainly neither as funny nor as ridiculous as the caricatures drawn by the cartoonists of the day; nor were they as formidable and omnipotent as their insistent propaganda must have led us to believe.

In 1919 the vanquished in Europe lost their Empires and dynasties and the map of Europe was redrawn. Working in haste the statesmen, the officials, the demographers and the

professors replaced the old régimes with others that were still, to
some degree, autocratic and unrepresentative. Long years of
tradition, precedence, habits and some degree of order and
stability were swept away; the discipline of religion, the
abstract loyalty to Kings and Princes, and the painfully
acquired rules of family and society were rent asunder. Bankruptcy and inflation in certain countries ruined the middle
classes who could have provided the social and administrative
stability of the new régimes. The field was open to the crack-
brained orators and the rabble rousers who could inflame the
usually disinterested masses with feelings of resentment or
hatred and, more serious for the peace of the world, instil
nationalistic ideas of military resurgence and revenge. It is rare,
if not impossible, for an abnormal personality to exert any deep
or lasting influence on a civilized, stable and sophisticated
society. Even an abnormal person may only appear to dominate
a disturbed population. It is more likely that a society in decay
spawns a short list of leaders with hypnotic and, seemingly,
divine powers who can sway their followers and exact blind
obedience. However, the soil must be ready for the seed: the
disturbed society may choose to be represented by a leader, who
could never conceivably be a member of a conventional government, but senses and perpetuates its baser desires and needs.

The instability of the Ottoman Empire at the turn of the
century allowed full scope for the rebellious tendencies of a
young Turk called Mustafa who was born in Salonika in 1881.
Tuition at a military academy did not dissuade him from
joining a revolutionary group but subsequently he rehabilitated
himself by distinguished service against the Italians in Tripoli,
and against the British and Dominion Forces in Gallipoli in
1915. Far from superintending the disarmament and demobi-
lization of the Turkish forces in 1919 he established a separatist
government and was elected President of a new Turkish
Assembly in 1920. Successful campaigns against the Greeks
were made easier by the incapacity of their Commander-in-
Chief who was mentally disturbed and refused to get out of bed
since he was convinced that his legs were made of glass and
would break.

It is not only in Great Britain that fame and fortune brings new names and new titles. After his victory at the Dardanelles, Mustafa became Mustafa Kemal Pasha and the title of Ghazi was added when he had defeated the Greeks. Finally after 1934 he chose the surname of Ataturk, which means Father of the Turks, and altered his first name; George Bernard Shaw was not entirely facetious when he referred to him as "Whataturk". It is strange that Kamal Ataturk, who was no less cruel and repressive than other dictators, should have been regarded in Western Europe with less abhorrence. His reforms certainly removed the last oriental vestiges of the Ottoman Empire. He abolished the fez, ended polygamy and emancipated the women; even more practical measures were the adoption of the metric system, a compulsory medical examination before marriage and the disinfection of certain buildings in Istanbul.

The details of his medical history were widely circulated even before his death. An attack of gonorrhoea in his youth may be forgiven and forgotten and it has been emphasized, as if in extenuation, that he did not contract syphilis. The nature of the kidney disease which afflicted him after 1917 is obscure. It led to bouts of severe pain which in turn have been adduced as the cause of excessive drinking, mental depression and even precipitate political action. Stones in the kidney could certainly lead to spasm of excruciating colic, although disorders of the spinal vertebrae, that crippled Lord Curzon and President Kennedy, must be considered as a differential diagnosis. We have no record whether it was the spur of nationalistic fervour or the whip of pain that drove Ataturk to confront the British at Chanak in September 1922. We only know that Curzon, the British Foreign Minister, had more to contend with than the spinal and sciatic pain which, with the aid of a steel support, he had born stoically for most of his life. An attack of thrombophlebitis in the veins of his leg had compelled him to stay in bed from May to July and temporarily to hand over the Foreign Office to Lord Balfour. Treatment by a hypnotist was unsuccessful but eventually he was able to hobble to a Cabinet meeting on 15 September. He was in no state to restrain those who were prepared to fight the Turks but with patient diplomacy he regained the support of the French; though the nervous strain was such that he burst into tears during discussions with

Poincaré, the French Premier. Curzon has been criticized for his passivity but it gained a breathing space during which the military leaders in Chanak averted the conflict.

For years Ataturk had had recourse to alcohol and even his iron constitution could not withstand its ravages. His liver became enlarged and hardened while itching and tingling in the legs signalled the presence of alcoholic peripheral neuritis. Worse still his brain was affected and he showed the characteristic changes of Korsakow's psychosis: "a disturbance of attention and memory which leads to the disorientation of the patient in space and time".[1] His mental faculties deteriorated and his powers of recall failed; after pronouncing an opinion he would alter it next day. Victims of this disorder fill the gaps in their memory with imaginary events; a particularly dangerous phenomenon in a man with autocratic power whose whims and fancies exact instant compliance. The last months before his death in 1938 were enlivened by the young Zsa Zsa Gabor, who thereafter held him in high esteem and later recalled the association with affection.

Benito Mussolini was less fortunate than Ataturk for in 1905 at the age of twenty-two years, he contracted syphilis. It was not until that year that the spirochaete, which had hitherto eluded the more conventional microscopic and staining techniques, was revealed as visible evidence of the cause of syphilis. In 1906 Wassermann described a blood test by which syphilis could be diagnosed in the laboratory and permitted a precise, rather than presumptive, diagnosis to be made in the later stages of the disease. As if these advances were not spectacular enough Paul Ehrlich, the father of chemotherapy, introduced his specific treatment for syphilis with organic arsenic compounds in 1910.

In the days before early and adequate treatment the physician was often the reluctant witness of latent syphilis spreading through the brain, spinal cord and other organs. "If you know syphilis, you know medicine" was an old maxim, for its depredations could mimic many other diseases. Syphilis had always to be considered as a possible diagnosis and medical students were advised to be suspicious and sceptical: after all the admiral had once been a midshipman and the bishop was once an undergraduate.

The various types of syphilitic involvement of the nervous system may be distinguished by physical examination and patients with these disorders provide an excellent test for those medical students undergoing a qualifying examination. In practice he will find that the signs are often less gross and that subtle changes in mental state create the first suspicion. However, poor judgement and reasoning, failing memory, emotional changes and delusions are not confined to syphilis; they may be found in patients with generalized arteriosclerosis, or with tumours, infections and abscesses in the cranial cavity. They can also occur after long forgotten, or recent head injuries, often of a trivial type, and in states of alcoholic excess and vitamin deficiency.

Even dictators cannot destroy all record of their past and elaborate attempts to ensure secrecy about health may even excite speculation and rumour in democratic as well as autocratic régimes. By 1939 there were grounds for suspecting that Mussolini might have syphilis of the nervous system. His comprehension of the English language and facility in that tongue had lapsed. This was the opinion of the American Ambassador who had an audience just before Mussolini met Chamberlain, Daladier and Hitler in Munich at the climax of the Czechoslovak crisis in September 1938. A few months later the French Ambassador stated that Mussolini was "in a period of intellectual decline".[2] The Chief of Police had no doubt about Mussolini; he told Ciano, the Foreign Secretary, that his father-in-law should have treatment for syphilis. It has never been proved that he had syphilis of the central nervous system. The records of his Wassermann reactions only include blood samples and no mention is made of any examination of his cerebrospinal fluid. Before the Second World War a blood sample was tested in two separate laboratories in London and found to be negative. After he had been rescued by Otto Skorzenny from the Allies, and taken to Germany in September 1943, yet another blood test for syphilis was apparently negative.

The rest of his medical history was humdrum. He vomited blood in 1925 and symptoms of peptic ulceration continued to trouble him. Enlargement of his liver could not be attributed to alcohol. Sir Aldo Castellani, a consultant in tropical medicine who practised in London for many years, considered that some infection contracted in the First World War had involved the liver. In 1942 he found not only a recurrence of peptic ulceration but evidence of amoebic infection in the bowel and infestation by worms. Treatment of this last condition led Mussolini to expel the largest round worm that Castellani had ever seen: "a real hypertrophic Fascist ascaris".[3] Professor Morell, Hitler's personal physician, overhauled Mussolini in the autumn of 1943 and reported "slight blood pressure", nervous exhaustion and weak bowels; this opinion exasperated Goebbels who exclaimed, "In fact, just about what we've all got."[4]

In proposing the motion, "Things are not what they seem", at the Oxford Union, G. K. Chesterton, a massive and rotund figure, convulsed the audience by loosening his trousers and extracting a cushion. Totalitarian and democratic propaganda can flatter the leader and deceive the people for, by careful selection and distribution of photographs, it is possible to create a distorted and untrue image. This was the picture of Mussolini that was seen outside the Rome – Berlin – Tokyo axis; vigour, virility and athleticism enhanced by the shaven head and the dark, protuberant jowl. Even an experienced official like Sumner Welles, armed with all the information that the State Department could provide, was shattered by what he saw as Roosevelt's emissary to Italy, Germany, France and Great Britain in February and March 1940.

"My first impression was one of profound astonishment at Mussolini's appearance. In the countless times I had seen him in photographs and in motion pictures, and in the many descriptions I had read of him I had always gained the impression of an active, quick moving, exceedingly animated personality. The man I saw before me seemed fifteen years older than his actual age of fifty-six. He was ponderous and static rather than vital. He moved with an elephantine motion; every step appeared an effort. He was heavy for his height, and his face in repose fell in rolls of flesh. His close-cropped hair was snow-white."[5]

Mussolini had already begun to degenerate at the time of the

Munich agreement in September 1938 when, for the first time
since July 1914, peace and war were poised in the balance.
Possibly in panic and out of self-interest he threw himself then
on the side of peace; in September 1939, when admittedly the
position was nearly irrevocable, he made no effort to intervene.

Adolph Hitler could hardly have hoped to avoid the accusation, so commonly levelled at public figures and as ubiquitous as
the spirochaete itself, that he had syphilitic involvement of the
nervous system in later life. When rumours about venereal
disease have been spread the best verdict that the victim can
expect is one of "not proven"; never can he receive the complete
exoneration of "not guilty". Reinhardt Heydrich, Himmler's
Deputy in the secret police and counter-intelligence, collected a
twenty-six-page dossier on Hitler's health. The sources were not
stated, the reliability of the contents could not be checked, but
its evidence cannot entirely be ignored. Himmler showed the
file to Felix Kersten, his masseur and confidant, in December
1942 who reproduced the details some years after the end of the
Second World War. Apparently Hitler had syphilis in his youth
which had not been completely cured. In 1937 and 1942
complaints of insomnia, dizziness and headache had presumably
suggested a diagnosis of "progressive syphilitic paralysis". Two
other pieces of evidence explain why syphilis may have been
mentioned in the file.

Professor Morell, Hitler's personal physician, had been in
charge of a venereology clinic in Berlin. His special interest
would have lead him to suspect syphilis and to consider this
diagnosis before others. In the light of his professional experience
he might have seen syphilis where it did not exist, though any
prudent general physician would have considered the diagnosis.
Heydrich had the ways and means of securing copies of Morell's
notes and may also have had access to a second piece of more
indirect evidence. Kurt Schuschnigg, the Austrian Chancellor,
was summoned to Berchtesgaden by Hitler in February 1938.
He made a strange remark before he left:

"You know, it would really be better for Wagner-Jauregg to
undertake the trip instead of me."[6]

Wagner-Jauregg was a celebrated Austrian neurologist who

first used malarial infections in the treatment of syphilitic general paralysis.

If syphilis of the nervous system could reasonably be a presumptive diagnosis, and certainly one to exclude until 1942, later events rendered it unlikely. Hitler developed a tremor in his left arm and left leg; he dragged his left foot, his gait became shuffling and his body stooped. In March 1942, Goebbels was appalled how Hitler had become grey and old and attributed these changes to the anxieties of the Russian campaign. Goering thought that Hitler had aged fifteen years in five years of war. In the last winter of the war Hitler's keen memory was blunted and his grip on events weakened.

Hitler had many of the symptoms and signs of the Parkinsonian syndrome whose varying entities are characterized by impairment of movements, rigidity and tremor in the limbs, a fixed and staring expression of the face and a slow shuffling gait. Paralysis agitans, first described by Dr James Parkinson in 1817, usually starts in the sixth decade of life and predominates in males. It is by no means associated with mental impairment which leads one to reflect if Hitler may have had another condition. A form of Parkinsonism may follow Epidemic Encephalitis Lethargica or Sleepy Sickness. Its onset is so insidious that the original virus infection may have been forgotten or unrecognized but, like the spirochaete, have persisted in the nervous system. The stiffness, rigidity and poverty of movement are not unlike the manifestations of paralysis agitans but post-encephalitic Parkinsonism can be distinguished by mental apathy and depression, together with characteristic movements of the eyeballs.

Oculogyral spasm usually consists of upward movement of the eyes and retraction of the lids although lateral, oblique or downward deviation may occur. When the patient looks ahead the eyes may remain fixed or turned inwards. A striking feature of Hitler, and one that impressed itself on many visitors, was the quality of his eyes. His glance was compelling and even hypnotic. A celebrated cartoonist wrote that they "popped and stared"[7] while one of Lloyd George's entourage described them in 1936 as "blue and slightly protruding eyes".[8] The generals were consistent in their views. Ironside wrote about "a watery, weak-looking eye"[9] and von Senger referred to eyes that were large, blue and watery "possibly due to his constant use of stimulating drugs".[10] Edouard Daladier, the French Premier from 1937 until 1940, provides a vital clue of clinical significance. He had every chance of studying Hitler at close quarters during the Munich conference in September 1938:

> "His dull blue eyes had a hard, strange look, and during the short greetings they suddenly turned upwards".[11]

Von Economo published the first description of Encephalitis Lethargica in 1917. At that time the illness was characterized by its severity and rapid spread but over the years the clinical picture has changed. The early, acute symptoms are milder or absent and the delayed or chronic manifestations, appearing after a latent period of twenty or thirty years, are more conspicuous. There is much that is obscure in Hitler's medical history but his exposure to poison gas on the Western Front with its sequela of "hysterical blindness" has by constant repetition been accepted as valid. Victims of gas attacks filled many hospitals in the First World War and concomitant infections could easily have been obscured by the effects of noxious fumes. Indeed Hitler's visual failure could conceivably have been due to the ocular disturbances that are associated with acute encephalitis. An unnoticed and unreported sub-clinical attack could leave the virus lurking in the central nervous system; and lead, twenty or more years later, to the mental degeneration, motor disorders and oculogyral spasms of post-encephalitic parkinsonism. His physicians became disturbed about Hitler in 1937 and suspected syphilitic disease of the nervous system. Yet this was just twenty years after the first epidemic of encephalitis, and Hitler's hysterical blindness, when the advent of chronic sequelae could be expected.

Professor Theodore Morell has been adversely criticized by lay historians and curtly dismissed as a quack. It is true that he employed a vast armentarium of remedies which were administered by mouth and by injection. Practical experience soon teaches the physician that the most humble patient cannot be denied the traditional bottle of medicine and that patients of higher social standing and intelligence are also not satisfied by

logical explanation and reassurance alone. Years before, Lloyd
George had become a devotee of the hormones and vitamins
that Morell prescribed for Hitler; and Churchill, despite wiser
advice to the contrary, reputedly had a medicine chest that was
full of pills, potions and ointments.

Morell has also been taken to task for administering a mixture
of strychnine and belladonna for the relief of a gastric disorder.
There is no real evidence that Morell prescribed it for this
condition, though such a mixture was used in the past as a
laxative. The critics have omitted to record that belladonna in
large doses is used to treat the muscular rigidity of the Parkinsonian syndrome. In the normal pursuit of his profession Morell
would have been justified in pushing the dose of belladonna to
the limits of tolerance and balancing its benefits against side-
effects such as restlessness, confusion, excitement, hallucinations
and delirium. In a practice that involves the care of a man who
could sway the destinies of nations the physician may find that
the drug that relieves the main symptom of his patient may
have an adverse reaction on comprehension, judgement and
decision.

Yosif Visarionovitch Dzhugashvili was born in 1879 and took
the name Stalin when he was indulging in undercover activities
against the Czarist régime. On accession to absolute power he
lent his name to cities and streets while, in the uncritical
idolatry of the war years, he was addressed with deference as
Marshal Stalin or with unaccustomed and unsought familiarity
as Uncle Joe.

The medical history of his early years is undramatic. It is true
that he was marked for life by the scars of smallpox and that
infection or injury to the left arm led to shortening and
instability. He was not the only leader to be supported by a
metal brace and to find every quirk of character or behaviour
attributed to injury in childhood. A birth injury to the left
shoulder and arm was said to account for the emotional outbursts and self-assertion of Kaiser Wilhelm II though a recent
review of the evidence suggests that the deformity neither in-
convenienced nor embarrassed him. Moreover, there are many
examples of birth injuries that leave no scar or deformity on
character and personality. Lord Halifax, Foreign Secretary and

Ambassador in Washington during the years of the Second World War, was widely respected as a man of integrity who practised Christianity in public life. The serenity and nobility of his temperament gave no grounds for suspecting that he was born without a left hand.

During the Second World War Stalin held court and summoned the statesmen and politicians of the other powers in the Western alliance to the presence. Invariably they paid unsolicited tributes to his remarkable efficiency, his grasp of military, technical and political affairs, and his skill in that hard bargaining, with human lives and less powerful nations, which is graced by the name of grand strategy. He treated his guests as if they were undergraduates at a bump supper, and forced them to drink endless toasts, although the alcohol content of the colourless fluid in his own glass was never determined. Some of the visitors at Yalta had to be carried from the banquet table but the long hours, the gargantuan meals and nocturnal conferences had no effect on Stalin's alertness or perspicacity. It is true that there were rumours of "heart trouble" but one is left with a lingering suspicion that this provided an admirable excuse to avoid flying or leaving Russia; and one that incidentally forced Churchill and Roosevelt, both of whom had "heart trouble", to exhaust themselves by arduous and dangerous journeys and to operate at some psychological disadvantage in a foreign environment.

Churchill and Roosevelt were seemingly so confused by Stalin and his Jekyll and Hyde performances that they have not given a convincing picture of him. It was left to Milovan Djilas, Tito's emissary, to furnish a vivid pen picture of Stalin and to trace his mental and physical decline over the course of three visits in 1944, 1945 and 1948.

Others had remarked on Stalin's stocky body with its stiff and foreshortened left arm but Djilas portrays his face, as if with the brush of an artist, and compels the reader to conjure up an image of flesh and blood that is more vital than the black and white photographs.

"He had quite a large paunch and his hair was sparse, though his scalp was not completely bald. His face was white, with ruddy cheeks. . . . Not even his moustache was thick or firm."[12]

Djilas considered that long hours in overheated and artificially lit rooms had given Stalin the typical "Kremlin complexion" though his description stirs clinical memory. A British official remarked incidentally that Stalin's complexion had a green tinge rather than the grey pallor that he had been led to expect. Nevertheless a yellow tint of the facial skin and red patches on the cheeks, conforming with Djilas's description, could constitute the "strawberries and cream" complexion that may be found in a form of thyroid gland deficiency called Myxoedema. Admittedly this condition is several times more common in women than in men but it is also associated with a gain in weight, sparse and dry hair, slow cerebration and defective memory. The mental changes may depend on the underlying personality and may proceed to the dramatic state of "myxoedematous madness" so aptly described by Dr Richard Asher. Mental hyperactivity and hallucinations can be present or even a psychosis characterized by feelings of suspicion and delusions of persecution.

On his last visit to Stalin in 1948 Djilas was shocked by the evident signs of senility. The mental celerity had gone and Stalin was suspicious and resented disagreement. Djilas was also appalled to find that weighty discussions about affairs of State were inextricably mixed with interminable bouts of eating and drinking; a convention, long associated with Russian life, but not unknown in the Western world.

There was one last purge before the end that was regarded by the frightened men in the Kremlin, and the "Kremlinologists" of the West, as a sinister overture to another and bigger cycle of fear, suspicion, treachery and murder. On 3 February 1953 nine Professors of Medicine, all of whom had professional connections with the inmates of the Kremlin, were named as agents of foreign powers and as instigators of murder plots against party and military leaders. None knew when next the blow would fall but Stalin took his secret plans to the grave. A profound mistrust of others is inevitable in an autocracy and is essential for self-preservation but other factors may have exaccrbated the fear and suspicion that dominated Stalin's last years. Alcoholic excess and the natural changes of senility can both lead to unfounded suspicions that verge on the pathological. The possibility that his mental state was influenced by the psychological changes associated with myxoedema should also be given some consideration. Nevertheless it may be unwise to explain Stalin's conduct on the grounds of an abnormal paranoid psychosis. He had every reason to fear the devious and untraceable tricks of an assassin for the suggestion that he personally precipitated Lenin's death in 1924 has never entirely been disproved.

Two months after the "doctor's plot" Stalin's daughter was summoned to his bedside for a cerebro-vascular accident had paralysed the right side of his body and rendered him speechless. A new team of doctors did what little they could under circumstances which could have imperilled their reputations and even their lives. Their efforts were in vain and after a second stroke he died on 5 March. 1953; though not before he had terrified the onlookers by emerging from a coma, fixing them with his gaze and lifting his left arm in a threatening manner. The medical treatment that he received illustrates the medievalism and modernity, the primitiveness and the sophistication, that still characterizes the Russian scene. His sick room was crowded with doctors and technicians who took electrocardiograms and chest X-rays although nobody could work the artificial respirator; yet in the midst of the modern equipment one physician, presumably from an older generation, was quietly applying leeches to Stalin's head and neck.

The dictators may have seemed grotesque caricatures to their critics in the democracies. It cannot be doubted that critics from the Rome-Berlin axis found much that was strange in the statesmen of the democracies. Leaving aside clinical considerations it is not unrewarding to study certain characteristics in personal history and habits that were common to both opposing groups of statesmen.

Roosevelt and Hitler both walked in their sleep. Although Ataturk must be described as a heavy drinker neither Churchill, Henry Asquith nor Stalin were total abstainers like Mussolini and Hitler. In common with Churchill, Hitler's vitality increased in the evening and his monologues transfixed his guests until the small hours.

Even professional actors are the first to admit that it is not what you say, or even how you say it, that takes hold of an audience; it is the person who says it that matters. Churchill's humour was of the earthy variety that twisted a Greek surname to "Plaster Arse". Many of Roosevelt's quips were of the schoolboy variety, that would not raise a smile if uttered by others, and this appreciation of simple fun may have led him to pay tribute to Stalin's "stalwart good humour".[13] The English reserve their greatest respect for the possessor of two characteristics which are in a sense interchangeable; a sense of humour and a sense of the ridiculous. In this connection Hitler has received scant recognition and justice. Only the unpredictability of the blast from an explosive saved him from certain death at Rastenburg on 20 July 1944. The remarks that he made shortly after he had staggered from the scene are reminiscent of British humour, coolness and insouciance. He had been pinned down by a wooden beam and in describing the after effects said that he had "a back side like a baboon" and lamented the cost:

"Oh my best new trousers! I only put them on yesterday!"[14]

Leaders all show glimmers of humour but these human touches should not prevent a light being turned on the darker aspects of their character and behaviour. None – not least those who persistently confine their condemnation to "fascists" – should be allowed to forget Stalin's multi-million murders. Hitler's atrocities, appalling as they were, pale in comparison and hardly merited the retribution that Henry Morgenthau, the U.S. Secretary of the Treasury, proposed to inflict on the German people. Roosevelt put his signature to the Morgenthau plan for the industrial dismemberment and pastoralization of Germany at the second Quebec conference in September 1944. Had not wiser counsel prevailed, and had not Roosevelt been persuaded by others to change his mind, the Secretary of the Treasury would have really earned his nickname of "Henry the Morgue".

A great man's jokes always appear to be excruciatingly funny; by the same exaggeration his peevishness or bad manners can exert a disproportionate influence. Rage may be spontaneous or simulated, rational or irrational, and is a weapon that is not despised or ignored by statesmen. The psychologist might quote theories of human development to explain why rage can transfix an adult as effectively as it can silence a child. The calculated arguments and the stiff-backed tradition of the German general staff collapsed in the face of Hitler's frenzy. Churchill was not above such primitive behaviour although carpet biting was excluded from his repertoire.

Nevertheless in the war years he strode around his office "like a beast of prey in the jungle sniffing the breeze". Lloyd George too was capable of a "terrifying malignity" and an unseen witness of one of his outbursts concluded that "this dangerous, fear inspiring quality is appropriate in great war ministers . . ."[15]

References

1. Lord Brain. *Diseases of the Nervous System* (Fourth Edition) p. 699. Oxford University Press.
2. Laura Fermi. *Benito Mussolini*, p. 372. University of Chicago Press.
3. Aldo Castellani. *Microbes, Men and Monarchs*, p. 169. Gollancz.
4. Christopher Hibberd. *Benito Mussolini*, p. 239. Longmans Green.
5. Sumner Welles. *The Time for Decision*, p. 69. Hamish Hamilton.
6. Gordon Brook-Shepherd. *Anschluss*, p. 40. Macmillan.
7. Emery Kelen. *Peace in Their Time*, p. 205. Gollancz.
8. Thomas Jones. *A Diary with Letters*, p. 199. Oxford University Press.
9. R. Macleod and Denis Kelly. *The Ironside Diaries*, p. 29. Constable.
10. F. Von Senger und Etterlin. *Neither Fear nor Hope*, p. 241. Macdonald.
11. Henri Noguères. *Munich*, p. 262. Weidenfeld & Nicolson.
12. Milovan Djilas. *Conversations with Stalin*, p. 59. Hart-Davis.
13. Max Freedman. *Roosevelt and Frankfurter: Their Correspondence, 1928-45*, p. 709. Bodley Head.
14. D. J. Goodspeed. *The Conspirators*, p. 184. Macmillan.
15. Ralph Furse. *Aucuparius*, p. 14. Oxford University Press.

CHAPTER 15

Statesmen and their doctors:
Quis custodiet ipsos custodes?

Scott Fitzgerald wrote that "the rich are different from you and me". He might also have added that great men are different from you and me. Great men are industrious; or compel their staffs and subordinates to work. They have outstanding intellects; or the capacity to assimilate and propagate the thoughts and ideas of others. They have unusual vitality; or are possessed and motivated by abnormal and obsessional compulsions. They have that magic and intangible quality that enables them to lead and inspire others; or an unhealthy ambition to dominate and manipulate their fellows. One quality alone is denied them and as a consequence in this one instance they stand in the ranks with their subjects. The characteristic that they share is a liability to illness.

There must be a latent period before many of the events of the nineteen sixties can be fully revealed or examined. Certain State papers are now made available to the British public after thirty years but, even where other sources can be tapped, historians are restricted by their reluctance to discomfort those personalities and their relatives who are still alive. Unless another Moran publishes his studies, anything resembling a full medical history of the majority of contemporary statesmen cannot be pieced together for another ten or fifteen years. Failing such a study the interested observer can only make use of incontrovertible facts that cannot be concealed or rumours that must be carefully sifted. Reports of illness may have some factual basis but may also be inspired by malice or designed to secure a denial or a revelation of some clinical detail that has been concealed hitherto. Even if the historian confines himself to the facts and ignores the rumours there is no doubt that illness in statesmen is as common and incapacitating in this present decade as it was in the first sixty years of the century. Frank disclosure has revealed a state of affairs that is as familiar as an old film that is seen again and takes the observer back to the days of Woodrow Wilson and Bonar Law. In August 1964 President Segni of Italy had a stroke which paralysed the right side of his body and rendered him speechless; the classification of his incapacity as temporary rather than total meant that Parliament could not be convened to nominate a successor. At about the same time Mr Ikeda, the Japanese Prime Minister, finally decided he could no longer run the country from the clinic where he was receiving treatment for cancer of the throat. Earlier in the same year Nehru, the Prime Minister of India, had a stroke but remained in office, and even tottered into Parliament where he clutched at the benches, until his death in June. Lal Bahadur Shastri, Nehru's successor, soon fell ill though the episode was attributed to the effects of prophylactic inoculations rather than to a recurrence of the heart attack which had occurred in 1959; within eighteen months he died suddenly. In April 1964 the non-existent "King of Cambodia" reserved a 6 ft 7 in. bed in a hospital for genito-urinary diseases in Paris. The patient turned out to be President Charles de Gaulle who underwent a prostatectomy.

It is never unreasonable to suggest that men after middle life might have an enlarged prostate, liver or kidney disease, diabetes or degeneration of the vascular or nervous system. Khruschev, Tito and Chairman Mao have all come under suspicion in the Western Press. As far back as 1963 it was said that General Franco had diabetes as well as Parkinsonism and certainly when he showed himself to the Spanish people in 1968, after a long period in seclusion, he "stared expressionlessly before him, his mouth slightly open".[1] However early in 1969 his personal physician made no mention of this condition but stated that his pulse, blood pressure and heart were normal. It has long been suggested that President Nasser has diabetes and the consequences of such an illness in a statesman could be serious. In August 1968 he received treatment in Russia for a disease affecting the arteries of the legs. One reporter considered that the scanty details suggested an obscure arterial disorder

called Buerger's disease although pain in the legs or discomfort
in walking could also occur with the arterial changes or the
neuritis which, though fortunately rare, may be serious accompaniments of diabetes if this disease cannot be properly controlled. It is the methods used to treat the disease, rather than
the disease itself, which may have grave repercussions in world
affairs. The modern treatment of the disease began in 1921
when Banting and Best isolated insulin which was shown to
supply the needs of those diabetic patients who are deficient of
this hormone. Without insulin these patients cannot utilize
sugar so, while their blood sugar rises, their body wastes; with
insulin they can make use of sugar once more. However, in
some patients, even with strict control of diet and insulin, the
level of blood sugar is irregular. If it is too high the patient may
go into coma. If it is too low, and such a state may occur if a
meal is missed or after undue exertion, the condition of hypo-
glycaemia may follow. The symptoms can vary from mild
sleepiness, fatigue, and hunger to intellectual impairment,
irrational behaviour, uncontrollable excitement and a state not
far removed from mania. The condition has to be differentiated
from acute alcoholism and is one, even in its early stages, that is
highly undesirable and dangerous in those who carry any grave
responsibility.

With the benefit of modern surgical and medical treatment,
anaesthesia, and resuscitation the statesman can now be
shuffled from bed to a summit meeting at unprecedented speed.
This approach defies the long established régimes, conceived
after extensive clinical experience, of rest, graded activity and
convalescence which were found to be necessary for a complete
restoration of health. Even the statesman in full possession of his
faculties may be exposed to unprecedented hazards as a result
of the capacity of modern aircraft to cross oceans and continents
in hours instead of days.

A daytime flight between the United Kingdom and the
United States of America confronts the passenger with a longer
day, due to the time change, and fatigue is naturally expected.
Even if the passenger sleeps well on a return night flight from
the United States to the United Kingdom, fatigue is still present
though the evening in the American zone has been shortened.

Such fatigue differs from our normal experience in the United Kingdom and the United States where we can miss a night's sleep or work a longer day without the protracted weariness and vague disturbance of bodily function that may be present for two or three days after prolonged east–west and west–east flights. Research work over several years provides an explanation. Vital processes such as sleep and wakefulness, brain activity, temperature control, urine production, hormone formation, gut activity, oxygen consumption and mineral metabolism are geared to a carefully adjusted schedule by day and night. If the body is rapidly transferred to a different time system its own carefully synchronized activities will be out of step with the new local time. Flights in a north–south axis do not, of course, involve the passenger in different time schedules.

What may have begun as an academic study has an important bearing on the fitness and, in particular, on the mental alertness of statesmen and senior officers and others with high executive and administrative responsibility.

Dr Hubertus Strughold, as chief scientist of the American aerospace medical division, observed that the changes which follow the disturbance of bodily rhythm:

"May have some significance in international conferences during the first few days of the meeting. The morning hours during the first few days after long-distance eastbound flights, and the later afternoon hours after westbound flights, are not the proper times for important negotiations or vital decision."

"It has been observed that actors, chess players, athletes and, last but not least, race horses were not at their intellectual or physical best the first few days after arriving from a region four or more time zones away."[2]

Recent work has confirmed these findings. The results of varying tests after a daylight flight of eighteen hours from Oklahoma City to Tokyo were described by McGirr:

"There was a marked and quite significant deterioration in psychological performance on the first full day in Tokyo as judged by both reaction time and decision time. It is worth ·

stressing here that these tests for reaction time and decision time, though scientifically valid, were of a relatively simple type and were not comparable to the delicate balance of sophisticated judgements required of a diplomat or a business executive."[3]

Statesmen and senior officers should be added to his list. The degree of their mental vigilance and efficiency is of prime and profound importance but changes in mental alertness, as distinct from changes in physical condition, may pass unnoticed. A further piece of research has shown that the incidence of errors in another group under observation was greatest at 3 a.m.; the incidence then dropped, rose briefly again about 4 p.m. and fell again until the peak in the early hours of the morning.[2] A long flight that lands an official or a commander at a conference or in a zone of operations when, whatever the local time, they are in a 3 a.m. and accident prone state may lead to political or military disaster.

The speed of adaptation is related to the age of the subject. In the Oklahoma City–Tokyo study a rapid return to normal behaviour was observed in young students. In contrast the older men showed impairment of reaction time and decision making for as long as five days.

Normally the secretions of the adrenal glands prepare the body for a day's activity by the beginning of the morning. Following a long flight they may be at peak activity at the local time for retiring and thus render sleep difficult or impossible. The opportunities for sleep may in any case be limited and active duties may further curtail rest. There are those who maintain that the mind and body can be trained to work with less sleep or that the fatigue which follows can be overcome by will power. Experimental work on volunteers suggests that, though subjects can stay awake for three or four days, a serious deterioration occurs. Visual disturbances lead to illusions and hallucinations. There are gross deviations in the awareness of time. Disorganization of mental processes lead to slowing of thought, impairment of concentration and incoherence. Furthermore there is inability to correct errors for these are not even recognized. Admittedly these signs are the results of laboratory experiments, carried out at the extremes of physiological tolerance, but the effect of sleep deprivation, in those responsible for weighty and far-reaching decisions, should be given serious consideration. The consequences are not lost on the secret police of totalitarian powers who depend on mental disintegration to extract confessions.

Reactions to travel may lead to more than physiological and functional impairment for overt psychological disturbance can occur. A consistent pattern of events predispose to the breakdown; the journey may have been undertaken with some reluctance and is one that has involved solitary travel for several days. Meals have been irregular, sleep interrupted and, though alcohol may have been consumed before the flight, the normal intake of customary drinks and beverages is often considerably reduced. Psychotic manifestations appear suddenly in the form of hallucinations, delusions and irrational fears of persecution or accusation. Recovery is quickly assured by mild sedation, rest and a correct intake of food and fluids; measures which if used before and during the flight would have probably prevented the breakdown.

Great men are different from you and me. When a great man fails it is difficult to decide when incapacity begins; difficult to assess the degree of incapacity; and even more difficult to tell him that he is incapacitated. The role of the doctor in regard to this small and select group of patients is unique and most practitioners have neither personal experience, nor second-hand knowledge from experienced colleagues, of the correct approach and of the special problems that are involved.

It is difficult enough even after years of practice, to decide the degree of incapacity in a manual labourer or to recommend with confidence the premature retirement of a bank manager or a business executive. The statesman presents a more daunting problem. What doctor would care to decide whether the crippled Woodrow Wilson was any less effective than his inept Vice-President?: a man whose place in history is ensured by his statement, "what this country needs is a good 5-cent cigar". Would any physician care to decide whether the crippled Churchill was more or less effective than the younger, but ailing, Eden? Certainly all three had disorders which, at a lower executive level, would lead most doctors to recommend rest, a change of occupation or early retirement.

The illnesses of great men present the doctor with two main dilemmas. The first relates to the behaviour of great men as patients for, owing to their exceptional personalities, fortitude and avidity for power, they are liable to cause special difficulties to the attendant physician and, since they are skilled in concealing their real feelings and thoughts, the taking of a clinical history may be a thankless task. They would not have risen to high office without the power, innate or acquired, to dominate others and for this reason the usual doctor-patient relationship may be reversed. Normally the patient accepts a doctor's special knowledge and authority during their personal relationship in the course of an illness. The doctor indeed dominates the majority of his patients but patients of the highest social or authoritarian status may dominate their doctors even during an illness; at some risk, it must be emphasized, to the efficacy of diagnosis and treatment and to the reputation of the unfortunate doctor. Churchill bullied his medical advisers and his humiliation of two fellows of the Royal College of Physicians, who failed to sustain their recommendations under pressure, can only be appreciated by those unsuccessful candidates who have undergone a comparable ordeal while seeking admission to the College.

It is true that some doctors, within the confines of their consulting rooms, can use autocratic methods to reinforce their medical authority for the ultimate benefit of their distinguished patients. Great men form an exceptional minority and the doctors who can dominate them are so few in number that they become legends in the profession.

At times it may appear that they impress by their oratory, flamboyancy or eccentricity rather than by familiarity with the minutiae of medicine and surgery; a combination of factors that leads doctors, with less fashionable practices, to mutter about fine bedside manners and even charlatanry. John Abernethey, that distinguished surgeon whose name is still revered at the Royal Hospital of St Bartholomew, enhanced his reputation at the same time as he insulted his patients irrespective of their rank or station. Otto von Bismark, the German Chancellor, was a man of blood and iron in the eyes of the rest of the world but nothing more to his intimates than an irritable and unstable neurotic who overindulged his love of food, alcohol and tobacco. In 1883, when Bismark was sixty-eight years old, a new doctor worked a seeming miracle. Under his régime, Bismark submitted to a stringent diet and ultimately, as his insomnia and nervous manifestations vanished, his capacity for work was restored. Dr Otto Schweninger needed to be more than an outstanding physician; he had to possess that power of dominance, instinctive, learned or simulated, which enabled him to bolster the powers of medical dominance which suffice for the average patient.

The second dilemma that faces the doctor, when he treats the great man, is one that occurs in the care of any patient although the more prominent his standing the more dangerous are the horns. There are occasions, fortunately unusual, when doctors find they are burdened with another ethical responsibility which differs from the normal one that he owes solely to his patient. Usually this involves nothing more than the notification to the local authority of certain infectious diseases, though his patients may subsequently regard a routine visit by the public health officials as an unwarranted and deplorable invasion of their privacy. In even less common, but potentially more serious circumstances, the confidentiality of the relationship cannot be blindly maintained if public safety is involved as it might be through the incapacity of a railway driver or an airline pilot.

Conditioned by the established traditions of the medical profession, and admittedly ignorant of political affairs, the average doctor understandably concentrates on his personal responsibility for the immediate welfare of his patient. Nevertheless, doctors cannot escape the political consequences of their actions for, by condoning incapacity, they may contribute to situations which have serious political implications. Little or no attention has been given to the attitude and personality of the few select physicians who are called upon to treat the elect. Their judgement or advice may be swayed, consciously or subconsciously, by factors that bear no relation to strictly professional or ethical considerations; and, as a consequence, they may exert more political influence than they realize or desire.

The accolade that is most valued by physicians is the title of "clinician"; the title that he fears is that of "politician", although unacademic and extra curricular activities may carry him far. The ivory towers of Académe contain research workers with political prejudices and even the true blue clinician can hardly be expected to exclude all but medicine from his life. The role of the doctor whose practice verges on the borderland of politics is worthy of examination for extraneous factors may influence the doctor-patient relationship. The function of all doctors is to serve their patients and enable them to make the best possible use of their functions. They must not act as a judge or an actuary; they must not play the part of God or even that of the Elder Statesman. Yet in treating the elect the doctor may be unable to avoid an element of self-interest which does not affect his relationship with more ordinary patients. If his patient remains in power he basks in reflected glory: if his patient resigns he may return to the shadows with his political master.

Many can be exonerated from any accusation of self-interest. Woodrow Wilson's physicians genuinely believed that removal from office would take away the purpose of life and living. Moran felt the same about Churchill and hoped that, by persuading him to take a seat in the House of Lords, the best of both worlds would be gained by his patient. Lord Dawson seems to have adopted the view that patients can and must be persuaded to face their responsibilities; an essential contribution to everyday living but one that makes general practice both exhausting and frustrating. What is sauce for the goose is sauce for the gander but the possibility that reluctant Prime Ministers could be goaded into activity by their physicians is unedifying and alarming. Lloyd George consulted Dawson in June 1921 and was deeply disappointed that a breakdown in health was only temporary and that he was soon put back on the saddle. By the same token, Dawson propped up Baldwin who, groaning and protesting, lasted until the Coronation of May 1937 which, somewhat arbitrarily, had been selected as the date of his retirement.

There are times when the physician is aware that a lust for

power, vanity, habit or ambition outstrip the mental and physical ability of his patient. The spirit may be willing but the flesh is weak or an active body is handicapped by a failing mind. He must be on his guard lest an ailing patient, an impressive figurehead but a travesty of a man, may be exploited by party or country. Doctors who practise in the corridors of power can be confused by their ethical responsibilities to their patients and to the community; and, as the Nazi doctors found to their cost, fail to differentiate between their medical authority as physicians and their acquired structural authority as part of a government or party machine. They should never forget the searing and haunting words of James Roosevelt as he recalled the fourth term nomination and election of 1944:

"I never have been reconciled to the fact that Father's physicians did not flatly forbid him to run."[4]

References

1. Richard Eder. *The New York Times*, 7 July 1968.
2. Life International. 7 December 1963.
3. P. O. M. McGirr. *Trans. Soc. Occup. Med.* (1967), 18, 3.
4. James Roosevelt and Sidney Shalett. *Affectionately, F.D.R.*, p. 313. Harrap.

Index